Peace before Increase

Dr. Amanda Kay Cruz

Dr. Amanda Kay Cruz

Peace before Increase

Hi, I'm Amanda. I'm a Jesus believer, I'm a wife, and I'm a mom. Those are my big rocks. I haven't always put these big rocks in the jar of life first. Too often they've been set aside so I could keep jar space available for smaller rocks like work, ministry, achievements, chores, friendships, trips, and finances. When my biggest idol--my career—recently took a turn I wasn't prepared for, I began following the Lord through an intense journey of learning to trust Him more than my own ability to make everything turn out okay. I had to unlearn investing myself into the places where my presence was being yielding highest returns of earthly praise and instead began investing myself into incorruptible heavenly treasures that can't be stolen from me such as my own salvation and that of my husband and children. The deconstruction has been messy, and is ongoing. I'm nowhere near perfect. I'm merely a person trying not to let the devil win by staying continuously in the Lord's presence. I resolve to resume this fight afresh every. single. day.

I wrote this book—God's book as my family endearingly calls it—to chronicle the daily decisions I've learned to make to see God as THE source, not a REsource, to talk TO God more than I talk ABOUT God, and to help me reverse an entire life's worth of damaging inner dialogue. One crumb at a time, the Lord has revealed ten necessary habits I've had to rinse and repeat over and over to become the vessel of answers I need instead of waiting for them to fall from Heaven.

Are you experiencing anything overwhelming right now? Are you in charge of your sin or is it in charge of you? Are you doing something each day to get closer to God? Before working on strengthening any other circumstances or bonds, the damage control needs to begin on your relationship with God. If you need some raindrops to fall on the parched desert sand of your faith, you picked up the right book. You can't have next-level living with now-level faith any more than you can have a marriage while behaving like you're single, or be a parent while living like you've no kids. It's time to level up.

It's laughable that I'm the person God convicted to write about peace BEFORE increase. In the past, I didn't understand that the Lord will bless you because of something, not BEFORE something, as God's Word expresses in Romans 6:16, Joshua 1:7-8, Genesis 46:1-4, and 2 Chronicles 7:14. Only God knew I was formerly the queen of if/then praying, like "God, if you give me this opportunity to make extra money, then I'll handle finances better" or "God, if you soften my husband's heart toward this family trip, then I'll stop worrying about maintaining control." I wasn't behaving as if the Word of God was Lord over my life. Until a change in circumstances forced me to press in. He has taken me from a wilderness to a garden before anything has changed in my earthly circumstances. If He can do it for me, He can do it for you, too.

Dedication

To my tribe and greatest earthly supporters—Husseim, Adam, Hannah, Emma, Isaiah, and Josie. Thanks for embodying Ephesians 4:2 by showing me that true humility is not thinking less of myself, but thinking of myself less. May we continue growing closer to God and each other, keeping our hope in His unfailing love as depicted in Psalm 147:11, knowing Isaiah 55:11 promises His Word does not return to Him empty!

Acknowledgment

All acknowledgement goes to almighty Elohim for the things I've put down, so my hands are free to pick up something greater! In Daniel 3, You didn't save Shadrach, Meshach, and Abednego from the fire. You saved them IN the fire. Others turned to You because they went through the fire. They were promoted because they went through the fire! Circumstances didn't steal their hope or mood! It's hard to describe in earthly words how grateful I am to get to abide in Your Holy splendor. Thank you for showing me so much more through the breaking than the blessings. Even on days like the one captured below, where I must faith it until I make it, I realize without the gift of this waiting season, this book would remain on my bucket list, I would still be sixty pounds heavier, and my salvation, marriage, and parenting would all continue taking the backseat to my career. No dollar can ever buy me what gratitude has bought me. My gratitude is the greatest wealth of all! Help me to bathe in it daily, inclining my ears to Your desires so that I can continuously reflect Your love to myself and to those around me.

Contents

Dedication 5

Acknowledgment 6

Introduction 8

Stride 1: Declutter 20

Stride 2: Roof Busters 52

Stride 3: Exercise 64

Stride 4: BIBLE! 82

Stride 5: PRAY 101

Stride 6: Internalize... 164

Stride 7: Raisin Cakes 199

Stride 8: Search 258

Stride 9: Fast 282

Stride 10: Lighten Up... 304

Conclusion 335

Notes 339

About the Author 351

Introduction

It's the dead of night. You are driving home from a visit with someone dear to you and your gas light turns on. You pull over, and each of the three gas pumps that you try isn't accepting card payments at this time (go figure), so you reluctantly drag your feet into the convenience store to pay the cashier inside. As you pull out your wallet, you set your car keys on the counter, and the person in line behind you reaches to grab them. "Uh, no," you say sternly. "Those are MINE!" The hand retreats even faster than it first appeared.

Wouldn't it be life-changing if we had this same reaction to the theft of our God-given strengths, assets, and gifts? Consider if, the next time an unexpected finding from a doctor clouds your view of the future, you respond by saying, "Uh, no. God's prosperity is MINE in the name of Jesus!" Or the next time hard news from work poses a threat to your financial security, you react this same way saying, "Uh, no, God's provision is MINE in the name of Jesus!" Or the next time a sharp-tongued relative comes to thrust their opinion where you didn't ask for it, thus attempting to deposit doubt in your mind, you respond by declaring, "Uh, no, God's virtue is MINE in the name of Jesus!" Sounds simple, yet astonishing, doesn't it? If you're not currently tapping into the full authority deposited within you by God's Holy Spirit, you're reading the right book. Just as an inserted key connected to your car engine gives it power, becoming more deeply connected to God will give you power and boost your faith.

Imagine you were debilitatingly sick, and someone gave you a pill that not only saved your life but made you feel better than you did before you fell ill. Would you just go about your life like business as usual? Of course not! You'd want to tell everyone who would listen about the miracle that saved your life so it could save theirs, too! That's how I feel about the blood donor that not only died and rose again so that I could receive all-encompassing forgiveness, but even more so, He died and rose again so that I could inherit 7,487 promises God made to humankind, plus eternal life in God's presence.[1] If you had ANY idea what Jesus has saved you from, you'd live EVERY second of your life for Him!

In order to pay the debt for their sins, Old Testament believers had to follow a system of sacrifices. Usually, they atoned for different sins by sacrificing perfect animals without blemish. But God knew this couldn't go on forever. He knew that since the fall of Adam and Eve, not a single one of us could live a perfect life without blemish, worthy of God on our own, so He sent His son, Jesus, to the earth to live a life without sin on our behalf. And then, in order to reunite us with God, Jesus died the painful death that our past, present, and future sins deserve. John 3:17 says, "God did not send the Son into the world to condemn the world, but so the world could be saved through him" (ASV). When Jesus, the "Lamb of God," sacrificed Himself on the cross, He took the punishment for ALL of our sins, once and for all satisfying God's demand for justice and permanently ending His wrath. GOD IS NOT MAD ANYMORE! With our sins, we killed Jesus, and yet He saved us. Pause and dwell on the magnitude of God's love for a moment. Despite all of our flaws, our misuse of His blessings, our focus on our wants instead of His, and our prioritization of wealth and power, He still cared enough to send His own beloved sacrifice so we could reconcile with Him. That blows my mind. Now, forever, instead of knowing our name but calling us by our sins like our enemies, God knows our sins and calls us by our name. What a beautiful gift that so many of us still struggle to receive.

Why is it so hard for us to trust that when God speaks a word, it WILL come to pass? When we meet a mountain, why don't we think its maker could move it? I think the answer is simple. We've let go of God's hand. In Psalm 116:6, the psalmist states: "The Lord protects the simple; I was brought low, and he saved me." Are you trusting God to not only save your life, but to make it worth living? Are you trusting Him to save you in every way a person can be saved? C.S. Lewis once aptly said, "I believe in Christ as I believe in the sun, not because I can see it, but by it, I can see everything else." I'm not here to brag to you about my love for God because I fail Him daily, but I'll certainly use this book to brag about His love for me because it NEVER fails!

Upon recently landing with our infant daughter Josie after her first trip in an airplane, my husband Husseim complimented her with a beneficent grin, for doing so well throughout the ride. "All of our kids fly so well!" I told him, "It's because breastfeeding is such a gift from God!" "No," he corrected me. "It's because YOU'RE a gift from God." In due time, you'll recognize what a triumph this brief conversation was for our own journeys to get deeper with God. Shortly after our return home from that trip—a brief visit to Charis Bible College—we engaged in this loving exchange:

If you knew what we were going through, you'd think our optimism made no sense! But God! In *Daring to Live on the Edge,* Youth With a Mission (YWAM) founder Loren Cunningham points out that impressions on one's spirit will come from one of four sources: (1) your own mind; (2) the mind of others (e.g., the world); (3) the mind of Satan (e.g., demons); or (4) the mind of God. I can honestly and truthfully tell you that as Husseim and I have grown a deeper connection with God, our minds have been trained to hear His whispers instead of what our own thoughts, others' thoughts, and Satan's attacks are constantly SHOUTING. This training came once we realized every single thing in this world could be taken from us except for Jesus. We made the conscious choice to only hold tightly to Him and His Word. We recognized that our minds were full of so many lies and we had to fight back by filling our minds with the Word of God.

"I've never seen you so happy in my entire life," my firstborn son Adam said to me three months into what I perceived to be the hardest season of my life to date. For the first time ever, my future at work was unforeseeable, as was my husband's health. We'd been told his body was fighting a tumor in his head that wasn't actually there. What a concept, right? I felt like I was fighting a fake tumor of my own: lies I'd been telling myself for years about my worth being dependent on my profession. "If they don't keep me," I'd think to myself, "I'll be a nobody. I'll lose my status, my ability to provide, my identity, my worth."

"Don't take this the wrong way, Mom," Adam continued, "but even though you used to always tell us you had to use your phone and computer for work purposes, us kids would rather be broke and have time to talk to you than have money and never see the real, unbothered you." My face began filling with tears, my heart hanging on his every word as he pressed on: "Lately you've spent so much time with me that you've been missing me when I'm not home, telling me the family's incomplete when I'm not there." Tears in his eyes too now, his voice beginning to crack, he recalled his sister Emma telling me I'm the peanut butter to her jelly, and his brother Isaiah telling me I'm the "best mommy indaho wide world" as he added ever so sincerely, "Mom, I know you see this as your darkest moment but I've never seen you in so much light." Wow.

Unbeknownst to my son, I'd been fighting so hard to find genuine contentment by not waiting for a certain desirable outcome and instead making the most of the moment that I'm in, with those I love most. Often during this season of waiting, I thought I was failing at that, too, but finally I was convinced otherwise. I was starting to grasp that waiting isn't passive like when you're in line at Starbucks. Waiting requires an aggressive pursuit of the Lord! Waiting is our chance to fix our self-dependence into God-dependence. It's our opportunity to respond positively to the bright future God has for us.

I realized that while I liked to think I was superhuman by serving with Husseim at church, working multiple jobs, homeschooling my kids, volunteering for multiple organizations, and Mom taxi-ing day and night, I was lost and I didn't even know it. "You know Mom," my daughter Hannah told me, "when you put God first, 100,000 other problems are resolved all at once." You're right about that my sweet girl. Thank you, Hannah.

If someone asked you to write a list of the five things you thought most about today, would they be galvanized by your sanguineness, or disheartened by your despondence? Would a trip through your mind's most prevalent stressors feel like a quiet walk beside a peaceful river or a nerve-wracking whirl on a vomit-inducing roller coaster ride? No matter how many weeds may or may not be growing in that fast-paced mind of yours, I assure you that with faith and effort, you'll get something worthwhile from the journey on which I'm about to invite you to embark. Not sure if your faith is where it should be? Questioning whether God's even there? Busy pouring the living water into others, yet not taking any time to receive it for yourself? I welcome you to be bold enough to admit these things! I want your days of half-heartedly lip-syncing through praise and worship after barely making it to a church service to be over. DONE. NO MORE. No matter how distant you may feel from God, know that anything begun in the Spirit shouldn't be questioned in the flesh.

If you dig deep enough, you know God's truth about you, and if you could flip a switch to be hopeful again, you would. You know there's an underlying reason why each time you lose your phone or stub your toes, you immediately lash out to find out whose fault it is other than yours. If you could put an end to those reactions, you would, but it's not that simple. You've tried so many times before. Despite your best efforts, you're falling into pit, after pit, after pit. I've got news for you: YOU ARE NOT A PIT DWELLER.

It's time to let the Word of God shape your identity instead of the word of man. It's time for God to take His rightful place as your top priority in life. It's time to gain control over your thought life. Whatever uncertainty you're feeling is pleasing to the enemy but displeasing to God. The mental anguish you've become all too familiar with IS NOT WHO YOU ARE! Hear me when I say this: you're made PERFECT in the presence of Jesus. The more time you spend in Him, the more time you'll be freed from stress and worries. An anxious heart has no room for healing, but a restful heart changes everything. It's not the circumstances you're up against that break you. It's how you carry them. You're not worthless. You're not unlovable. You're not helpless.

You might be surprised to learn that 75-98 percent of mental, physical, and behavioral illnesses come from one's thought life,[2] or that 60-80 percent of visits to primary care physicians have a stress-related component.[3] Your mind works your body like a computer. If a doctor diagnoses you with something egregious and tells you that you only have six months to live, if you believe them and thus program that in your head, you'll die in six months. But if in faith you tell yourself this is not your diagnosis and you tell your body it will fix itself in the name of Jesus, you will live!

This book is going to help you change your perspective of the world through a bottom-up approach. We'll work from your feet to your head. For years, I tried achieving spiritual healing to no avail with various top-down approaches mainly using my eyes, ears, mind, and mouth. I've seen and heard many powerful messages, and I've even spoken about them to encourage others, but those messages usually booked a one or two-night stay up top, in my head, and never ventured down to my heart, or my feet. As Tony Evans says "Faith is measured by your feet, not your feelings. It's measured by what you do, not by what you say you are going to do."[47] A ha! It's no wonder why I lost my zeal for the Lord. For years, I felt empty during prayers and altar calls. I knew the sacred responsibility I held as a Christian spouse, I knew what Biblical principles I needed to instill in my kids as a Christian parent, but I lacked a real relationship with God myself. Was He really there?

Perhaps you can relate. Maybe you know what it's like to make all the right choices for everyone else but none of the right choices for yourself. Maybe it seems like your whole world is collapsing on top of you and at times you find it hard to breathe. You know better than to end your own life, but at the moment, you're finding it hard to live through another tomorrow. You don't know if you can endure this wait another day. Friend, you're not alone. John 16:33 guarantees you will have trouble in this life, and there are three reasons why: because you've sinned and it's a consequence, because it's an attack from the enemy trying to stop you from doing right, or because it's a God-led trial and He's taking you through the wilderness for a reason. But I have good news for you: the promise the Lord renders in Psalm 71:20-21 to restore you and turn things around for your good is the SAME FOR ALL THREE.

God's grace will turn any scenario around for the good of His believers. If you're anything like me, you hear this and think, "Cool, sign me up!" You want the Lord's goodness, but you get in your own way of receiving it. You think His commitment to forgive those who have repented and remember their sins no more as relayed in Hebrews 10:12-17, applies to others but not to you. Ahem. Wrong. You're forgivable. And God's forgiveness was yours before the moment you asked for it. Now we just need to get you walking, feeling, and believing in that forgiveness for yourself.

RIGHT HERE. RIGHT NOW. In the name of JESUS, declare refreshed endurance over yourself. Follow your inhale and exhale from start to finish. As thoughts try to push their way in to discourage or distract you, just observe them without analysis or judgment and let them drop to the floor. Focus on what an amazing gift it is to have breath in your lungs! Anchor your thoughts to this prayer from Ephesians 3:16-20 as you receive it aloud:

> God I pray that you'll unveil within me the unlimited riches of Your glory and favor until supernatural strength floods my innermost being with Your divine might and explosive power.
>
> Then, by constantly using my faith, the life of Christ will be released deep inside me, and the resting place of His love will become the very source and root of my life. Then I will be empowered to discover what every holy one experiences—the great magnitude of the astonishing love of Christ in all its dimensions. How deeply intimate and far-reaching is Your love!
>
> How enduring and inclusive it is!
>
> Endless love beyond measurement that transcends my understanding—this extravagant love pours into me until I am filled to overflowing with Your fullness, God! Never will I doubt Your mighty power to work in me and accomplish all this. God, You will achieve infinitely more than my greatest request, my most unbelievable dream, and exceed my wildest imagination! God, You will outdo them all, for Your miraculous power constantly energizes me (TPT).

You can't drift toward holiness, but you can work toward it. This work will require strides instead of steps. Steps are easy. I want to ensure you know from the jump that the kind of life changes I'm talking about in this book require all-in work, not baby steps. Think of some of the best athletes of all time like Bo Jackson, Mia Hamm, or Babe Ruth. These individuals are humans just like you and me but what separates them apart from anyone else is how much skin they put in the game. When average humans are at home relaxing, or binge-watching a favorite Netflix series, these above-average humans are putting in hours upon hours of work. They prove to the rest of us that strides are hard, but beneficial. Strides get you to your end goal quicker than steps. While others bask in the comfortability of their wishes and desires, you'll be thriving in the indisputable hope ignited by REAL change.

In the strides that follow, I'm going to give you ten foolproof ways to find God, and yourself. If they worked for me, they'll most certainly work for you. Each will be prefaced with a Bible story, and closed with a life application challenge plus lyrics to a worship song prayerfully chosen by myself, Husseim, or one of our five arrows—Adam, Hannah, Emma, Isaiah, and Josie. Buckle up and get ready to ride.

<u>Stride 1: Declutter</u>

Matthew 14:22-31

Walking on Water

Jesus sent His disciples to get into the boat and go on ahead of him, while he dismissed the crowd (many whom He's just healed and then out of five loaves and two fish, fed five thousand). After he had dismissed them, he went up on a mountainside by himself to pray. Later that night, he was there alone, and the boat was already a considerable distance from land, buffeted by the waves because the wind was against it. Shortly before dawn Jesus went out to them, walking on the lake. When the disciples saw him walking on the lake, they were terrified. "It's a ghost," they said, and cried out in fear. But Jesus immediately said to them: "Take courage! It is I. Don't be afraid."

"Lord, if it's you," Peter replied, "tell me to come to you on the water." "Come," he said. Then Peter got down out of the boat, walked on the water and came toward Jesus. But when he saw the wind, he was afraid and, beginning to sink, cried out, "Lord, save me!" Immediately Jesus reached out his hand and caught him. "You of little faith," he said, "why did you doubt?" (NIV).

Distraction. What a sneaky card the enemy plays. We're all struck by it, but we're too distracted to see our need to be helped from being distracted! Here, as Peter wants to challenge his faith by walking on the water to Jesus, he steps out of the boat but once he is distracted by seeing the wind and averts his gaze away from Jesus, he starts to sink. This beautifully heart wrenching story mirrors so many of my own. Often, I've felt an impulse to take a leap of faith, and I take it, only to quickly fizzle back to where I was because something or someone caught my eye over Jesus. Tell me you've been there too. Tell me you know what it's like to focus on the *how* of your calling over the *who*.

Tell me you know what it's like to be focused on the water (the circumstances you're in) instead of the One who is calling you to look past them. Or that deep down inside you know that you're keeping busy to avoid doubting! Yep, I went there because I've been there. You might be doing tons of things "for God" or "His kingdom," yet barely meeting *with God*. It could be that you're ashamed to face Him, or that you're uncertain about hearing from Him, or it could even be that you're scared of the work He'll have you do like repenting for losing it with your kids, making amends with someone you haven't spoken to in ages, honoring a commitment you made to someone in need, etc. Paying attention to the quality of our lives or even more simply, our days, is hard work. Certainly, it's easier to ignore internal work than to correct it.

Perhaps like me, you feel overwhelmed by all the things in you that need fixing. Maybe you don't want to be reminded that God knows about it all, or dare I say, maybe your busyness is saving you from taking the risk of pursuing God and hearing nothing back, thus deepening the doubt in Him that you never voice to others. Enough is enough. Finished are the days that you get in the way of your own blessings by filling your time with meaningless things. Busyness is NOT a badge of honor, nor is it a measure of success!

God stands ready to provide blessings beyond what we can imagine if only we'll give Him His rightful place in our lives! Jehovah-Jireh—a name He is given in Genesis 22:14–shows us this. Jehovah-Jireh means the Lord is our provider! Let us not forget that! WE are not the ones holding Him up, so there is nothing, NOTHING we can do to let Him down. Imagine seeing Jehovah-Jireh in Heaven when you pass away from this earth and at his feet are hundreds of present boxes. More than you ever saw in your very best memory of Christmas. You ask Him, "My Lord, what are all of these boxes?" to which He replies, "My beloved, these are all the gifts you never asked me for!" We serve a limitless God who wants so much more for us than we, and our busy schedules, allow room for!

Maybe you have a hard time believing that. Or maybe you're still questioning if I'm another goody two-shoes Christian whose life is too close to Heaven to relate to yours. This I must confront head-on. I've undoubtedly seen the undeserved grace and favor of God in my life. But I am no greater than you and I am no stranger to hardship. A daughter of divorce and dysfunction, I craved stability throughout my upbringing. My parents moved often since they were both on active duty in the United States Air Force. Add to that mix their post-divorce decisions to live as far away from one another as possible and complications were inevitable. My life's path took more twists and turns than a cheap garden hose. I saw more than I wanted to see, heard more than I wanted to hear, and endured more than I wanted to have the capacity to endure.

After attending six elementary schools, four junior high schools, and three high schools in order to have both a mom and a dad present in my life, I was desperate to know a love that my parents or stepparents could never give me. I began having sex out of wedlock at the tender age of fourteen and birthed my first miracle at the age of fifteen. I remember vividly the day that I sat in a teenage parenting class as a freshman in high school and learned that according to various studies, less than half of all teenage mothers receive their high school diploma, and less than 2% of all teenage mothers earn their college degree by the age of 30.[4] As I sit here writing this for you, my praiseworthy reader, (actually laying here, typing on my phone, nursing my youngest daughter as we moms do), I am 30 years old. And I am delighted to report that God completely obliterated those statistics in my life.

Like my girlhood, the story the Lord wrote for me prior to getting here to age 30 was tangled, yet invigorating. I graduated from high school two years early and started earning my undergraduate degree when I was sixteen years old as a mom to, by then, a toddler. The hustle of working minimum wage jobs while also going to school full-time exhausted me but I leaned on God and reaped from it all that I could. He gave me dreams of using a gift he'd placed in me as a little girl who used to set up make-believe lessons in her aunt's classroom. A gift to teach and to motivate others.

Through faith and elbow grease, I graduated a year early with my bachelor's degree and began my first high school English teaching job at the age of nineteen, while my son was still not yet old enough to start school or to remember the mess my life was before he entered it. I must say I felt pretty content with that feat. But God wasn't done. Remember, He measures our faith by our feet, not our feelings. I kept walking.

Once I married my life's greatest accomplishment, my husband Husseim, my faith grew faster than a California redwood! Together our dreams multiplied. The Lord spoke life and encouragement into my heart through my husband and with his support, I went on to earn a master's degree in educational leadership at the age of twenty-three with five years of teaching experience already under my belt. Then, in a record shattering two years after that, the Lord equipped me to earn my doctorate degree in English with an emphasis in Rhetoric and Composition at age twenty-five. Only five months lapsed from the proposal to the final defense of my nearly 150-page dissertation—the fastest completion of a dissertation that my committee had ever seen. The same month that I received my PhD, I joined our local university as full-time faculty. Only God could move a young teacher (of special education at that point) from a middle school to a university in an instant. Just. Like. That. I remember being the youngest lecturer hired by the university's English department that year, the only new hire without any connections to the department, and the only one with my doctorate, let alone also being a married mom of three miracles at the time. Fast forward to five years later, my husband and I now have five miracles—three daughters and two sons.

What's life like now for a mom of five? Like some of you, I was forced by Covid-19 to homeschool our children around three years ago, but through prayer we eventually converted that "force" into a passionate choice because we believe firmly that God will hold my husband and I accountable for the education that we provide for our children. He will ask both of us, "What did you do with these children I loaned you?"

I'll never forget a fellow homeschooling momma helping me through that conversion by asking me, "If your own K-12 experience left you so woefully lacking that you don't feel confident in your abilities to teach your own children K-12, why are you putting your kids through that same system?" And not long after this, a sister in church begged me to stop looking for a calling to teach my children. She said the calling was rendered the moment the Lord entrusted my husband and I with each of our five miracles! What strength we draw from Psalm 127:4 which reads "Like arrows in the hand of a warrior are the children of one's youth" (ESV).

From the depths of our souls, we declare Psalm 144:12 which reads "Lord may our sons flourish like well-nurtured plants, our daughters like graceful pillars, carved to beautify your palace. Make our sons in their prime like sturdy oak trees, our daughters as shapely and bright as fields of wildflowers (NLT).

Now here's the part of my testimony where—deep sigh— God wants me to get real. Cue the mic drop. I'm a firm believer that people don't care what you know until they know you care. So here's my heart on a platter, only for God's honor. I know if it wasn't for my failures, I wouldn't know the depth of His grace. What I've just shared are some highlight reels from what God has done with my life but nothing behind-the-scenes. I've not told you of my struggles with insecurities, dishonesty, stealing, greed, pride, unforgiveness, wrath, envy; need I go on? I could fill a longer book than this with past shame and regret. I'm a whole mess of a human. And yet, here I am certain God wants to use my circumstances to advance His Gospel. In truth, I'm not writing to you from a mountain top as you might think. But I'm not writing from a valley either. As I lay here typing, I'm facing a huge Jericho, for I am not spending this season in a classroom for the first time since the birth of my firstborn son fifteen years ago.

Although getting to homeschool without also working full-time has long been a secret consideration of mine hidden in the deepest recesses of my heart, as a two-income household, I assure you I did NOT plan this pause. God did. Be forewarned fellow ambassador for Christ. God may supernaturally suffocate your supply so you have to renew your dependence on him! As we learn in Matthew 10:39, whoever finds his life will lose it, and whoever loses his life for the Lord's sake will find it (ESV). I draw strength from the eloquent words of Miriam James Heidland who once proclaimed, "God has allowed things in my life for His own providence and they have broken my heart open to love like Him and I would never come close to loving like Him had those things not happened to me." I gather from this that there is a purpose for my pain. Actually, more purposes than I can count.

Just after beginning my tri-annual mental abandonment of my husband and children so I could go above and beyond to prepare the Taj Mahal for each of my university classes—even though a simple cubical skeleton would work just fine—I rang in the new year with floods of tears. The reality was hitting me that I would soon have to leave our newborn daughter to resume working. Or not. The university where I have lectured for the past five years didn't schedule me to teach for the first time ever, yet, as God would have it, has continued paying my contract. Maybe unexpectedly staying home post-delivery would be a welcomed opportunity for anyone else, but for me, this was unsettling. I mean, we're talking about my dream job, the best job I've EVER had, the job I based my value as a human off of, and I'm taking a semester off? What about the future? When could I go back? Am I still valued as a teacher?

Woah.

My heart became a blender, combining a toxic mixture of fear, relief, anguish, gratitude, and sadness. Oh, how I wish I could tell you I didn't look to my feelings for affirmation of my purpose but nope. After so many years with this job that truly has meant more than the world to me, to the ears of my heart, it felt I was told, "We're going to take some time to decide if you're worthy of taking another contract here." I didn't consider at that point that I'd just had a baby, and my family needed my undivided attention more than ever before. I also did not think I had the authority to throw lies about my abilities to the pits of hell where they belong. I was shaken to my core! And yet in moments, I also felt a bizarre sense of solace.

I had to acknowledge the hand of God rested heavily on my family and I, for I've been given a gift of rest and I'm still being paid. This is a miracle from above. It defies all logic! "Thank you, Jesus," I said repeatedly the day the news was first rendered. That gratitude would carry me through news just one week later that the symptoms of the Idiopathic Intracranial Hypertension (IIH) Husseim had been diagnosed with a year prior had worsened. The cerebrospinal fluid (CSF) his body was overproducing was causing intolerable pain on his skull, eyes, neck, etc. He'd never known a low like this. Nor had I.

Where my faith has wavered with unbelief in God's provision, Husseim's hasn't. Where Husseim's faith has wavered with unbelief in God's healing, mine hasn't. I thank God for Husseim and his embodiment of the earnest love that 1 Peter 4:8 talks about. Husseim's the spice to my pumpkin and I'm the tacos to his Tuesday. To this very moment, though I'm learning to trust that seeds of hope for my professional future have been planted in the spiritual realm, and though Husseim's learning to trust that seeds of his physical healing have been planted in the spiritual realm, we are waiting together eagerly and expectantly to see them fully manifest in the flesh. How wonderful that through the unexpectancy of spending a semester at home, God's sovereignty reigns, enabling me to be by Husseim's side, prioritizing him instead of chasing my career goals, which, according to Revelation 20:12-15, won't even be recorded with my name in the book of life!

Before receiving this update—let's dub it a gift—from my employer, I was struggling to picture how I would survive another semester of busyness. I attribute this to why inexplicable tranquility initially consumed me in those first moments after I perceived my whole world to be flipped upside down. Within a few hours after learning about my gift, the Lord gave me and a dear friend of mine a sweet word at the same exact time that I needed to "pause and pray." I recalled learning how intimidating Jericho and its barbaric inhabitants were and how the walls of Jericho crumbled without

Joshua or his soldiers ever lifting a single hammer, dislodging a single brick, or prying loose a single stone. God did it all for them.

God didn't tell Joshua to go take the city. In Joshua 6:2, He said, "Joshua, receive the city I have taken" (ESV). I was totally down to believe God has already won in my situation too, until my husband reminded me how much our standard of living relies on my income, not just his. He thought if I stopped teaching, I'd probably have to stop homeschooling and we'd probably have to give up our home. Once we sat under the weight of that reality, we allowed toxic thoughts to successfully cripple us with consternation. I won't mince words about that. We were going downhill, fast.

Do you remember what Peter did after Jesus died on the cross? The same Peter who we just read about walking to Jesus on water and who, despite denying knowing Jesus three times prior to the crucifixion, eventually became the leader of the apostles, traveling through Palestine and Asia Minor converting countless souls and working countless miracles? In John 21:1–25, we see that along with some of the other disciples—or learners, as I prefer to call them—after the death of Jesus, Peter and his doubts resumed doing what they had always done—fishing. But he caught nothing, for returning to his old fisherman ways was not the will of God.

I admit that after discovering I'd be sitting out from teaching for the first full semester in fifteen years and wholeheartedly believing I let down my husband and children, I experienced doubts like Peter, and I, too, returned to my old ways—controlling what would happen next. I let my mind run rampant with worries about when I would get to return to work or if I needed to hunt for a new opportunity. I could not shake panicking off of my head. Fear of unemployment ate through my stomach faster than a McDonald's Big Mac. I started searching for job after job and contacting connection after connection to uncover potential prospects so that no matter what the outcome from my employer after this semester, I would have peace of mind that my family wouldn't go hungry. That was all me, of course, not God. And if I could return to those first few days after the being given this gift, I would tell myself defeat does not align with the Word of God! I would tell myself to interrupt every single "WHAT IF" with "BECAUSE GOD ________" and every single "I CAN'T" with "SO I'LL TRUST GOD TO ________." I would remind myself to stand on His promises and trust Him to make all things new. Despite this not being a path I would have chosen, I would tell myself to accept that stumbling through it was okay.

The waiting isn't over, but my trust in myself over God is. A few nights ago, at about 2am, I awoke to nurse my Josie girl and heard the Holy Spirit gently say "You can't see the shore, but I can. Trust me." This prompted me to read Isaiah 26:3 which says, "He will keep in perfect peace those whose mind is stayed on Him, because we trust in Him" (NIV). So still, in this exact moment, next steps are unclear to me in my natural eyes and yet I know here in the middle is exactly where I need to be. And I securely believe that it's where you, brave reader, need to hear from me. God knows you don't need to hear from another Christian author who has already reached the top of their mountain. (Hallelujah! So thankful for that for them!) He knows you're yearning to hear joy can be found in the middle of the hardest times of your life, BEFORE you can see victory with your natural eyes. It can, kind soul.

I never thought I would find myself saying this wait is the best thing that could have happened to me, but spiritually, it is! I am thanking God for it every day! Sometimes with eyes blurred by tears, but still, I thank Him! If you look hard enough, dignified child of the king, you will also find hope that your glory days still lay ahead of you, not behind you! Your miracle is in motion. Flex those faith muscles and prepare to trust.

Before I learned I wouldn't be teaching this semester and thus before my spiritual restoration began, I was a Mrs. Jones in the eyes of others, including those who I would consider my closest family members and friends. Surely you know what I mean. A Mrs. Jones is the epitome of the ideal woman.

A Mrs. Jones does what no one else can fathom doing. She leads Bible studies for her church, she volunteers with the young and old, she's well-kept and educated, she has a well-established career, yet also manages to keep her dishes clean, picks up around the house, regularly dates her husband, keeps him sexually satisfied, prepares home cooked meals every night, potty trains all of her youngins by age two, has them reading by age four, homeschools her kids in all of the other academics without assistance from others, and resolutely raises them to be God fearing commissioners. One might pride themselves on the respect that comes with maintaining such a front. People would always bathe me with compliments like "Amanda you're extraordinary! You're a superhuman! There's no one like you!" and questions like "Amanda how do you do it all?" "Not well!" I should have told them! People's perceptions of me did not at all match the reality of my circumstances.

I was doing all of those things, but I was DROWNING. In the days and weeks immediately following the birth of our fifth miracle Josie, in addition to my full-time role lecturing, I picked up a part-time lecturing role for another department to earn extra coins. Nothing short of the exemplary "yes girl," I also assisted and/or sponsored every university committee and organization that ever sought my involvement, I led with my husband as co-marriage ministry specialists for our church, I helped Teach For America with nationwide transitions of preservice teachers into the K-12 classroom, I homeschooled each of our children except for our oldest who I drove to/from a private Christian school half an hour away from our home, I tutored for our homeschool community, and I taxied each of our children to a slew of extracurricular activities, all while trying desperately to maintain intimacy with my husband plus a cleanly and orderly home with filling meals for our growing brood.

I was LOSING IT! I thought maybe I should take up yoga, start my days by swimming in cold water, change my diet, get outside more, lift weights, or get some Botox. I often thought of escaping to one of my best friends' houses for a week since they live a good four hours away from my reality. At my worst, I even wondered if I belonged in an insane asylum. "I'm stressed" and "I'm overwhelmed" were my most commonly used phrases. I remember telling my husband many times that I was concerned about my mental health. But I did nothing about it.

Stress was crippling me, and busyness was ruining me. Yet if you asked me how I was doing, I would casually tell you everything was fine. Am I ringing any bells for you yet, fellow believer? I got used to people thinking I was sensational. I got used to doing more than most because I knew I could, even though could and should are two very different words. I was too distracted all the time to see that busyness was not a virtue to be applauded. Busy was the greatest enemy of my spiritual life! Busy was KILLING me spiritually, physically, AND silently. While busy being busy, I didn't even notice it was a problem!

Peace before Increase

About two months before receiving the gift of waiting from my work, just three weeks after giving birth to our youngest daughter, busy reared a new ugly head. I fell down our stairs trying to tend to our youngest son Isaiah after he awoke from a bad dream and I fractured my coccyx—a painful butt injury I wouldn't wish on anyone. Looking back on this now, I realize that God allowed that fall to give me a chance to wake up and clear some things off of my plate. But I didn't listen. The very next day, I sat on my injury to get my Adam to school. Business as usual. I continued seeking busyness instead of my Savior.

I was so distant from the Lord. I treated Him as an accessory, as salt that was sprinkled here and there in whatever small crevices I could squeeze Him into, but certainly not as the meat in my life, not as my everything. I made Him a homeschool subject for my other four children and ensured they learned about Him, but I didn't seek a personal intimate relationship with Him myself. And no one knew this except for He and I. I faithfully shared morning devotionals with various souls the Lord brought into my life over the years so I could encourage them but in my own heart, I didn't behold many of the things I shared. I was in sheer distress. I would begin each day with the same scripted prayer as the day before, not expecting any interaction with the Lord. Wanting a good life, but not working on my spiritual relationship. Sure, I would say a quick popcorn prayer sporadically throughout the day, but robotically, not faithfully.

And my marriage? It was hanging on, mostly because as Christians my husband and I know God hates divorce, but as I look back on it now, albeit gradually, I realize our marriage was dying too. My husband and I had become passing ships, more like roommates than soulmates.

We weren't praying together, or reading the Word together, we stopped desiring quality time with one another, we didn't so much as acknowledge one another many times when coming to/from our home, we usually ate supper separately and on the go, we kept up with our sex life out of obligation instead of passion, I made all of the decisions regarding our children, and we quarreled like cats and dogs over money. We always said if we were to part ways, it would be because of money. My husband is a saver, and I am a spender. We knew this from the beginning of our relationship, but I always thought three, five, or ten years down the road, it would remedy itself. Eventually we would figure it out. Wrong. After all these years we have been together, I was still fighting my husband tooth and nail for purchases, almost always revolving around the kids. "They don't need that" he would say. "I work too, and I want to get it for them" I would bark back. I'm sure at some point my husband stopped praying I would change in this area because I had proven plenty of times that I wouldn't. Thankfully, even when we forget our prayers, God doesn't. And I don't believe He ever forgot Husseim's desire to live in financial peace. Likewise, I believe God remembered my half-hearted prayer in the midst of the busiest time of our lives when I asked him to help me be a better Christ follower, a better wife, and a better mom.

What unknowingly intrepid prayers we once prayed. I'm already finding clarity only a couple weeks into my waiting for word on what will happen next with my career. The answer to our prayers came dressed like a problem. In our own strength, it looked like the worst thing that could have happened, but it was the best! God doesn't want us sulking in a corner, wrought with worry. It's our harvest time! And that means we have work to do. The spiritual corn ain't gonna pick itself—don't worry, that's about as Texan as this Cali-raised girl gets. I know God doesn't want me to waste this waiting, nor does He want you to waste yours, diligent reader.

He is getting us ready, teaching us, ensuring we depend on Him like never before. Because *waiting is where faith becomes necessary*. Serving a God of immediate gratification would require no faith at all. Waiting is where faith develops. Waiting is the training before a fight. It's the backstage dress rehearsals before a show. It's the practices before a game. It's the saving before a purchase. It's the studying before an exam. Do you know what the three days between Jesus' crucifixion and His resurrection teach us? Or what we should draw from the eight days between Thomas screaming his doubt and God actually appearing to Him? The presence of silence NEVER means the absence of God OR His miracles! So challenge yourself to TRUST that on the other side of this wait, you'll have a deeper, richer, livelier faith than you did before! Let's be encouraged by 1 Peter 5:7 which tells us "Trust Him with your every concern! He deeply cares for you (NIV)!"

About three days after receiving the gift from my work, I accepted God's fight to save me, my marriage, and our children. At last, I passed the baton to God and stopped running. For years I didn't fully trust He would carry the baton where I wanted it to go, but now, with no other option, I had to submit to His will. Finally, I said "It's all in Your hands God. Yes, even our finances" and I meant it.

So far in this wait, I have seen more breakthroughs in my spiritual life than I have experienced in years. No one wants a savior until they need one, right? I cannot wait to share with you the faith boosters that have helped me so they can help you, too. By the end of this, I pray you'll fill your spiritual arsenal with weapons to take to battle with you as you undergo your own spiritual restoration. I encourage you to learn to apply one stride per week in a small group so you can discuss your progress with people who will hold you accountable to grow.

The first stride, ***decluttering***, requires you to carve some time out of your day to pick yourself up. We'll do this by writing an escape letter. I call it this because before you can change anything in your life, you must escape the dark hole you've dug for yourself in your mind. You can only minister to others from the overflow of your cup, so you need to make sure you are constantly refilling your cup.

You will use the blank pages that follow to write an *encouraging* escape letter to yourself, grounded in the character of God, without succumbing to guilt or fear. Pour out the very things you know you need, that no one ever poured into you. Choose a Bible story or lesson to include in it, and hang it up somewhere that you'll see it often. Especially on your hardest days. Early on in my wait, the Lord convicted me to stop searching for a person to tell me what I needed to hear. No person knew better than me what I needed to be told!

The one who controls the folded tissue AKA brain between my ears is me, so I have to be my own best influence. I have to BE the adviser I always wished I had instead of looking for someone who would fill such a role. For my own escape letter, on paper I drew a stick-figure of myself, smiling brightly, and beneath it, this is what I wrote. On the days that I'm too distraught to read it aloud to myself, I have my husband, or a trusted friend read it to me. Sometimes the added layer of support that comes from hearing my words from someone else's voice brings me deeper solace:

You're going to be okay. You've made mistakes but that doesn't mean YOU are a mistake. Do NOT be mistaken! You can sit there lamenting forever about how bad you've been, feeling guilty until you die, but not one tiny slice of that guilt will do anything to change a single thing in the past. God has already forgiven you. It's time to forgive yourself once and for all. The chains weighing you down are no bigger than the small chains that attach circus elephants to wimpy stakes in the ground. Their memory of impossibilities in the past are stronger than the real possibilities of the present.

Aren't you tired of getting in your own way? Aren't you tired of looking at others, secretly coveting the seemingly uncomplicated lives they live? As long as you are drawing breath, there is a new beginning and a new chance. Believe that joy IS coming. Open your door, sit with the son in the sun and whisper His name: JESUS! Boom, all you have to do is mention His name and the presence of God will be with you!

The Lord is building you into a person of character, integrity, and honesty. His grace is as boundless as His love! Stand on His promise in Exodus 14:14 that He will fight for you! You need only stay still! God is conforming you in His image! He's reigniting your love for Him and His Word! You're the head and not the tail. You're above and not beneath. You're a leader and not a follower. You're the temple of the Holy Spirit, a conduit of the living water, who can stand against the schemes of the devil. You're going to make the devil regret the day that he ever pointed a sword at your family! Inhale God's presence and exhale praises for what He's already done! If everything in your world at the moment is hurting but your big toe, praise the Lord that your big toe isn't hurting!

You've prayed for change, but you are the change! Your heart is the change! God is strengthening you and your sweet family. He is making you lose the taste in your mouths so what you want most is wholeness and righteousness! He's flooding your hearts, minds, bodies, and souls! Watch His glory flood every area of your life, your husband's life, and your children's children's children's lives! Don't be afraid. Only believe! Allow the little girl inside of you to arise, fully cured of insecurity, so the world can see that GOD is still performing miracles and GOD still has all the power Your jovial, youthful spirit is being returned to you in this season, but you have to choose to wear it. Every. Day. Who are you? You're an unstoppable creation from a limitless God!

He loves you and He is more than enough to fill ALL of your gaps! At the mention of His name, the name that is the way, the truth, and the life, every lie has to bow! When you allow yourself to look back, you'll see a pattern, but when you look forward, you'll see a future and a hope! It's time. It's time to set your heart on the Father and move forward in confidence. Do not wallow. Do not retreat to your comfortable corner. If you do, you won't ask for God's unlimited resources. Tell Him how you feel and ask Him for His help! You know you're not strong enough to endure this in your own strength. You know you need Him to hold your hand through this fire. You need Him to shut the mouths of lions and bring your dry bones to life! Believe in yourself and seek God's wisdom! You need IIis counsel! Quit giving Him multiple choice quizzes where you only want Him to tell you whether to choose this or to choose that or to select from option A, B, C, or D! No more! Desire only Him and His ways! Jesus, Jesus, Jesus!

Surround yourself with the best people who will best activate your mirror neurons. While they sing a song of praise, you'll feel victorious! When they shout a victory, you will too! If you don't have faith today, you can borrow some of theirs!

You WILL MAKE IT! Just as contagious as faith is, so is cynicism. If you have cynical people holding your mirror, you'll always feel small. You'll feel smaller than your challenge, smaller than your giant, because you're not looking at your God but when your mirror is your fellow upward bound disciples and your MAKER, whose mercies are new with every rising of the sun, you'll trust that He who began a good work in you will be faithful to complete it! Think of how a mirror always shows you an image in reverse. God knows how your situation works out. He knows how your story ends. He knows what He put in you! When your mistakes are your mirror, you stay on the outside of Canaan like the people of Israel refusing to enter the Promised Land in Deuteronomy 1:19-45 because of fear of future things falling apart. They don't refuse to enter because they lack the strength to go in, just like you aren't stuck because you are small, but because you are seeing small! Be reminded of the Bible story of Elisha and the Floating Ax Head in 2 Kings 6:1-7:

> *The disciples of the prophets said to Elisha, "The place where we're staying is too small for us. Let's go to the Jordan River. Each of us can get some logs and make a place for us to live there."*
>
> *Elisha said, "Go ahead."*
>
> *"Then one of the disciples asked, "Won't you please come with us?"*
>
> *Elisha answered, "I'll go."*
>
> *So, he went with them. They came to the Jordan River and began to cut down trees. As one of them was cutting down a tree, the ax head fell into the water. He cried out, "Oh no, master! It was borrowed!"*
>
> *The man of God asked, "Where did it fall?" When he showed Elisha the place, Elisha cut off a piece of wood. He threw it into the water at that place and made the ax head float. Elisha said, "Pick it up." The disciple reached for it and picked it up" (NIV).*

Sweet self, you are a branch of the true vine! When did you lose courage in God's plan for your life? When did you drop an ax head of your own and become wrought with regret as a result? When did you lose blessings spoken over you by others? What stained your heart? No matter how many times the Lord tells you to rise up and move on from your past life, if you don't have courage to believe Him, you won't move on. Remember Elisha. He doesn't just get the lost ax head and deliver it to the disciple. He asks the disciple to first show him where he lost it. In your mind, take yourself back to the time that you lost your bravery. Go there and take it back! Take it back from whatever person/job/circumstance stole it from you. The Lord was able to return the ax head to this disciple, but only after he went back and acknowledged where it fell!

Write your own escape letter here:

Hardships are like holy sandpaper. They'll expose every flaw and weakness you have—and that's a GOOD thing if we give our detriments to the Lord and ask Him to conform us to His image. So let me ask you: how close do you feel to God? Writing an uplifting escape letter to yourself should have made you more aware of your need to dedicate time to building up your faith, thus lessening the distance between you and your heavenly father.

If you ever feel like you are just going through the motions of praying at meal and bedtime, attending Sunday service at church, looking up a feel-good Scripture on your phone from time to time, and replying "good" wherever someone asks you how you're doing, even though "meh" would be a more accurate response, I more than understand you! I was you before the Lord allowed my entrance into this intensely needed waiting season. It is not my hope that you face an unanticipated waiting period like I am right now, however I do hope, in your own strength, you can decide to fix your personal relationship with Jesus. Work on aligning your heart with His on the inside and He will take care of everything on the outside!

Whatever it is that you're holding onto, be it unforgiveness, unworthiness, guilt, worry, resentment, pride, you name it, realize it is your cross to bear, no one else's. Not your spouse's or your kid's or your neighbor's or even your cranky coworker's. As part of His punishment, Jesus was forced by the Romans to carry His own cross to the place of his crucifixion. When you're ready to die to self and live all-in for Jesus, you'll do the same. You will carry to Him your cross so He can spiritually resurrect you!

Do not look to another person to fix something in you that only God can. When I learned tides were changing with my job, aside from a couple of brief words I spoke to Jesus in my mind, I took the weight of the news to my husband before I took it to God. I hadn't talked personally with God in a long time. What would I say? Unfortunately, my husband's clapback was not one you'd see in a romantic Hallmark movie. His reaction wasn't void of worry because it turns out, he's human! And he has human feelings! But not God. Aren't we glad that all of God's emotions are rooted in His holy nature and are always expressed sinlessly?!

As I'm writing this paragraph, it's been almost three weeks since receiving the gift of waiting from my work and I can confidently say I've ingrained the meaning of Matthew 5:3-8 in my mind and heart: "You're blessed when you're at the end of your rope. With less of you, there is more of God and his rule. You're blessed when you feel you've lost what is most dear to you. Only then can you be embraced by the One most dear to you. You're blessed when you're content with just who you are—no more, no less. That's the moment you find yourselves proud owners of everything that can't be bought" (MSG).

In such little time, I've gone from a level four faith to a level twenty faith all because I've stripped away the busy, and reignited my passion for God and His will. I'm sure you want to know how. Let me tell you: PARROTS WITH BIG COWS. This stands for Prayer, Worship, Bible, and Community. My oldest son Adam came up with the mnemonic. It's wacky enough to be memorable! In the pages that follow, I'll expand on becoming the vessel of the answers you seek by applying more than just these four components, but I consider these to be the core. This is where you must start. As you'll soon see, once I could handle more, I did more.

Parrots (Prayer), Worship (With), Big (Bible), Cows (Community) equals the four legs of a believer's table. One falls without just one! God's voice will break through all the noise in your life if you maintain your table! Like with any relationship, over time you'll inherit more treasures and memories, but this table has to be your foundation. If ever your daily schedule becomes too full to fit in prayer, worship, Bible, and community, you're busier than God wants you to be. Take another look at the escape letter you wrote to yourself. What leg of the believer's table does your self-advice remind you that you're missing the most? Prayer? Worship? Bible? Community? Whichever leg emerges as most cumbersome to incorporate into your life is likely the one you should declutter for.

Life Application Challenge 1: *If you've already written your uplifting escape letter, you're ready to subtract one and add one! To make room for a new routine using more prayer, worship, Bible, or community, take something big off of your plate. Imagine you got a call from your employer just like I did, fueling an unforeseen change in your career trajectory. Even if you have to call it "temporary," at least you'll try life without busyness prioritized over Jesus. Galatians 6:9 says, "And let us not grow weary of doing good, for in due season we will reap, if we do not give up."*

Lyrics to Amanda's pick: "Take Courage" by Kristene DiMarco

Self-Chosen for its reminder that to God, patience isn't about how long we can tolerate waiting, it's about how well we trust while we're waiting. 2 Timothy 2: civilian pursuits, since his ain (NIV).

Slow down, take time
Breath in He said
He'd reveal what's to come
The thoughts in His mind
Always higher than mine
He'll reveal all to come
Take courage my heart
Stay steadfast my soul
He's in the waiting (x2)

Hold onto your hope
As your triumph unfolds
He's never failing (x2)
Sing praise my soul
Find strength in joy
Let His Words lead you on
Do not forget
His great faithfulness
He'll finish all He's begun
Take courage my heart
Stay steadfast my soul
He's in the waiting (x2)

Hold onto your hope
As your triumph unfolds
He's never failing

He's never failing (x2)

And You who hold the stars
Who call them each by name
Will surely keep Your promise to me
That I will rise in Your victory
And You who hold the stars
Who call them each by name
Will surely keep Your promise to me
That I will rise in Your victory
Take courage my heart
Stay steadfast my soul
He's in the waiting (x2)

Hold onto your hope
As your triumph unfolds
He's never failing (x2)

Take courage my heart
Stay steadfast my soul
He's in the waiting (x2)

Hold onto your hope
As your triumph unfolds
He's never failing (x2)
He's in the waiting (x7)

Peace before Increase

He's never failing
Take courage my heart
Stay steadfast my soul
He's in the waiting (x2)

Hold onto your hope
As your triumph unfolds

Stride 2: Roof Busters

Mark 2:1-12

Jesus Forgives and Heals a Paralyzed Man

A few days later, when Jesus again entered Capernaum, the people heard that he had come home. They gathered in such large numbers that there was no room left, not even outside the door, and he preached the word to them. Some men came, bringing to him a paralyzed man, carried by four of them. Since they could not get him to Jesus because of the crowd, they made an opening in the roof above Jesus by digging through it and then lowered the mat the man was lying on. When Jesus saw their faith, he said to the paralyzed man, "Son, your sins are forgiven."

Now some teachers of the law were sitting there, thinking to themselves, "Why does this fellow talk like that? He's blaspheming! Who can forgive sins but God alone?"

Immediately Jesus knew in his spirit that this was what they were thinking in their hearts, and he said to them, "Why are you thinking these things? Which is easier: to say to this paralyzed man, 'Your sins are forgiven,' or to say, 'Get up, take your mat and walk'? But I want you to know that the Son of Man has authority on earth to forgive sins." So he said to the man, "I tell you, get up, take your mat, and go home." He got up, took his mat, and walked out in full view of them all (NIV).

What a remarkable story of Jesus restoring the faith and health of a paralyzed man. The man unquestionably could not walk, or even reach for Jesus himself. Four selfless others brought him all the way to the feet of Jesus. Mind you, this was no easy task. Picture your favorite celebrity coming to town and being swarmed by fans who all want their chance at a moment with this person. Only multiply that mental image by a million plus because Jesus has abilities no celebrity could ever possess. The power of the Lord to heal the sick was bestowed upon Jesus. Everyone wanted to get to him. Everyone. The house he was in was jam-packed! Getting in was impossible for even one more, but four with a paralyzed man on a mat? Even more impossible!

Thank God the four mat bearers didn't take no for an answer. Since the crowd prevented them from getting the man to Jesus, they dug an opening in the roof above Jesus and lowered the paralytic man down on the mat he was lying on. Why? They wholeheartedly believed Jesus could and would heal him. They did the unthinkable for this man and then, so did Jesus. In Luke 5:17-20, He shocks everyone in the crowd by first forgiving the man of his sin.

As relayed in 1 Maccabees 9:55, at the time, Jews believed certain sins caused paralysis (NIV) and so the man should still have been unable to walk. They thought only God had the spiritual authority to forgive sins and certainly no human could do that. As a matter of fact, this is the central issue religious leaders ultimately held over Jesus. Luke 22:66–71 elaborates that in their eyes, He claims spiritual authority that is only God's to hold, so they essentially think he's going against God and this will be the justification behind their push to eventually have Jesus crucified.

As the scribes struggle to see past the connection between Jesus' claim to forgive the man and the man's continued state, they raise two challenging questions: "Who is this?" and "Who can forgive sin?" If you were there, unsure of what authority Jesus had, what would help you believe? Hearing Jesus proffer forgiveness that no one but God could see, or actually seeing right in front of you that a man went from paralyzed to walking in one moment? Obviously, the latter, right?

Not only is it miraculous that Jesus simultaneously revived the man's spiritual *and* physical body, but it is also downright astonishing that Jesus instructed the no longer paralyzed man not to leave his mat behind. If this story happened in modern times, when everyone only wants others to see the closest to perfect version of themselves, you better believe that mat would have gone in the trash, never to be seen or heard of again. But Jesus didn't want that. He wanted that mat to serve as a testimony of what he did in response to the man's faith and that of his four mat bearers.

Can you think of any mats in your life that God could use to show off His faithfulness? Are any past sins coming to mind that you've long kept buried out of fear of others' judgment? Can I tell you God doesn't see you through the lens of your mistakes? I used to keep a mental list of what I considered to be my worst offenses. And I would repeat that list to myself every time I was discouraged. Misery loves company, right? But in this waiting season, our gracious God is teaching me that we can't walk in full forgiveness for our past sins until we have the power to share them with trusted others. Think about it. Would you rather be stranded on a deserted island alone or with a tribe of others? Wouldn't hardships be easier to overcome with trustworthy support? And wouldn't others be encouraged to know freedom from their own sin exists?

Ultimately, we're as sick as our secrets. When we hold onto sin as secrets, the enemy still has a hold on us, smothering the mud of guilt all over us repeatedly. We think thoughts like "They don't know what I've done" or "if they knew XYZ about me, they'd be horrified," but once we let those secrets out, they die a fast death. Imagine them as balloons that our Lord immediately deflates for us as soon as we break through our shame of having lived through them. Once we share aloud our sins from a place of triumph instead of regret, we can be washed new as we fall into the loving embrace of our Savior! The remnants of the balloons remain, but only as evidence of God's goodness and what He has helped us to overcome.

It's irrefutable that without the four men who carried him to Jesus, the man on the mat wouldn't have been set free. Psalm 133:1 says, "How good and pleasant it is when God's people live together in unity" (NIV)! There are things we, too, will not be able to bring to the Lord on our own in this life. Let's remember the encouragement in Proverbs 27:9 which says, "Sweet friendships refresh the soul and awaken our hearts with joy, for good friends are like the anointing oil that yields the fragrant incense of God's presence." Walking through any season feels more approachable with others by your side. The dark loses its power.

God Himself exists in community, as Father, Son, and Holy Spirit. Following the example of His Trinity—the perfect community—God designed us to *need* community, too. And yet we dare to regard this as a suggestion instead of an instruction. Romans 12:4-5 tells us we're better together than we are alone (NIV). It can be astoundingly difficult for some of us to commit to community, especially if we're guarded, living dangerously busy lives, or self-preferencing solitude. But God desires integrated living for us—and consistently committing to such is a sign of a mature faith. Notice I didn't say every once in a while committing. I said consistently committing. Like the centenarians in Okinawa, Japan who daily or at least weekly cultivate their lifelong friendship circles called "moais" (mo•eyes). Not pushing community aside whenever the going gets rough.

If you needed to take a particular medication to keep your body functioning, would you push IT aside in tough times? I would hope not! Consider time in fellowship with other believers to be even more important than any medication could ever be. It's so essential to your mental, emotional, and even physical health. Strong social ties have been associated with a lower risk of dementia, as well as lower blood pressure and longer life expectancy.[6]

Are you aware that your character is built from the most dominant traits possessed by those closest to you? Whom you spend your time with in this life is CRITICAL. So, tell me. Do you know four Jesus-loving friends who would bust through a roof to help you catch your healing? Four people with faith even bigger than yours? I want you to go through the rest of this book with a group of people who inspire and challenge you. We'll call them roof busters. Commit to meeting with these roof busters once per week continuously. They'll help change your life. You'll learn from their mistakes, and they'll learn from yours, so you all don't have to make as many. Each of you has treasure on your life that needs to be shared! If you're married, you and your spouse might choose another couple or two to work through the rest of the material in this book with. Otherwise, gendered groups are best. Men busting roofs for men, women busting roofs for women.

If married, you won't want to create any room for your heart to wander into dangerous waters with someone of the opposite sex, no matter what they look like or how unattracted they may be to you or you to them. Just the potential for that to happen can be perceived by our partners as dishonoring, whether anything inappropriate actually occurs or not. Like buying insurance on a rental car even though you're 99% sure you won't get in an accident, you can think of joining your married heart only with same-gendered friends as a wise precaution. Affairs are much more common than you think, and they don't "just happen" as we often hear partners say.

Picture a frog in a pot of cool water. If we gradually increase the temperature of the water, death will sneak up on the frog before it even notices a problem. Making an opposite sex friend a trusted advisor in your life if you're married is like putting yourself in a pot of cool water. It's certainly not risky on the onset but the environment of your heart can change ever so subtly and gradually in ways that eventually can destroy your marital relationship. Jeremiah 17:9 says "The human heart is the most deceitful of all things, and desperately wicked. Who really knows how bad it is" (NIV)? In Matthew 15:19, Jesus Himself adds, "For from the heart come evil thoughts, murder, adultery, all sexual immorality, theft, lying, and slander" (ESV). Need I say more? Don't follow your heart, please. Follow Jesus. If you're married and working through this book solo and even if you're not married and just want to recenter your focus on Jesus, why not do so without the distraction of potential mates? Selecting opposite sex roof busters is not a risk worth taking.

With that said, if four roof busters have already come to your mind, get a hold of them at once and ask them to go through the rest of this book with you! And be sure to tell them you are so thankful for the people like them that God has brought into your life. People who haven't gotten tired of you going through battles. Thank them for their obedience to the heart of the Lord, who wants us to do life together, "carrying one another's burdens" as relayed in Galatians 6:2 (NIV).

On the other hand, maybe you're one of the 61% of young adults that a mental health report from the Harvard Graduate School of Education concluded are experiencing "serious loneliness" and therefore you can't think of who to reach out to.[17] Or maybe you have friends, but you know their faith isn't what it needs to be to sharpen yours. Either way, it's okay! Your four friends can be found in church! After all, the church is God's primary instrument of salvation! Try praying these words aloud:

Lord, I know I'm not meant to walk in this world without solid Godly friendships. Help me break the stronghold of inadequacy off of my life. Help me to stop feeling inferior to other believers and to see myself just as important and complete as you see me. As Your Word says in Psalm 101:6, I will search for faithful people to be my companions (ESV)! I want to be like Jesus, who modeled intimate friendship with His disciples. Reveal to me the new friends you desire for me. Friends who fit all the criteria David outlines in Psalm 101 as he too looks for faithful friends, seeking Your ways. In your name I pray. Amen!

Now, a Godly friend is a Godly friend, but a Godly friend sharing similar circumstances with you is a double blessing! Don't withhold the areas of your life in greatest need of decluttering as identified in the first stride. If you're planning to get married, don't shy away from asking new friends if they're in serious relationships also. Or if you're already married, you'll want to know if new friends are married. If you're a parent, ask if they're a parent. I'm not saying this to disqualify anyone who does not share these commonalities with you, but do be aware of them because they can certainly help speed up the bonding process!

How quickly you choose your four roof busters really depends on your eagerness. If you want to start this study immediately, then, the next time you attend a church service, ask the Lord to guide you to the right four believers, or one to start, and you can ask that one to invite three others! It is that simple! Alternatively, you could ask one believer to join your study each time you attend church. If you attend church twice a week, your mission will be accomplished in two weeks! If you attend church once a week, then after one month, you'll be ready to go! However it happens, if you're leaning on the Lord for guidance, He won't lead you astray!

Don't pay any mind to the devil when he attempts to convince you that no one wants to befriend you. If someone declines your invitation to the study for whatever reason, declare 2 Chronicles 15:7 to yourself: "Be strong and do not give up, for your work will be rewarded" (ESV). Be equally encouraged by Isaiah

41:10-13: GOD'S Hand is not upon you to push you down but to lift you up (NIV)! God is for you, NOT against you! Don't forget that he intends for YOU to make half of any friendship! So, you will want to be the same light to your newfound friends as they are to you! As they pray and fight for you, be sure you pray and fight for them, too! Psalm 145:18 promises, "The Lord is near to all who call on him, to all who call on him in truth." When we remain in Him, we amplify the power of prayer!

Life Application Challenge 2: Start meeting at least once per week with four or more Jesus loving roof busters with faith even bigger than yours. Go through the rest of the strides together, preferably one per week. Don't stop! Ecclesiastes 4:9-12 reminds us: "Two are better than one, because they have a good return for their labor. If either of them falls down, one can help the other up...Though one may be overpowered, two can defend themselves." Once you finish this book, turn your meetings into a weekly Bible study!

<u>Lyrics to Amanda's Pick: "Different" by Micah Taylor</u>

Again self-chosen, this time because it proves that a comfort zone is a beautiful place, but nothing ever grows there. Let us live out Romans 12:12 as we rejoice in hope, remain patient in tribulation, and persist constantly in prayer (NLT).

I don't wanna hear anymore, teach me to listen
I don't wanna see anymore, give me a vision
That you could move this heart, to be set apart
I don't need to recognize, the man in the mirror
And I don't wanna trade Your plan, for something familiar
I can't waste a day, I can't stay the same
I wanna be different
I wanna be changed
'Til all of me is gone
And all that remains
Is a fire so bright
The whole world can see
That there's something different
So come and be different
In me
And I don't wanna spend my life, stuck in a pattern
And I don't wanna gain this world but lose what matters
And so I'm giving up, everything because
I wanna be different
I wanna be changed
'Til all of me is gone
And all that remains
Is a fire so bright
The whole world can see
That there's something different
So come and be different, oh
I know that I am far from perfect
But through You, the cross still says I'm worth it

So take this beating in my heart and

Peace before Increase

Come and finish what You started
When they see me, let them see You
'Cause I just wanna be different, yeah
I wanna be different
I wanna be changed
'Til all of me is gone
And all that remains
Ooh, is a fire so bright
The whole world can see
That there's something different
So come and be different
I just wanna be different
So could You be different
In me

<u>Stride 3: Exercise</u>

Genesis 22:1-18

Abraham Tested

Some time later God tested Abraham. He said to him, "Abraham!"

"Here I am," he replied.

Then God said, "Take your son, your only son, whom you love—Isaac—and go to the region of Moriah. Sacrifice him there as a burnt offering on a mountain I will show you."

Early the next morning Abraham got up and loaded his donkey. He took with him two of his servants and his son Isaac. When he had cut enough wood for the burnt offering, he set out for the place God had told him about. On the third day, Abraham looked up and saw the place in the distance. He said to his servants, "Stay here with the donkey while I and the boy go over there. We will worship and then we will come back to you."

Abraham took the wood for the burnt offering and placed it on his son Isaac, and he himself carried the fire and the knife. As the two of them went on together, Isaac spoke up and said to his father Abraham, "Father?"

"Yes, my son?" Abraham replied.

"The fire and wood are here," Isaac said, "but where is the lamb for the burnt offering?"

Abraham answered, "God himself will provide the lamb for the burnt offering, my son." And the two of them went on together.

When they reached the place God had told him about, Abraham built an altar there and arranged the wood on it. He bound his son Isaac and laid him on the altar, on top of the wood. Then he reached out his hand and took the knife to slay his son. But the angel of the LORD called out to him from heaven, "Abraham! Abraham!"

"Here I am," he replied.

"Do not lay a hand on the boy," he said. "Do not do anything to him. Now I know that you fear God, because you have not withheld from me your son, your only son."

Abraham looked up and there in a thicket, he saw a ram caught by its horns. He went over and took the ram and sacrificed it as a burnt offering instead of his son. So Abraham called that place The LORD Will Provide. And to this day it is said, "On the mountain of the LORD it will be provided."

The angel of the LORD called to Abraham from heaven a second time and said, "I swear by myself, declares the LORD, that because you have done this and have not withheld your son, your only son, I will surely bless you and make your descendants as numerous as the stars in the sky and as the sand on the seashore. Your descendants will take possession of the cities of their enemies, and through your offspring all nations on earth will be blessed, because you have obeyed me" (NLT).

What faith Abraham proved he had when he obeyed God's commandment to sacrifice he and his wife Sarah's first and only son together, Isaac, whom Sarah waited until age ninety to finally have! When Abraham demonstrated his devotion, the Lord spared Isaac and provided a ram stuck in some shrubs as a sacrifice instead—as conveyed in Leviticus 4:35 and 5:10 of the Old Testament, God required animal sacrifices to temporarily cover sins and to foreshadow the eventual complete, perfect, and final sacrifice of Jesus Christ. Before this ultimate final sacrifice, Hebrews 9:22 tells us, "Without the shedding of blood there [was] no forgiveness" (NIV). The Lord then confirmed the covenant He had previously made with Abraham—the promise of land, the promise of descendants, the promise of blessing and redemption. (Shout out to fellow Classical Conversations families who memorize that covenant for Cycle 1/Week 7 of the Bible memory work.)

God wants our whole hearts. Not pieces that aren't already devoted to other people and things. He doesn't want His followers to see Him as a hobby, He wants us to see Him as everything. And therefore, He wants us to be *willing* to sacrifice everything to follow Him. If you think about it, submitting our *will* to the Lord is the only unique thing we really have to offer Him because anything else we think we "give" to Him is something He has already loaned or given to us.

Alas, this brings me to stride three. When you spend intimate time with the Lord in prayer, worship, and His Word, are you all in like Abraham? Are you approaching Him with such devotion, coherence, and reverence that you can honestly say you surrender all? Do you find that you have a threshold that must be met before you are finally willing to let go? Or other resources that must be exhausted before you'll face your Heavenly Father?

If you're tired of being tired as you take mundane trips through Scripture apps, praise playlists, or the same ol' same ol' prayer routines, stride three is for you: EXERCISE! Would you believe me if I told you your physical posture reflects your state of mind? Consider how you are sitting right this moment, as you and your fellow roof busters have plunged into reading this book. Are you slouching? Are your shoulders hunched over? Is your chest caving in? Is your chin up, or down? How straight is your spine? Your answers to these questions are an excellent reflection of the condition of your soul. George Müller once explained it this way:

> The first great and primary business to which I ought to attend every day was, to have my soul happy in the Lord. The first thing to be concerned about was not, how much I might serve the Lord, how I might glorify the Lord; but how I might get my soul into a happy state, and how my inner man may be nourished.[5]

Getting your soul happy in Christ doesn't happen as easily as snapping your fingers. I wish it did. You're going to have to be intentional. Like all believers past and present, you have to learn to make a fresh choice daily to pick up your cross and die to self. One way I've learned during this season of waiting to give the Lord His rightful place in my life is how I spend the first moments after my alarm clock goes off. As I first wake up each morning, I thank God for the gift of a new day and I ask Him to fill me with His Holy Spirit so I don't waste it. Next to my bed I keep two jars: one called "fruits in waiting" and one called "fruits in use." Before I stand to my feet for each new day, I pull out a slip of paper with one of the fruits of the spirits as relayed in Galatians 5:22-23 and declare it over myself, my husband, and each of our children. I also name the opposite of the selected fruit in order to declare what I desire none of us to be plagued with that day. Here is what each slip of paper says:

1. God, I receive your love, and release my insecurity.
2. God, I receive your joy, and release my unhappiness.
3. God, I receive your peace, and release my stress.
4. God, I receive your patience, and release my impulsiveness.
5. God, I receive your kindness, and release my inconsideration.
6. God, I receive your goodness, and release my control.
7. God, I receive your faithfulness, and release my disloyalty.
8. God, I receive your gentleness, and release my inflexibility.
9. God, I receive your self-control, and release my sinful nature.

This never fails. The fruit of the Spirit I pull sets just the right tone for my day. And once my "fruits in waiting" jar is emptied, the jars trade places so the pattern can continue. I keep the movement of the papers from left jar to right jar, so I never lose my place. I've also done this with different Scriptures, prayer templates, declarations, etc. I'm now constantly changing things up to keep my soul happy, not stagnant, in Christ. Plus, I find writing on the slips of paper to be therapeutic. It stretches my faith. Whereas when I rely on beginning my day by rote, I run the risk of my prayer life becoming meaningless repetition.

After this, I invite the Holy Spirit to anoint my feet as I apply pure olive oil mixed with an essential oil scent I enjoy—right now cinnamon as cited in the recipe God gave to Moses in Exodus 30:22-24 (NIV). My husband and I learned we can make these oils ourselves and keep them on hand in roll-on vials that cost under $10 on Amazon, so we can bless others with them too, as God prompts.

To the ancient Israelite, there was no oil or fat with more token meaning than olive oil. It was used as a moisturizer, a fuel for lighting lamps, for nutrition, and for countless other purposes. Scented olive oil was chosen to be a holy anointing oil for the Israelites. In Exodus 27:20, the Word says, "You shall charge the sons of Israel, that they bring you clear oil of beaten olives for the light, to make a lamp burn continually" (ESV). I want to burn continually for the Lord, for my whole body to be filled with light as referenced in Matthew 6:22-23 (NLT), but I must choose to ignite that light daily and this is how I do so. As needed, I'll ask the Holy Spirit to anoint other parts of my body that I use most to sin. (Come up with your own too!) This is not an exhaustive list; all Scriptures are from the NIV:

- My knees, so the Holy Spirit can anoint my humility as I serve Him. With my knees I will worship and bow down, I will kneel before the Lord, my Maker, as He is named in Psalm 95:6.

- My belly, so the Holy Spirit can anoint my gut with discernment and my soul with strength. I trust in the LORD with all my heart, and I do not lean on my own understanding. In all my ways I acknowledge Him, and He will make straight my paths as avouched in Proverbs 3:5-6.

- The top and bottom of my hands, so the Holy Spirit can anoint my work ethic and empower me to be a helper to my family and to others. I desire to lay these elder hands of mine on all who need to be reminded not to neglect their gifts as instructed in 1 Timothy 4:14. I need God to equip me to practice what I preach to my children daily: "Hands are for helping, not for hurting!"

- My heart, so the Holy Spirit can anoint my emotions with victory over any wounds that may not show up on an x-ray but can show up at any moment in my sinful nature if not resolved. I know from Proverbs 14:30 that my heart at peace gives life to my whole body, but envy rots the bones.

- My chin, right under my mouth, so the Holy Spirit can anoint the words I speak to build others up, not to destroy. I'll embody Proverbs 13:3, by being careful with what I say and thus protecting my life. A careless talker not only destroys others, he destroys himself.

- My cheeks, under my eyes, so the Holy Spirit can anoint my sight to be void of filthy scenes or traumatic memories while fully hearkening value in others as well as appreciation of God's inexplicable miracles all around me. I will see more right than wrong in people. Following the example set in Matthew 7:3, I won't look at the speck that is in another's eye, but not notice the log that is in my own eye.

- My ears, so the Holy Spirit can anoint my hearing to be sincere and receptive. For Proverbs 18:15 proclaims that the ear of the wise seeks knowledge.

- My forehead, so the Holy Spirit can anoint my mind's choices and visions, as detailed in Ezekiel 3:9. I trust God to make my forehead like the hardest stone, harder than flint. I am strong! I am not afraid of my enemies.

- My head, so the Holy Spirit can anoint my brain with healing, memory, and proper regulation of my body as God designed. God is the lifter up of my head. He delivers me from being consumed with myself and my troubles. He delivers me from being my own god. He lifts up my head so that, by faith, I can see HIM. As His Word says in Psalm 3:3, the Lord put His Spirit in me so that I desire to serve others.

Let's face it: for many of us seeing is believing. As

instinctively visual creatures, seeing these acts of receiving God's anointing by faith stops us from hindering it and makes us more likely to let it flow. It chips away our sinful desire to be in control and enhances our dependence on the Lord, ultimately teaching us to believe from rest. Believing from rest doesn't mean from ease. We still have legwork.

Rest is trusting that God's got this, even if we mess up every. single. day. Our souls are His to cultivate! I am finding that to take so much pressure off of me. I'm not the source. My job is not the source. My marriage is not the source. My children are not the source. GOD IS THE SOURCE. Everything else is a resource He aligns for our good. My friend, our Heavenly father is so worthy of our trust. He just IS. And aren't we glad He IS the same yesterday, today, and forever, as Hebrews 13:8 reminds us (NLT).

Seeking the Holy Spirit to anoint my feet is a daily commitment I've devoted myself to. It keeps me grounded literally, figuratively, and spiritually. I use it as my quick chance to voice to the Lord all the things I have planned for the day so He can grant me the grace to endure them. I tell Him that I want to walk with courage in His ways and on His paths. The other anointing examples shared above, I only use situationally, as needed.

As a mom of five, I know how quickly the day fills, and I am by no means suggesting that God requires you to have a full-on deliverance service every time you wake up to a new day. He loves you and takes you as you are. Start small. Don't burn out. My declaration of one of the fruits of the Spirit and my invitation for Him to anoint my feet are two quick popcorn prayers that rarely take me more than a minute. I primarily do this to ensure the prefrontal cortex of my brain is focused on the Lord—and nothing else—as I begin my day. Despairingly, I began forming this habit after taking an inventory of my spiritual weapons and using them to fight off the tears I was waking up with as I worried about securing another contract from my employer in the future.

Once I've received the Holy Spirit's anointing of my feet, it's GO TIME! Through much trial and error throughout this gifted wait, I've learned the surefire way to receive from the Lord is to get the body warmed up! Just like any athlete practices before the big game, prayer warriors should get moving before spending time with the Lord. The way to ready your mind and heart for the intake of Scripture is to WAKE UP!

Maybe you've tried the usual "devo" routine. You might have an app you like to read sprinkles of Scripture from, although if you're honest, no matter how beautifully woven together the words are, you spend about as much time reflecting on them as you do brushing your teeth. I don't want that for you! YOU shouldn't want that for you! Since you presumably have some available time now (you're reading this book, aren't you?), let's give it a whirl.

Go outside to love on your body. Do it! Do it now. For other days ahead, you can be more proactive. You can set out your tennis shoes/socks/water bottle where you see them. If it's out of sight, it's out of mind, right? But if it's in sight, it's in mind. So merely taking a small step of preparing ahead like this, yields results. For now though, I say just GO. Don't regard the time, agenda, or to do list. This is vital! If you've little ones and they're awake, bring them too. There's a million and one devices out there for them to sit in for a bit. A blanket and a bowl of flour works wonders too. Pick an exercise you can do for ten minutes and ACTUALLY DO IT. Not just because it's good for you physically, but even more importantly because of the benefits this will give you spiritually. I suspect after you experience the blessing this is, you'll want to do more than ten minutes, but ten minutes is plenty enough!

As my kids and I always chant when it's "PE time" during our homeschool day, exercising makes you alive, alert, awake, and enthusiastic! It helps elevate your state of being. The better you feel physically, the better you'll experience your spiritual life and sense of well-being! Not only does "exercise promote the production of neurotrophins, leading to greater brain plasticity, and therefore, better memory and learning, [but also] on top of neurotrophins, exercise results in an increase in neurotransmitters in the brain, specifically serotonin and norepinephrine, which boost information processing and attitude."[49] Translation: God designed exercise to be just as good for your brain as it is for your body!

When you exercise, your decision making sharpens and your daily life becomes so much more manageable! It's easier to walk up and down stairs, carry groceries, keep up with the younger ones, lift things, or take on whatever curveballs come your way without losing control over your emotions. Regular exercise increases the number of tiny blood vessels that bring oxygen-rich blood to the region of the brain that is responsible for thought! Likewise, regular exercise increases the connections between brain cells (synapses) and spearheads the expeditious development of new nerve cells. Ultimately, this results in brains that are more adaptive, efficient, and plastic, which spawn better performance as we age! Exercise also improves cholesterol levels, aids in blood sugar balance, lowers blood pressure, and reduces mental stress, all of which can help your brain AND your heart.[15]

But don't just take my word for it. In Romans 12:1 Paul validates the push to take care of our bodies when he avows: "Therefore, I urge you, brothers and sisters, in view of God's mercy, to offer your bodies as a living sacrifice, holy, and pleasing to God—this is your true and proper worship" (NIV). Torturing yourself to slim down for an event or trip is the wrong aim. Change your perspective. See that exercising is an act of worship, a way that we strive for holiness. God wants us to surrender every part of ourselves–body, soul, heart, and mind into His loving hands.

For your ten minutes, you can try walking, marching in place, throwing some alternating punches, back squats, cossack squats, jumping jacks, mountain climbers, burpees, lunges; it doesn't matter what you do. Just pick one exercise and stick with it for ten minutes, or, if you're not the timer type, play 3-5 songs from Christian artists that get you PUMPED like Disciple, Pillar, Phinehas, August Burns Red, Social Club Misfits, Aha Gazelle, or any of the 116 rappers! I strive to make sure whatever I listen to glorifies God, not because I'm uptight or overly religious but because I know I'm vulnerable.

The old adage "You are what you eat" should more appropriately be "You are what you hear." Music is one of a few things on this earth that gets in our minds with or without our permission. That's why sometimes you catch yourself singing a song you were only exposed to for a brief moment. It's also why some songs you heard when you were a young child, you still know as an adult. As parents, my husband and I have always found music selection to be hugely important. I often credit Christian hip-hop with helping us raise our oldest son who is now fifteen. Unlike the trash music that shaped my character growing up, from Christian hip-hop, Adam has learned God's grace, respect, gratitude for life, integrity, drive, and grit.

Dr. Vanita Rahman—clinic director of a nonprofit organization that promotes preventive medicine—asseverates that exercising for at least ten minutes each day slows the effects of aging and muscle loss, and benefits "virtually every organ system in our body. It helps us sleep better and improve our mood, sense of well-being, and quality of life."[6] Rahman further reports that if adults ages 40 to 85 would engage in just ten minutes of moderate to vigorous physical activity a day, it would prevent 110,000 deaths a year! If the same groups increased their exercise by twenty minutes, it could save 209,459 lives, and thirty minutes of daily exercise could ward off 272,297 deaths.[6] Just don't obsess over the recommended thirty minutes. Often the thought of dedicating that much time to exercise is why people forgo any exercise at all. Ten minutes a day may seem small, but over the course of a whole year, it adds up to many hours of exercise!

Most significant of all, exerting energy for ten minutes incomparably improves your oxygen uptake, thus heightening your cognitive focus before receiving the Word of God, hard truths and all. When you're done exercising, dedicate two minutes to preparing to enter God's presence with an authentically happy soul. Stand confidently with your hands on your hips like a superhero for this part. Puff your chest out and lift your head up, keep your feet apart, and say cheese! That's right. I want you to *smile* for the whole two minutes so play a short song or set a two-minute timer. Stick a pencil in your mouth to force the smile if you must. Smiling—even fake smiling—has a positive impact on mood.[51] Essentially, triggering certain facial muscles by smiling "tricks" your brain into thinking you're untroubled, even when you are!

Smiling for two minutes straight while standing in this superhero pose will help your body release cortisol and endorphins that provide numerous health ameliorations, including improved blood circulation, boosted immunity against diseases, increased endurance, reduced pain, reduced stress, a prolonged life.[54] The more you do this, the easier it gets, I promise. Over time, you'll learn you have a lot of reasons to naturally smile. ;-)

Life Application Challenge 3: *Get outside and do any exercise you choose for just ten minutes a day, and spend two minutes a day in your most confident superhero pose, smiling. Proverbs 15:13 says "A glad heart makes a happy face."*

Lyrics to Husseim's Pick: "Champion" by Dante Bowe

Peace before Increase

My heroic husband Husseim resembles Christ in character and conduct. In the blink of an eye, he'll oil a lock or adjust AC piping entirely on his own, without complaint, even if he's fighting inexplicable pain. Watching Husseim triumphantly persevere through his health battles reminds me that the less we see ourselves as separate from God, the more we'll be amazed! In the book of John, some disciples reported that more people were beginning to seek Jesus for baptism rather than John the Baptist, who preceded Jesus' arrival to earth by about six months. John is unscathed by this news. In John 3:30, he humbly replies, "He must become greater; I must become less" (NIV). Our purpose in this life is to exalt Christ, not ourselves.

I've tried so hard to see it
Took me so long to believe it
That You'd choose someone like me
To carry Your victory

Perfection could never earn it
You give what we don't deserve and
You take the broken things
And raise them to glory

You are my champion
Giants fall when You stand Undefeated
Every battle You've won

With the One who has conquered it all
I know who I am, because I know whose I am, Hallelujah
There's nothing left to prove
There's nothing left to prove
He freely gave it to us
Rejoice, rejoice, rejoice
Freely He gave
When I-, come on sing

When I lift up my voice and shout (come on)
Every wall comes crashing down
I have the authority (Jesus

I am who You say I am
You crown me with
confidence
I am seated
Undefeated
With the One who has
conquered it
all, It all, it all, it all, it all

When I lift my voice and shout
Every wall comes crashing
down
I have the authority
Jesus has given me

When I open up my mouth
Miracles start breaking out
I have the authority
Jesus has given me

When I lift my voice and shout
Every wall comes crashing
down
I have the authority (yes, I do)
Jesus has given me
When I open up my mouth
Miracles start breaking out
I have the authority
Jesus has given me

You are my champion
Giants fall when You stand
Undefeated
Every battle You've won

has)
Jesus has given me
When I open up my mouth
Miracles start breaking out (it
starts to break out)
I have the authority
Jesus has given me (2X)

You are my champion
(Sing it out, come on, giants)
Giants fall when You stand
Undefeated

Every battle You've won (I am)
I am who You say I am
You crown me with confidence
I am seated
In the Heavenly place
Undefeated (by the power,
come on)
By the power of Your name
I am seated (in Heaven)
In the Heavenly place
Undefeated
With the One who has
conquered it all

In the Heavenly place
Undefeated
With the One who has
conquered it all

Now I can finally see it
You're teaching me how to
receive it
So let all the striving cease,
oh

Peace before Increase

I am who You say I am
You crown me with
confidence
I am seated
In the Heavenly place
Undefeated
By the power of Your name
I am seated in the Heavenly
place
Undefeated

This is my victory

You are my champion
Giants fall when You stand
Undefeated
Every battle You've won

I am who You say I am
You crown me with
confidence
I am seated
In the Heavenly place

<u>Stride 4: BIBLE!</u>

Acts 8:26-39

Philip and the Ethiopian

Now an angel of the Lord said to Philip [one of the twelve apostles He specifically chose to spread the Gospel], "Go south to the road—the desert road—that goes down from Jerusalem to Gaza." So he started out, and on his way he met an Ethiopian eunuch [castrated man placed in charge over a king's harem of wives and concubines], an important official in charge of all the treasury of the Kandake (which means "queen of the Ethiopians"). This man had gone to Jerusalem to worship, and on his way home was sitting in his chariot reading the Book of Isaiah the prophet. The Spirit told Philip, "Go to that chariot and stay near it."

Then Philip ran up to the chariot and heard the man reading Isaiah the prophet. "Do you understand what you are reading?" Philip asked.

"How can I," he said, "unless someone explains it to me?" So he invited Philip to come up and sit with him.

This is the passage of Scripture the eunuch was reading:

"He was led like a sheep to the slaughter, and as a lamb before its shearer is silent, so he did not open his mouth.

In his humiliation he was deprived of justice. Who can speak of his descendants? For his life was taken from the earth."

The eunuch asked Philip, "Tell me, please, who is the prophet talking about, himself or someone else?" Then Philip began with that very passage of Scripture and told him the good news about Jesus.

As they traveled along the road, they came to some water and the eunuch said, "Look, here is water. What can stand in the way of my being baptized?" And he gave orders to stop the chariot. Then both Philip and the eunuch went down into the water and Philip baptized him. When they came up out of the water, the Spirit of the Lord suddenly took Philip away, and the eunuch did not see him again, but went on his way rejoicing (NLT).

I'm not a betting woman, but I'm reasonably certain that you'd be hesitant to act if you came across a stranger reading the Bible and the Holy Spirit convicted you to assess that stranger's understanding of it. Heck, you'd probably be pleased enough to see a person reading the Bible in public! In this story, God reveals there is more to the Bible than just our reading of it. It has to be understood to produce change in us. Once the apostle Philip explains to the Ethiopian who Jesus is and what He did for us, he's sold! He immediately wants to be born again! And then Philip, whose mission is now complete, vanishes into thin air!

God wants us to have the same miraculous encounters with Him as Philip and the Ethiopian. He'll meet our faith wherever it is! In Matthew 9:29, Jesus says, "You will have what your faith expects" (TPT)! But this is more than a choice. Like the Ethiopian, once you decide to go all in with Jesus, you must follow up with action. Jeremiah 29:13-14 says we are to seek Him and we can find Him when we seek Him with all our heart. "I will be found by you," declares the Lord (NIV). That's a promise!

In his book, *Science Speaks*, Peter W. Stoner takes curiosity about the promises of God to a whole new level. He outlines the mathematical likelihood of one person in the first century coincidentally fulfilling just eight of the most easily digested prophecies rendered in God's Word. Mind you, he points out that about one third of the Bible is made up of prophecies, and in the Old Testament alone there are roughly 332 prophecies which Jesus fulfilled. The scientific material he presented with his mathematical analysis is described by other scientists in the forward of his book to be "conservative," "dependable," "accurate," and "thoroughly sound."[7]

In *Evidence That Demands a Verdict*, Josh and Sean McDowell share this quote from Professor Stoner: "We find that the chance that any man might have lived down to the present time and fulfilled all eight prophecies is 1 to the 17th power (1 in 100,000,000,000,000,000)."[8]

I don't even know how to say that number. For comparison, they add that in October of 2018 the Mega Millions had a $1.6 billion jackpot, and the odds of winning that were merely 1 in 302,575,350. It's probable that your jaw is dropping as much as mine did when I first learned about this and the existence of the Dead Sea Scrolls—pre-Bible prophesies about Jesus that were fulfilled despite being written one hundred years prior to His birth. And that's not all: the likelihood Stoner calculated of one person fulfilling 48 prophecies would be 1 in 10 to the 157th power. It would take a whole page for me to type that many zeroes! If this doesn't arouse your belief in God's Word, I don't know what will!

Amid the gift of this waiting season, my family and I have adopted the mantra: "A Bible story a day keeps the devil away." Bible study does NOT have to be complicated, as we've learned in a weekly "Soup & Story" we were invited to by angels on earth Nathan and Melinda Bell—a fellow homeschooling couple whose path crossed ours during the waiting. The Bells taught us to prayerfully pick a Bible story, read it twice, retell it without looking at it, and then answer three simple, yet lifechanging questions: 1.) What does the story teach us about God? 2.) What does the story teach us about man/ourselves? And 3.) How can we apply what we've learned to our daily walk?

We've been so impacted by this manageable approach to Bible study, that we've begun replicating it in our own weekly "Soup & Story" in our home, and like a domino effect, many of our friends have been inspired to do the same. God's Word is spreading like a wildfire! On the pages that follow, I'll share our favorite single-sitting Bible stories that we have used so far for family or "Soup & Story" Bible study. The stories come from both testaments, and are listed in no particular order:

- Mark 4:1-20 (The four soils)
- Luke 12:13-21 (Is the rich man a fool?)
- Ezekiel 37 (Dry Bones)
- Judges 3:12-31 (Ehud and Shamgar)
- Acts 12:1-19 (Peter's Miraculous Escape from Prison)
- Mark 11:1-11 (Jesus rides into Jerusalem)
- Luke 2:1-38 (Jesus' birth and revelation to the shepherds)
- Mark 2:1-12 (Jesus heals a paralyzed man)
- Acts 12:1-17 (God releases Peter from prison)
- Matthew 2:1-18 (Harod and the wise men)
- Luke 8:40-56 (Jesus raises Jairus's daughter)
- Mark 12:41-44 (Jesus and the widow's offer)
- Luke 19:1-10 (Jesus and Zacchaeus' offer)
- Mark 15:1-15 (Jesus before Pilate)
- 1 Kings 21 (Elijah, Ahab, and Naboth's vineyard)
- Mark 4:35-41 (Jesus calms the storm)
- 2 Kings 5:1-17 (Elisha and Naaman)
- Esther 2-7 (Esther the queen)
- Judges 6:1-16 (Gideon and the Midianites)
- Genesis 25; 27; 32; 33 (Jacob and Esau)
- Exodus 2:11-23 (Jethro and the Midianite)
- Mark 15:16-23 (Jesus carries His cross)
- Jonah chapters 1 and 2 (Jonah and the big fish)
- Mark 5:25-34 (Jesus cures a sick woman)
- Genesis 37:18-36 (Joseph and his brothers)
- Ruth chapters 1 and 2 (Ruth and Naomi)
- Genesis 41:1-44 (Joseph and Pharaoh's dreams)
- Luke 17:11-19 (Jesus and the lepers)
- Acts 8:26-39 (Philip talks to the Ethiopian)
- Genesis 6:13-9:29 (Noah and the ark)
- Exodus 17:1-7 (Moses and the miracle water)
- Genesis 22 (Abraham tested)
- Luke 18:1-8 (Widow and the unjust judge)
- Jeremiah 38 (Jeremiah and Zedekiah)

- o 2 Samuel 6:3–8 (Uzzah killed for disobedience)
- o Mark 12:13-17 (Jesus and the Roman tax)
- o Exodus 1 (Midwives Shiphrah and Puah)
- o Acts 28:15-24 (Paul's disappearance)
- o Luke 15:11-32 (The prodigal son)
- o 2 Samuel 5:1-9 (King David captures Jerusalem
- o Acts 13:4-12 (Paul and Elymas)
- o Mark 10:17-23 (Jesus and the rich young man)
- o Acts 27 (Paul and the shipwreck)
- o Luke 4:14-24 (Jesus speaks in Nazareth)
- o Acts 14:8-20 (Paul and Barnabas)
- o John 13:2-15 (Jesus washes the disciples' feet)
- o Luke 3:1-16 (John the Baptist)
- o Acts 4:1-22 (Peter and John heal a lame man)
- o Acts 4:32-37 (Barnabas)
- o 1 Samuel 18:6-11; 19:9-18 (Michal's rescue of David from King Saul)
- o Acts 24:27-25:12 (Paul appears to Caesar)
- o Exodus 2:1-15 (Moses and the Egyptian slave master)
- o Acts 17:1-10 (Paul escapes from the mob)
- o 2 Corinthians 11:32-33 (Paul escapes in a basket)
- o Acts 25:13-26:29 (Paul speaks to Agrippa)
- o Acts 16:16-36 (Paul, Silas, and the earthquake)
- o Luke 24:13-43 (Jesus seen on the road)
- o Mark 11:15-17 (Jesus and the money lenders)
- o Acts 10:9-28 (Peter's friendship with Cornelius)
- o Judges 15 (Fox Arson)
- o Matthew 13:1-9 (The parable of the sower)
- o Judges 16:4-30 (Samson Delilah)
- o Luke 15:11-32 (The parable of the prodigal son)
- o 2 Samuel 21 (Goliath's Son killed by David's Brother)
- o Mark 29-46 (The last supper and Jesus' arrest)
- o Luke 5:5-11 (The miraculous catch of fish)
- o Exodus 18:13-27 (Advice from an In-Law)

- o Numbers 16 (Korah)
- o John 12:9-11 (Lazarus' Unwanted Attention)
- o 2 Samuel 9 (Mepiboshet)
- o Mark 12:1-9 (The parable of the tenants in the vineyard)
- o Luke 10:30-37 (The parable of the good samaritan)
- o 1 Samuel 25 (Stingy Nabal)
- o 2 Kings 4:42-44 (One hundred men fed)
- o Matthew 18:10-14 (The parable of the lost sheep)
- o Acts 8:4-23 (Philip and Simon the sorcerer)
- o Exodus chapters 8-14 (Moses and the Exodus)
- o Acts 9:1-18 (Saul on the road to Damascus)
- o Mark 15-24-37 (The crucifixion)
- o Acts 2:1-21 (The first Pentecost)
- o Matthew 7:24-29 (The house built on rock)
- o Luke 24:1-31 (Jesus resurrected)
- o Matthew 26:17-30 (The last supper)
- o Joshua 2 (Rahab)
- o Judges 5 (Jael and the peg)
- o Isaiah 6 (Isaiah's Vision of the Lord)
- o Luke 2:41-52 (Jesus in the temple as a boy)
- o Matthew 10:5-20 (Instructions for service)
- o John 5:1-17 (Lame man healed)
- o Numbers (Quail before plague)
- o Daniel 3:1-27 (Shadrach and the furnace)
- o John 6:1-15 (Jesus feeds the five thousand)
- o Exodus 20:1-17 (Moses and the ten commandments)
- o 1 Samuel chapters 9 and 10:1-16 (Samuel annoys Saul)
- o Exodus 16:11-26 (The desert trek and mana from Heaven)
- o Mark 8:22-26 (Jesus heals a blind man)
- o 1 Samuel 1:1-28; 3:1-19 (Boy Samuel and Eli)
- o John 4:46-54 (Jesus heals official's son)
- o Mark 10:35-45 (James/John want to be with Jesus)
- o Mark 10:46-52 (Jesus gives Bartimaeus Sight)

- o 1 Samuel 18:5-9 (David and Jonathan)
- o 2 Samuel chapters 4 and 9 (David and Mephibosheth)
- o 1 Kings 3:16-28 (Solomon's wisdom with a baby)
- o 2 Samuel 23:13-17 (David and three soldiers)
- o Acts 2 (Pentecost)
- o 1 Samuel 26 (David spares Saul's life)
- o Luke 16:1-13 (The Shrewd Manager)
- o 1 Samuel 17:1-51 (David and Goliath)
- o Acts 19:11-41 (Riot of Silversmiths)
- o 2 Kings 4:1-7 (The woman with olive oil)
- o Daniel 6:1-24 (Daniel and the Lions' Den)
- o 1 Samuel 16:14-23 (David the Musician and King Saul)
- o 2 Kings 2 (God's Power through Elijah)
- o 1 Kings 16-39 (Elijah and the Prophets of Baal)
- o Exodus 4:24-26 (Circumcision of Moses)
- o 1 Kings 17:1-16 (Elijah and the poor widow)
- o 2 Kings 61-7 (Elisha and the floating ax head)
- o Luke 36-50 (Jesus anointed by a sinful woman)
- o 1 Kings 13 (Deceptive Prophet)
- o Matthew 25 (10 virgins parable)
- o Amos 7:10-27 (Amos speaks out)
- o 2 Samuel 14 (A Woman's Gift the Speak)
- o Genesis 38 (Tamar)
- o Acts 36-42 (Peter prays Tabitha back to life)
- o Luke 5:18-25 (Man on a mat healed)
- o Genesis 18:1-15 (Abraham and three strangers)

It is easiest to incorporate a new habit into your routine by attaching it to something you already consistently do, such as dinner time, laundry time, bath time, as soon as you walk in the house at the end of the day, etc. As I often tell my students, first we read to enjoy, then we read to destroy (meaning to pick apart/gather meaning). According to Srinivas Rao, who runs the Unmistakable Creative Podcast, reading something twice, as the Bells have demonstrated, helps to remember more information, miss what we learned the first time around, actually take action on the information we read, and have the information last. [9]

(AFTER EXERCISING), consider reading a Bible story solo, between you and God, and then at dinner or sometime before bed, you could gather your people to read the story again with them. When you return to it, it'll feel like treading a path you've already walked. You'll be like a tour guide leading your people through God's truth and in my experience, Bible time is less likely to be skipped because of this. When we stay ready, we don't have to get ready. When we have to get ready, we look less forward to this time in God's Word, perceiving it as one more thing on the to do list.

Daily I pray for a radical increase in Bible consumption among others in waiting, and that the Holy Spirit will point those in waiting to just the right words that their souls need to hear. Another meaningful way to interact with the Word as I learned from Celebration Church in my hometown of Clovis, California is CEPS which stands for Claim, Example, Promise, Sin. In question form, these four thought generators become: What command should you obey? What example should you follow? What promise should you claim? What sin should you avoid?

Peace before Increase

In the long run, you do you for Stride Four. Read it, watch it, hear it, experience it, just get the Bible in you! As 1 Colossians 17 so beautifully attests, God's Word must be before all things, for IN Him, all things are held together (NLT)! It wasn't until the beauteous waiting that I'm presently in that I started seeing the Bible as sustenance. I never understood the full weight of others calling it that until now. We need God's Word in us even more than food! So my encouragement to you is to get the Word in your system by whatever means possible!

We live in a time when absorbing the Word of God is easier than ever! You can listen to it by downloading a free audio Bible app, and you can watch Bible stories acted out in many free apps too. When reading it yourself, please read a version you understand. Picking the right Bible is more important than picking the right house. If the Bible you're rocking is a King James Version (KJV), unless you're furthering your poetic or writing abilities, I encourage you to try another version like Amplified (Amp), New Living Translation (NLT), New International Version (NIV), or the New American Standard Bible (NASB). I love the Passion Translation (TPT) too but you can only read the New Testament in that version, not the Old Testament, and they're both important.

Some experts say sitting with pen-in-hand and reading the Bible yourself is the only way to interact with God's Word, and I don't disagree that we can gain much from studying a readable Bible and taking notes. In fact, I love the SOAP (Scripture, Observation, Application and Prayer) method, but there are many other ways to engage with the Bible that I don't think are wrong. Sure, you should be careful with some devotionals because they may feature way more of the writer's experiences and only a little bit of Scripture sprinkled in here and there, but you can judge that for yourself.

Personally, I love hearing Bible stories on Spotify (yes, even the ones that were intended to be told to children) because I am an auditory learner. I'm also a visual learner so anytime I can watch a Bible story told in a film or a show, I do that too. Here is where I'll insert a shameless plug for Pureflix instead of Netflix. I had no idea how much TV had a hold of my life and my family's life until this restoration began. Nighttime especially used to be filled with show after show after show, most often with each of us in different rooms viewing our different preferences. In their *Conquer Series: The Battle for Purity*, Jeremy And Tiana Wiles say nighttime is actually when we should watch the least TV because it is the time we should be preparing for the battle while we sleep. It's most common for those who struggle with anxious thoughts, pornography, and sexual addiction to masturbate before they go to sleep at night or when they wake up in the morning.

To protect yourself from the nighttime battle, the Wiles suggest that you turn off all electronic devices thirty minutes before you go to sleep, spend ten minutes practicing deep diaphragmatic breathing to help calm your limbic system (which is what Scripture refers to as your heart), and spend twenty minutes doing something edifying in the Holy Spirit like meditating on Scripture and allowing the Holy Spirit into your heart each night. The overarching purpose behind these actions, as concluded by the Wiles, is this:

> According to neuroscience, ten percent of your brain works when you're awake, and ninety percent works when you're not. Your brain cleans itself out when you sleep- pruning old neural connections that aren't being used. So if you're not dabbling with [toxic thoughts or desires], your brain will start to prune the synapses associated with [toxic thoughts or desires]. Therefore, this exercise of preparing for the battle each night - meditating on Scripture before bed - is crucial. Why? Because God's Word has the power to physically restructure our brain. Most of the conscious decisions we make will continue to operate on an unconscious level- while we're sleeping. Developing this discipline will help you start winning the battle each night, allowing you to dream of who God has called you to be.[10]

As a family, we are being much more careful about the selection and the timing of our TV intake now and our output is so much more meaningful. We don't get out of balance anymore. We consume more of God's Word than the world's, which is what's primarily projected in shows and films. The peace we've received from this commitment is worth more than any series. I wouldn't change it for anything! I have come to realize that my own longing for TV was to distract myself from doubts about God's presence in my circumstances. I would think I was fine as long as I stayed distracted instead of believing the instructions in James 4:8 to "Draw near to God, and he will draw near to you" (NKJV). I'd learned that "me" time was acceptable; I hadn't yet internalized the message from Psalm 84:10: "Better is one day in [His] courts than a thousand elsewhere" (NIV). When you're spending so much time watching TV, it's easy not to know what a day in God's courts is truly like.

If you need explicit Bible reading directions (I did, but was always too proud to ask for suggestions), dig into Psalms, the biggest book in the Bible. With the exception of Psalm 119, which happens to be the longest chapter in the Bible, each Psalm is fairly short, taking five minutes at most to read, and therefore they're easy to digest and meditate on. When I first read the book of Psalms, I read one Psalm a day for 150 days. On the first day of the month, I read Psalm 1, on the second day of the month I read Psalm 2, on the third day of the month I read Psalm 3, and so on and so forth. My husband first introduced me to this approach of using books of the Bible with around the same number of chapters as there are days in a given month like Proverbs, Matthew, Acts, 1 Chronicles, 2 Chronicles, 1 Samuel, Deuteronomy, Numbers, and Leviticus. This gives me accountability because if I miss a day, the date makes me aware of just how much I missed.

Another suggestion is to read the book of John one or two stories at a time. I love the stories in John because they document the life, death, and resurrection of Jesus, including many miracles

Jesus performed while here on earth. Whenever someone asks me where to start reading the Bible, I always say John!

If you're not presently part of the estimated 13% of American Christians who are regularly reading their Bible[46], endeavor to fall in love and curiosity with the Word. You might seek first to understand the key themes of the New Testament in four parts:

- Part 1: What God has done: how and why? Read Romans, Galatians, Colossians, 1 John, and Mark.
- Part 2: How to live it out: Read 1 Corinthians, Ephesians, 2 Corinthians, Philippians, James, Jude, and Luke.
- Part 3: The Church and authority: Read Acts, 1 Timothy, 2 Timothy, Titus, 1 Peter, 2 Peter, and Matthew.
- Part 4: God's love and our future hope: Read Hebrews, 2 John, 3 John, Philemon, 1 Thessalonians, 2 Thessalonians, John, and Revelation.

In whatever order you decide to read, just remember to prioritize quality over quantity. Allow the Word of God to dictate your experience, instead of forcing the Word of God to be colored by your experience. I'm not a big fan of reading the Bible in one year plans because rules without a relationship equals rebellion. If you're reading because you have to, it won't be long before you decide you don't have to.

Think of reading the Bible as eating a meal. If you don't eat for three days, when you do eat, you wouldn't be able to eat nine meals or if you could, you certainly couldn't savor them. The same is true with Bible reading. When you try to read too much too fast, you miss out on so many golden nuggets the Lord wants you to enjoy! Unlike eating food physically though, which makes you ravenously hungry the longer you go without it, the quotient of your spiritual hunger gets less and less, the longer you go without reading the Word.

It's all too easy to become spiritually malnourished! The only solution for this is force feeding! Did you know 52% of regular church goers don't believe objective moral truth about Christianity?[46] This means they doubt the realness and applicability of the Gospel. Calamitously, the vast majority of church goers today don't even know the books of the Bible. They've been replaced by a lot of secular humanism that's driving believers away. I pray America's not on our way to shutting down Bible apps or banning Bibles from being purchased online like China has. As it is, over the past five years the percent of American hotels allowing Gideon Bibles in hotel bedside tables went from 90% to 48%![46]

We *cannot* compromise Biblical truths. We cannot question the Bible and thus lose our heritage. Either we believe ALL of it, or we believe NONE of it. Personally, I'd rather die believing something rather than believing nothing. Eugene Peterson believes that the way we read the Bible is as important as the very fact that we read the Bible. If we read a translation that is difficult for us to understand, we will remain answerless and that is not where God wants us. God is not a God of confusion. If what we're reading does not bring clarity, conviction, courage, comfort, or confirmation, it is not from God.

How long should you read? That's almost as hard for me to answer as it is for me to tell students a minimum number of words to type in their essays. "As much as it takes to get the job done" I always say. The same principle fits here. Read for as long as it takes to digest the Scripture into your spirit. Chew it, meditate. Allow space for the Holy Spirit to speak to you. Sometimes I get what I need after just two minutes of reading. Other times it may be half an hour before I find it. Set reading methodology aside and simply persevere and persist. In *Honor's Reward*, John Bevere frames Biblical reading this way:

> Often God will send us what we need in a package we don't want. Why? To let us know He's God and we cannot second-guess Him. We cannot search for answers merely with our heads; we must seek Him and His provision with our hearts. Scripture cannot be interpreted from our limited human mental understanding. There must be a breath of the Spirit of God. He alone gives wise counsel and correct application. [12]

Recently in my waiting I figured out that it wasn't what I read that had so heavily impacted my own restoration—although that definitely has—it was the fact I've been doing it every day that has made the difference. The battle is new every morning and all the strength I accumulated the day before seems to expire each night at midnight. So each new day, I must start anew with a fresh Bible munch. It is my spiritual food that grants me grace to endure.

Life Application Challenge 4: After exercising, concentrate on your Word intake. Remember Romans 10:17 which tells us "Faith comes from hearing, and hearing through the Word of Christ" (NIV). Consider adopting the family mantra: "A Bible story a day keeps the devil away." Any consumption of the Bible works. Read it, watch it, hear it, experience it, just get the Bible in you and your loved ones, daily! You'll receive much more after being jolted with energy from briefly exercising!

Lyrics to Husseim's Pick: "Remember" by Bryan & Katie Torwalt

I'll never forget crying with my best friend and husband Husseim as we heard this song for the first time together while attending the Cure at Charis Bible College in Woodland Park, Colorado. Together we realized the human soul is the power and core of who a person is. Thus, we have a tremendous responsibility to feed it

well. We must ingrain deep inside the belief that with the power of God within us, we need not fear the powers around us. 2 Chronicles 10:15 says the battles are not ours, but God's (NIV). And let me tell you: when God is all you have, you quickly learn He is all you need. Instead of fixating on puddles of negatives, strive to look only to oceans of positives!

How quickly we forget the
God
Who lives in every day
How easy to lose sight that
You
Reside in the mundane
How quickly we forget the
power
That's running through our
veins
The kind of power that empties
graves

And oh my soul
Remember who you're talking
to
The only one who death bows
to
That's the God who walks
with you

And oh my soul
You know that if He did it then
He can do it all again
His power can still raise the
dead
Don't tell me that He's

And oh my soul
You know that if He did it
then
He can do it all again
His power can still raise the
dead
Don't tell me that He's
finished yet

If You broke through the
oceans
You can break through
these chains
If Your word made the
mountains
It can move them all the
same
If death fell before You
And it's still on its face
Then the power that raised
You
Is about to move again

If You broke through the
oceans
You can break through
these chains

finished yet

Lest we not forget the voice
That's holding back the waves
Was once the voice that told
the skies
To pour them into place
Let us join the endless song of
everlasting praise
The only God who empties
graves
Oh my soul
Remember who you're talking
to
The only one who death bows
to
That's the God who walks
with you
And oh my soul
You know that if He did it then
Then He can do it all again
His power can still raise the
dead
Don't tell me that He's
finished yet
He's not finished yet

And oh my soul
His power can still raise the
dead
Don't tell me that He's
finished yet

If Your word made the
mountains
It can move them all the
same
If death fell before You
And it's still on its face
Then the power that raised
You
Is about to move again
Is about to move again

Oh my soul
Remember who you're
talking to
The only one who death
bows to
That's the God who walks
with you

<u>Stride 5: PRAY</u>

Ezekiel 37: 1-14

The Valley of Dry Bones

The hand of the LORD was on me, and he brought me out by the Spirit of the LORD and set me in the middle of a valley; it was full of bones. He led me back and forth among them, and I saw a great many bones on the floor of the valley, bones that were very dry. He asked me, "Son of man, can these bones live?"

I said, "Sovereign LORD, you alone know."

Then he said to me, "Prophesy to these bones and say to them, 'Dry bones, hear the word of the LORD! This is what the Sovereign LORD says to these bones: I will make breath enter you, and you will come to life. I will attach tendons to you and make flesh come upon you and cover you with skin; I will put breath in you, and you will come to life. Then you will know that I am the LORD.'"

So I prophesied as I was commanded. And as I was prophesying, there was a noise, a rattling sound, and the bones came together, bone to bone. I looked, and tendons and flesh appeared on them and skin covered them, but there was no breath in them.

Then he said to me, "Prophesy to the breath; prophesy, son of man, and say to it, 'This is what the Sovereign LORD says: Come, breath, from the four winds and breathe into these slain, that they may live.'" So I prophesied as he commanded me, and breath entered them; they came to life and stood up on their feet—a vast army.

Then he said to me: "Son of man, these bones are the people of Israel. They say, 'Our bones are dried up and our hope is gone; we are cut off.' Therefore prophesy and say to them:

'This is what the Sovereign LORD says: My people, I am going to open your graves and bring you up from them; I will bring you back to the land of Israel. Then you, my people, will know that I am the LORD, when I open your graves and bring you up from them. I will put my Spirit in you and you will live, and I will settle you in your own land. Then you will know that I the LORD have spoken, and I have done it,' declares the LORD" (NLT).

Ezekiel teaches us that God is not far off, but nearby, constantly yearning for us to draw strength from His inexhaustible supply. Would you believe me if I told you God answers EVERY prayer that is according to His Word? If not, why? Is receiving whatever we ask, seek, and knock for as promised in Luke 11:9-10 not true? What about John 14:13? It promises us that whatever we ask in Jesus' name, that He will do, so that the Father can be glorified in the Son (NLT). The more time we spend in Him, the more attuned our prayers become to His character and will. We shouldn't pursue him only with "God gimme this" and "God gimme that" as if He's some sort of a cosmic vending machine waiting on our every beck and call. However, He does freely and lovingly give us everything we ask for in accordance with His will, which He reveals through unchangeable decrees in the Bible.

Some months into my wait, I called Andrew Wommack Ministry's 24/7 prayer line for help praying about my career trajectory. I told the representative that I didn't know if I should be asking God to keep me in my current role, or if I should be neutrally asking Him to place me anywhere that He wills so our family can continue to homeschool and be provided for. The prayer minister told me a story about a time he bought some cinnamon pop tarts for his daughter Reagan but upon arriving home, he realized she had specifically asked for cookies and cream pop tarts. Out of his love for her, he gladly and willingly returned to the store to get the specific pop tarts that his little girl wanted. "And I'm her earthly father," he pondered, "How much more do you think our heavenly father wants to bless us, His children?" This helped me turn an important corner in my prayer life.

Finally finished fearing improper wording while praying, I audaciously told God that I long to resume working as a better, balanced version of myself. At the same time, I elicited His Holy Spirit to search my heart in accordance with James 4:3 (NLT). I yearned to pursue the Lord with the right motives, instead of being led by my passions. I know God loves me too much to be used to serve my envy and ambition. I'm learning to bring my desires to Him with a spirit of trust and humility.

Perhaps you can relate. Trusting that God has SO MUCH good to gift us in His perfect timing is easier said than done. Maybe there was a time that you earnestly prayed for something, and you didn't see the outcome you desired. Maybe you've spent entire seasons praying for someone's health, or someone's finances, or even their salvation and you never got to see answers to your prayers come to pass. Andrew Wommack explains, "The problem is you think you can perceive what God does or doesn't do with your five senses. If you can't see, taste, hear, smell, or feel it, then that's 'proof' God didn't do it. The answer to this dilemma lies in understanding the existence of the spiritual realm."[11] When we pray, we're conversing with God's Holy Spirit, in the Heavenly realm—which in its original Greek means "the sphere of spiritual activities" and appears five times in the book of Ephesians: 1:3, 20; 2:6; 3:10; 6:12. John Stott constructively depicts the heavenly realm as "the unseen world of spiritual reality."

Because we cannot experience the Heavenly realm using the five senses of our flesh, we can only glean insight about it from God's Word. When you pray, "although it's a done deal in the spirit, whether or not you see it manifest in the physical really depends much more on if you know how to receive it than if God answered your prayer."[11] How to receive in the natural realm what God has already given you in the spiritual realm is as easy as 1, 2, 3:

1. Fall in love with God's Word until it becomes who you are. Romans 10:17 says, "So then faith cometh by hearing, and hearing by the Word of God" (NKJV). Consume the Word of God like the answers to your prayers depend on it, because they do! Memorize Scriptures, meditate on Scriptures, pray Scriptures, sing Scriptures, and post Scriptures using paper and tape to be read aloud throughout your house so they're always visible.

2. Believe that you receive while you pray, as we are instructed in Mark 11:24 (ESV). Close your eyes and imagine yourself exactly as you're praying to be. Your imagination can unlock your belief quicker than a wink. Set time aside to imagine daily until your desire comes to pass in the physical realm. Then, it's time to ask God to reveal a new dream!

3. Disrupt thoughts of unbelief. Feed your love for God until your fears starve to death! Romans 12:3 says God has given everyone the same measure of faith (NIV) until fear enters the equation. Fear is the basis for all unbelief. Its depth and breadth is different for everyone, but no matter its size, if you don't deal with it, it will begin to consume your mind and cause you to question the Word of God. Hold tightly to 1 John 4:16, knowing and believing in the love that God has for you (NIV)! Look for God's love all day every day. When you see it, proclaim to Him aloud that you receive it like, "God I see your love in that little girl enjoying her candy bar. I receive your love deep in my heart!"

God doesn't want you to have to depend on your job, the government, or your family. He wants you depending solely on Him and His unending love! The more you abide in Him, the more others around you will also be blessed by a radical change in your countenance. Your character is a magnet in your home. Are you drawing goodness or stress out of those you love most? To remind ourselves of how rich we are in Christ, my kids and I wrote down several of the deposits God placed in us since conception. We proudly hang this on our living room wall at home:

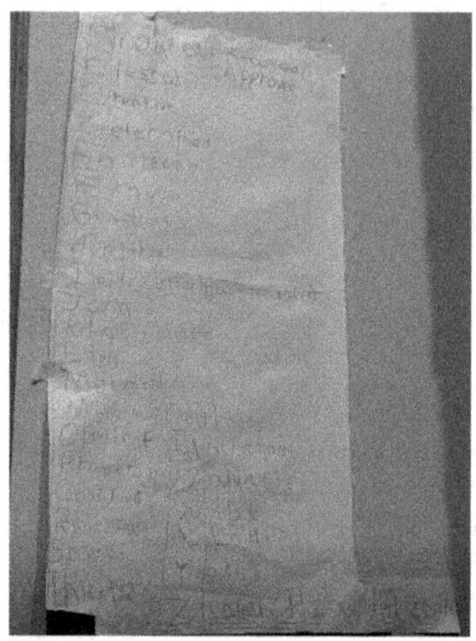

During the waiting, this list has evolved, dramatically. In alphabetical order for easier memorization, here are 100+ Scripture-based character qualities, and accompanying fiery verses, all from the English Standard Version (ESV) of the Bible, that you can prayerfully shepherd into your heart to tackle unbelief by simply proclaiming "I receive _________ in the name of JESUS":

A: Anointing, Acceptance, Approval, Appointing, Alertness, Attentiveness, Availability

I am anointed to preach of God's Kingdom and heal the sick (Luke 9:2)

I am aware of that which is taking place around me so I can have the right response to it

(Mark 14:38)

I show the worth of a person by giving undivided attention to his words and emotions

(Hebrews 2:1)

I make my own schedule and priorities secondary to the wishes of those I am serving

(Philippians 2:20–21)

B: Boldness, Blessings, Bravery

I believe what I have to say or do is true and right and just in the sight of God

(Acts 4:29)

I have no fear of bad news; my heart is steadfast, trusting in the LORD

(Psalm 112:7)

C: Cautiousness, Compassion, Contentment, Confidence, Creativity, Christ-likeness

Knowing how important right timing is in accomplishing right actions

(Proverbs 19:2)

My assurance comes from the Lord, not people, circumstances, or things. As I do God's will, I'll be richly rewarded with all He has promised

(Hebrews 10:35-36)

I invest whatever is necessary to heal the hurts of others

(I John 3:17)

I realize that God has provided everything I need for my present happiness

(I Timothy 6:8)

I'm able to approach needs, tasks, and ideas from a new perspective

(Romans 12:2)

D: Decisiveness, Deference, Dependability, Determination, Diligence, Discernment, Discretion

I have the ability to finalize difficult decisions based on the will and ways of God

(James 1:5)

I limit my freedom in order not to offend the tastes of those whom God has called me to serve

(Romans 14:21)

I ensure I fulfill what I consented to do even if it means unexpected sacrifice

(Psalm 15:4)

I set my purpose to accomplish God's goals in God's time regardless of the opposition

(2 Timothy 4:7–8)

I visualize each task as a special assignment from the Lord and use all my energies to accomplish it

(Colossians 3:23)

I have the God-given ability to understand why things happen

(I Samuel 16:7)

I have the ability to avoid words, actions, and attitudes which could result in undesirable consequences

(Proverbs 22:3)

E: Endurance, Enthusiasm, Equipping

I have the inward strength to withstand stress to accomplish God's best

(Galatians 6:9)

I express with my soul the joy of my spirit

(I Thessalonians 5:16,19)

F: Faith, Forgiveness, Friendship, Flexibility, Fairness, Fearlessness, Fortitude

I visualize what God intends to do in a given situation and act in harmony with it

(Hebrews 11:1)

I don't set my affections on ideas or plans which could be changed by God or others

(Colossians 3:2)

I clear the record of those who have wronged me and allow God to love them through me

(Ephesians 4:32)

G: Generosity, Gentleness, Gratefulness, Gratitude, Grace, Gifts

I realize that all I have belongs to God and I use it for His purposes

(2 Corinthians 9:6)

I show personal care and concern in meeting the need of others

(I Thessalonians 2:7)

I make it known to God and others in what ways they have benefited my life

(I Corinthians 4:7)

H: Hospitality, Health/Healing, Humility, Honesty, Honor, Hope

I cheerfully share food, shelter, and spiritual refreshment with those whom God brings into my life (Hebrews 13:2)

I recognize that it is actually God and others who are responsible for the achievements in my life

(James 4:6)

I am healed and delivered

(Psalm 107:20)

Jesus took away my sickness and gave me peace

(Isaiah 53:4-5)

I can speak to the mountains that are in my way, and whatever things I ask for in prayer, if I believe, I will receive (Matthew 21:21-22)

I will not waver, for God is faithful and He always fulfills His promises

(Hebrews 10:23).

I: Initiative, Improvement, Intelligence, Inquisition

I recognize and do what needs to be done before I am asked to do it (Romans 12:21)

With an intelligent heart, I acquire knowledge, and develop a wise ear seeking knowledge (Proverbs 18:15)

J: Joyfulness, Justice

How I love the spontaneous enthusiasm of my spirit when my soul is in fellowship with the Lord

(Psalm 16:11)

I hold a personal responsibility to God's unchanging laws

(Micah 6:8)

K: Kingdom-minded, Kindness, Knowledge

I won't be conformed to this world, but transformed by the renewal of my mind, that by testing I may discern what is the will of God, what is good and acceptable and perfect

(Romans 12:2)

Have this mind among yourselves, which is yours in Christ Jesus

(Philippians 2:5)

I encourage and build up others

(1 Thessalonians 5:11)

L: Love, Loyalty, Learning, Level-headedness

I give to others' basic needs without having as my motive personal reward

(I Corinthians 13:3)

I use difficult times to demonstrate my commitment to God and to those whom He has called me to serve

(John 15:13)

M: Meekness, Motivation, Modesty, Mercy

I yield my personal rights and expectations to God
(Psalm 62:5)

As I wait on the Lord, He shows me graciousness, justice, blessings, and mercy

(Isaiah 30:18)

N: Nimbleness in mind and body, Nurturing spirit

I am quick to hear, slow to speak, slow to anger

(James 1:19)

I am not easily angered and my heart is not foolish (Ecclesiastes 7:9)

O: Obedience, Orderliness, Obedience, Observantness, Optimism

I have freedom to be creative under the protection of divinely appointed authority

(2 Corinthians 10:5)

Preparing myself and my surroundings so I will achieve the greatest efficiency

(I Corinthians 14:40)

P: Patience, Persuasiveness, Punctuality, Prosperity, Prudence, Persistence, Purity, Peace

I accept difficult circumstances without giving God a deadline to remove them

(Romans 5:3–4)

I guide vital truths around another's mental roadblocks

(2 Timothy 2:24)

I show high esteem for other people and their time (Ecclesiastes 3:1)

Q: Qualifications, Quiet in spirit, Quick to obey

I am God's handiwork, created in Christ Jesus to do good works, which God prepared in advance for me to do

(Ephesians 2:10)

I am equipped with all I need for doing God's will. He is producing in me, through the power of Jesus Christ, every good thing that is pleasing to him. All glory to Him forever and ever!

(Hebrews 13:21)

I acknowledge there is "a time to keep silent, and a time to speak"

(Ecclesiastes 3:7)

R: Resourcefulness, Redemption, Righteousness, Responsibility, Reverence

I make wise use of that which others would normally overlook or discard

(Luke 16:10)

I know and do what both God and others are expecting from me

(Romans 14:12)

But seek first the kingdom of God and his righteousness, and all these things will be added to you

(Matthew 6:33)

I am aware of how God is working through the people and events in my life to produce the character of Christ in me (Proverbs 23:17–18)

S: Security, Self-Control, Submission, Sincerity, Sensitivity, Servant-leadership

I structure my life around that which is eternal and cannot be destroyed or taken away

(John 6:27)

I maintain instant obedience to the initial promptings of God's Spirit

(Galatians 5:24–25)

I exercise my senses so I can perceive the true spirit and emotions of those around me

(Romans 12:15)

I am eager to do what is right with transparent motives

(I Peter 1:22)

T: Thoroughness, Thoughtfulness, Tactfulness, Thriftiness, Tolerance, Truthfulness, Talents

I know what factors will diminish the effectiveness of my work or words if neglected

(Proverbs 18:15)

I do not let myself or others spend that which is not necessary (Luke 16:11)

I accept others as unique expressions of specific character

qualities in varying degrees of maturity

(Philippians 2:2)

I earn future trust by accurately reporting past facts (Ephesians 4:25)

U: Unbrokenness, Understanding, Uniqueness, Unity

I am hard pressed on every side, but not crushed; perplexed, but not in despair; persecuted, but not abandoned; struck down, but not destroyed

(2 Corinthians 4:8-12)

My patience gives me great understanding; I'm not quick-tempered

(Proverbs 14:29)

V: Virtue, Value, Victory, Valor

I believe moral excellence and purity of spirit radiate from my life as I obey God's Word

(2 Peter 1:3)

My victory rests with the Lord

(Proverbs 31:21)

W: Wisdom, Wonderment

I see and respond to life's situations from God's frame of reference

(Proverbs 9:10)

I believe all signs and wonders come to pass

(Deuteronomy 13:2)

X: Xenialness, eXcitement, eXploration, eXpertise, eXcellence

I maintain xenial communication relations, letting my speech always be gracious, seasoned with salt. I know how I ought to answer each person

(Colossian 4:6)

I don't give answers before I hear

(Proverbs 18:13)

I'm enthusiastic to serve the Lord, keeping my passion toward Him boiling hot! I radiate with the glow of the Holy Spirit and let Him fill me with excitement as I serve him

(Romans 12:11)

I pursue learning about the character of God, in whom are hidden all the treasures of wisdom and knowledge (Colossian 2:3)

Y: Youth, Yearning

I trust Him to renew my youth like the eagles

(Psalm 103:5)

I yearn to have God's exceeding grace within me

(2 Corinthians 9:14)

Z: Zealousness, Zappiness, Zestfulness

I put on righteousness as a breastplate, and a helmet of salvation on my head; I put on garments of vengeance for clothing, and wrap myself in zeal as a cloak

(Isaiah 59:17)

I labor, striving according to His power, which mightily works within me

(Colossians 1:29)

Like Ezekiel in the Bible story shared at the beginning of this stride, you, too, can *prophecy*! Stand ready for God to use you as you are! You don't need a seminary degree to be qualified. Any Christ believer can use the prophetic gift to speak insights or application of Scripture to the life of another as God inspires. See 1 Corinthians 12, Exodus 31:3, and Acts 2 (NLT). Prophesying can be understood as spontaneous preaching. Whenever you feel inclined to share a good word from the Lord with someone, you're prophesying to them!

1 Corinthians 14:31 tells us "For you can all prophesy one by one, so that all may learn and all be encouraged," (NIV). We're to see this gift as regulated by love, as relayed in 1 Corinthians 13 (ASV). It does not always work out in the form of speech, as noted in 1 Corinthians 12 (NIV), but per Ephesians 6:17, it often does (NIV). When I get the impression that I should share particular encouragement with someone, I ask God if I'm to stay or pray. Sometimes praying is all God wants us to do with an inclination we harbor. At other times, He'll use our words in an exact moment as instruments for His glory. The more we absorb His Holy Word, the more comfortable we'll feel unleashing it in the lives of others.

Stocking our spiritual arsenals with Scriptures begets confidence.

God's spirit isn't reserved just for Ezekiel either. His spirit resides within anyone whose trust rests in Christ as our savior, but like a muscle that only grows if you exercise it, your connection with the Holy Spirit will only increase if you spend time prayerfully growing your relationship with Him. The more you learn about His goodness and kindness, the closer to Him you'll want to be! And the closer you get to Him, the easier it is for sin and distraction to fall off of your life.

I picture Ezekiel like a boxer in a boxing ring with God as His coach, holding his head with both hands on his cheeks and forcing him to look only at Him, His Father. When we increase our narrow vision on God, and only God, we can't be distracted by any doubt. As God tells Ezekiel what to prophesy, he wastes no time obeying. He fixates on the Lord and allows not a single "what if" to cloud his judgment. This is how we overcome ANY and I mean ANY obstacle in life. Focus on God and converse with Him before anyone else! Fill your thoughts with His Word. Don't vent. Allow me to shed more light on Ezekiel's own grave circumstances so you can better appreciate his example of relentlessly focusing on God.

In case you're inquisitive like me about the discord in the middle east that remains even now, here's a quick history lesson for you. To this day, much disputation, political tension, and military conflicts exist between Arab countries and Israel—the Arabs versus the Jews. We can root *why* all the way back to Sarah's impatience to conceive a child which led her to convince Abraham to first have a son, Ishmael, with her handmaid Hagar, who was Egyptian-born. (Egypt is an Arab country.) Eventually, Sarah does birth her own son in Canaan, as God promised she would, and Sarah proclaims she does not want Ishmael to be a co-heir so, after God okays him doing so, Abraham banishes Ishmael and Hagar into the desert and the twelve Arab tribes descend from Ishmael's twelve sons: Nebaioth, Kedar, Adbeel, Mibsam, Mishma, Duma, Massa, Hadar, Tema, Jetur, Naphish, and Kedemah. Arabs—93% whom are present day Muslims—trace their lineage to Hagar and Ishmael.[20]

Still, the Jews descended, as God promised, from Abraham's and Sarah's only son together, Isaac, who bore two sons, Esau and Jacob. Isaac was tricked partly by His own wife Rebekah to bless Jacob, his second born, instead of Esau, his first born, whose five sons Eliphaz, Reuel, Jeush, Jaalam, and Korah would eventually have Roman descendants—and it is the Romans who at long last crucify Jesus on the cross. God renamed Jacob, Israel, born from whom are twelve sons, after which the twelve tribes of Israel are named: Reuben, Simeon, Levi, Judah, Dan, Naphtali, Gad, Asher, Issachar, Zebulun, Joseph, and Benjamin.

Unfortunately, these twelve tribes didn't remain one big happy family. A schism over taxation led them to divide Israel into two kingdoms: the northern kingdom and the southern kingdom. The northern kingdom nosedived immediately into idol worship. Because people and kings alike refused to return to Yahweh, God ended up allowing the powerful and merciless empire of Assyria to overthrow the northern kingdom of Israel. 2 Kings 17:1-23 tells us the Assyrians took the people captive and sought to pretty much destroy every remnant that this was once a nation (NIV).

As the northern kingdom (Israel) neared its complete demise, the smaller southern kingdom (Judah) flip-flopped between the worship of foreign gods and Yahweh. Good kings pulled the people away from the worship of false gods, but bad kings didn't. Back and forth, back and forth. One of the bad kings was Nebuchadnezzar, who took 10,000 Jews into exile in Babylon. The prophet Ezekiel was among those captives. As you can imagine, it was a pretty hard set of circumstances to believe from, when God shows him the revival of dry bones, signifying God's plan for the future national restoration of Israel which, at this point was as dead as a doorknob, completely deprived of its land, its king, and its temple. Israel had been broken for so long that restoration seemed impossible, BUT GOD.

Through Ezekiel, God expounds in Ezekiel 37:24 that Israel WILL be restored under the leadership of "David, [God's] servant [who] shall be king over them" (NIV). This means the restoration would occur when God sends Jesus Christ the Messiah, a descendant of David, as per Isaiah 7:14/9:6–7, and Luke 1:31–33 (NIV). I don't know what kind of trials you're up against, friend, but I want to assure you that the same fierce God who spoke to Ezekiel wants to speak to you too. Do you have room in your life to hear from Him? He wants you to let His Word, not the world, paint a picture of what's possible. He wants you back in touch with the hidden desires of your heart. He wants to insert this question in your heart: "Can these things live again?" He wants you to focus so much on your faith that you can't see anything contrary to it. He wants you to grow your imagination and renew your mind!

Private prayer leads to public power all the day long. Once you have taken however long you need to get the Good News in your system, it's time to hear from God! Is the terrain of your soul ready to listen? Or are there any weeds blocking God's ability to get through to you? Before getting into prayer, I encourage you to mow the **<u>W</u>EEDS**—an acronym I made to represent the top hindrances which get in our way of hearing God's voice. You may have also heard them called "prayer stoppers" or "voice blockers":

<u>W</u>orry. When your heart is overcrowded with fears, stresses, and what-ifs, there is no room for God to minister to you. Consider where your focus is. If God logged how much time a day you spend with Him, would it pale in comparison to how many hours your phone tells you you're using it per day? Where are you getting the majority of your daily information from? The news? Social media? TV shows? Movies? Are you more eager to get into these distractions than alone time with God? He knows if you are. And He longs to be pursued with diligence, NOT passivity. How would the closest person to you feel if you only passively and predictably communicated with them things like, "Let it be a good day" or "Let this food be nourishing"? They wouldn't exactly feel pumped, nor respected. The same is true of God, who wants us to hold Him in reverence, meaning profoundly honoring and adoring Him. Immersing yourself in God's Word daily as we discussed in Stride Four will show God how highly you think of Him, and will help prepare your heart to receive *and believe* God's truth more than the world's.

What this sounds like: *God, I am taking steps to think more about your Word than my worries. Help me to get rid of my doubts which have become like trash bags weighing me down wherever I go. I want to dance like these weights have already been lifted, because they have been! Your Word says so!*

<u>Ego</u>. What do you want more? Your wishes or God? I'm not talking about something here that is black and white in the Bible, like God's seven promises for our eternal life, soul protection, the supplying of all needs, power for the repentant, victory in health, protection from end-time persecution, and adoption into God's family, as is laid out for us in Revelation 2, 3, 11, 13, 17, 22, and 29 (NLT). I'm talking about liminal spaces, or those gray areas when you need to choose to go left or right, like pivoting careers, ending a toxic friendship, or utilizing limited resources, and you're not sure how to pray about it. Here's how. Set your ego aside so you can talk to God with a neutral heart. I know it's hard to convince ourselves of this sometimes, but He knows infinitely more than we do. We can see only what is in front of us. He can see around every corner!

What this sounds like: *God, I want your will, not my own. I know my will is the only unique thing I can offer you, since everything else I have was given or loaned to me by you, anyway.*

Envy. Remember the tenth commandment! Stay in your lane and don't covet! I know it's hard not to feel small when you see others acquiring success, health, wealth, material possessions, etc. seemingly with ease but don't compare your life to theirs. That's such an easy way for the enemy to distract us. The only person you should be better than is the person you were yesterday.

What this sounds like: *God, I close the door to all thoughts of wanting to have anyone's life but my own. I desire to keep my heart in a state of thanksgiving, for I know that is the cure against covetousness. Show me how much you love me today. I am fully living in every moment, looking for evidence of your goodness.*

Disobedience. Read 1 Timothy 6:10 and consider how your relationship is with material wealth. Have you ever focused so much on the things of this world that you ignore and/or displace God, as was the case in Deuteronomy 8:11-18 and Job 31:24-28 (NLT)?

We all do wrong, daily, but we don't have to deliberately do wrong and justify it like "I know I was short-tempered with my colleague, but he botched the project," or "I get that I didn't scan that one item in the grocery store's self-check-out, but at least I scanned all the rest." We must learn to repent sooner by immediately admitting to God and ourselves when we've sinned, receiving His forgiveness, and doing whatever we can to make it right, like apologizing to that colleague, or walking back in the store to pay for the item we missed.

The more we practice faster repentance, the closer we'll get to God and sin-free living! Maybe you're dealing with a deeper-rooted sin right now, one you'd tell me has been dominating you for years. To you I'd say the same thing! Do you control your sin or does your sin control you? Repent to the Lord and make it right! Once you ask for God's forgiveness, dwell on it no longer! Your past is behind you, but if you don't *feel* forgiven, you'll keep repeating it. In Isaiah 43:25, God says He "blots out your transgressions, for [His] own sake, and remembers your sins no more" (ESV).

What this sounds like: *God, I refuse to let sin or shame harden my heart. Either I'm going to believe your Word or not. I'm choosing to believe it. Even when my head is trying to remember my sin, I'm choosing to focus on you, and your love, and I will think of my sin no more! Soften my heart through my repentance!*

<u>Slander</u>. Psalm 101:5 avouches, "Whoever slanders his neighbor secretly I will destroy. Whoever has a haughty look and an arrogant heart I will not endure" (ESV). Strive not to put others in a bad light no matter how awful their conduct may be. Proverbs 18:21 explicates that "the tongue has the power of life and death" (ESV). We can use our words to build others up or tear them down. I don't know about you, but I'd rather be remembered for doing the latter. John 13:34 shares God's solution for slander: to love each other (ESV).

When we harbor unforgiveness, offense, resentment, bitterness, or anger toward another person it blocks our prayers. In Mark 11:25-26, Jesus said, "Whenever you stand praying, if you have anything against anyone, forgive him, that your Father in heaven may also forgive you your trespasses. But if you do not forgive, neither will your Father in heaven forgive your trespasses" (NLT). When we want to slander, our hearts are not right with God because in order to slander, we must step out of the path God designed for us.

What this sounds like: *God, today I choose to focus on my tongue. I want my tongue to be gentle. As I study your Word, illuminate for me revelations of how to love others like you love them.*

Once your weeds have been cut, don't just think to yourself

that you'll make a point to spend time in prayer with God. Schedule it, and honor it. Whatever time of day or night that you make an appointment with God and for however long you make it doesn't matter as much as honoring your commitment. Take your daily God appointments seriously. Don't cancel on Him. Does He cancel on you? If you had to meet with the United States president, would you miss it? How much more regard should you hold for the one true God? When you sit down with Him, be sure to seek Him confidently and expectantly, yet reverently. His Spirit dwells wherever He is treated as holy. Worship Him for His awesomeness like, "My God, you made the mountains, oceans, sun, moon, stars, planets, and on and on with YOUR hands!"

While in awe of Him, you can lucidly tell Him, "Father, your servant is here. Your son/daughter is here, listening." God will converse with those who eagerly pursue Him. John Bevere compares this diligent pursuit to a man going after a woman and going out of his way to win her over. He says "Similarly, we are to passionately seek God with all our heart, mind, and strength. God desires to be pursued and wanted."[12] Speaking with God can't be at the bottom of our to do list. It can't be something we *might* get to after we let 10,000 other things steal our attention. We're going to have to take the initiative to pursue Him without being fearful of not hearing from him. Why not shoot the shot?! Like Wayne Gretzky once wisely proclaimed, "You'll miss 100% of the shots you don't take!" In prayer, we get what we believe!

Aim to make your prayers less about petitioning God and more about deepening your own spiritual growth. Don't think praying doesn't matter because it does. Austerely saying God is in control is a cop-out. YOU have the ability to speak the Word of God into your circumstances. Don't wait for God. God's waiting for you!

<u>Prayers should be solution-focused instead of problem-focused.</u> The lifesaving power of God's Word is released when you pray it, whereas complaining in prayer about your circumstances only energizes and catastrophizes your problems. You can pray to receive revelations, wisdom, empowerment, character changes, and even impartation of spiritual gifts, but don't plead for things that God already gave you over 2,000 years ago when He sent His son Jesus to die on the cross for you!

In *the Blessings Bible*, Mike Murdock cites the following Scripture-based gifts that we inherited thanks to the shed blood of Jesus: salvation, Heaven, healing, forgiveness, dominion, mercy, fruitfulness, favor, family, provision, power, fellowship with God, longevity, abundance, understanding, grace, restoration, prosperity, authority, faithfulness of God, deliverance, security, promotion, and the ability to grow in Christ likeness by the work of the Holy Spirit.[13] As Andrew Wommack says in *A Better Way to Pray*, "prayer is not trying to twist God's arm to make Him do something. Prayer is receiving by faith what He has already done."[11] Understand that Jesus's death fully satisfied God's wrath! So quit praying as if you're begging Him not to be mad at you! He's not! Even in interceding for others, try to remember that the war between God and man is over. That's what the angels ecstatically proclaimed at the birth of Jesus in Luke 2:14 as they sang "Glory to God in the highest, and on earth peace, good will toward men" (NIV).

Nowhere in the Bible does God command a specific amount of time to be allocated for meeting alone with Him in a prayer closet. The recommendation to achieve a daily focus moment with Him is purely for your own benefit of recentering, not His. Do you go on a special date night with your spouse daily? Likely not. Yet are you in constant conversation with your spouse? Hopefully so. The same should be true of your constant communion with God. Wommack provokingly asks his readers to consider what would be left of their prayer lives if we no longer asked for things, repented for sin, and interceded—especially in those kind of intercessory prayers that sound *like pleading with an angry God to turn from His impending judgment and bestow mercy upon His people.*[11] Woah. That hit me hard.

Most of my prayers prior to the gift of this waiting season have sounded something like "Forgive me God for doing this again. Please help me to overcome this. Give me strength to be better." With an occasional "Bless so & so with grace to endure their trials" mixed in. Until I was reminded by Wommack that Adam and Eve prayed for NONE of these things! He reminds us "[Adam and Eve] had nobody to intercede for, no demons to cast out, and no kingdoms to tear down. They had no clothes, food, houses, or even jobs to believe for—no petitions at all—yet they met with God every evening in the cool of the day and communed with Him. Their conversations with God had nothing in them concerning sin, lack, need, problems, repenting, begging, or pleading. Yet they prayed—communing with God—every single day."[11]

The opposite of fear is not faith; it is certainty. For me, prayer has been a much needed tool to take me from wondering to certainty that every promise God gives us is, irrefutably, true. Here are some of my favorite Biblical promises to declare in prayer. All were extracted from the English Standard Version (ESV) of the Bible:

- I am in Christ Jesus, blessed with every spiritual blessing, chosen by God to be holy and blameless, predestined for adoption through Jesus, accepted in the beloved, forgiven of all my sins, and lavished with His wisdom to know His will.
  (Ephesians 1:1-9)
- I am predestined according to His purpose.
  (Ephesians 1:11)
- I am filled with the fruit of the Spirit: love, joy, peace, patience, kindness, goodness, faithfulness, gentleness, and self-control.
  (Galatians 5:22-23)
- I am receiving exceedingly abundantly above all that

I ask or think.
(Ephesians 3:20)
- I am strong in the Lord to fight off all Satan's attacks.
(Ephesians 6:10-17)
- I am confident of His finishing the work in me unto perfection.
(Philippians 1:6)
- I am a citizen of heaven.
(Philippians 3:20)
- I am becoming mature, growing in the measure of the stature of the fullness of Christ.
(Ephesians 4:13-15)
- I am rejoicing in the Lord always.
(Philippians 4:4)
- I am able to do all things through Christ who strengthens me.
(Philippians 4:13)
- I am having all my needs met according to His riches.
(Philippians 4:19)
- I am filled with the knowledge of His will in all wisdom and understanding. I am able to walk worthy of the Lord, fully pleasing Him, being fruitful. I am strengthened with all power according to His might unto all patience and joy.
(Colossians 1:9-11)
- I am anxious for nothing and guarded by God's peace; my mind has no turmoil.
(Philippians 4:6-7)
- I have been delivered from the domain of darkness and transferred to the Kingdom of God.
(Colossians 1:13)
- I have been presented to God – holy, blameless, and beyond reproach.
(Colossians 1:22)
- I am filled with God's power that works mightily in me.

(Colossians 1:29)
o   I am indwelt by Him in whom all fullness dwells.
(Colossians 1:19)
o   I am complete in Christ, filled with God, the possessor of everything.
(Colossians 2:10)
o   I am blameless.
(Colossians 2:12-15)
o   I am growing because my nourishment and strength come from God.
(Colossians 2:19)
o   I am not given a spirit of fear, but of power, and of love, and a sound mind.
(2 Timothy 1:7)
o   I am adequate, complete, and equipped for every good work.
(2 Timothy 3:17)
o   I am delivered from every evil deed and will be brought safely to His Kingdom.
(2 Timothy 4:18)
o   I am being renewed to true knowledge according to the image of Jesus.
(Colossians 3:10)
o   I am chosen.
(1 Thessalonians 1:4)
o   I am able to come boldly before the throne of grace to find mercy and grace.
(Hebrews 4:16)
o   I am confident that He will never leave me and I fear not what men can do to me.
(Hebrews 13:5-6)
o   I am lacking no wisdom.
(James 1:5)
o   I am loved and have been washed from my sins by His blood.
(Revelation 1:5)

- o I am the salt of the earth and the light of the world.
  (Matthew 5:13-14)
- o I am set free.
  (John 8:31-33)
- o I am kept by the power of God.
  (1 Peter 1:5)
- o I am His disciple because I have His love for others.
  (John 13:34-35)
- o I am filled with joy.
  (John 17:13)
- o I am united with God and Christ, and God's gift to Christ.
  (John 17:23-24)
- o I am protected by the power of His name.
  (John 17:11)
- o I am a saint.
  (Romans 1:7)
- o I am justified, reconciled, and awaiting more blessing from God that is available to me.
  (Romans 5:9-10)
- o I am now reigning as a king because of Jesus Christ within me.
  (Romans 5:17)
- o I am made right in God's sight by faith; I am at peace; I am privileged; I am confidently and joyfully looking forward to becoming all God has in mind for me; I am rejoicing in troubles because through them, God is building me up and making me strong.
  (Romans 5:1-5)
- o I am dead to sin and alive to God in Christ Jesus.
  (Romans 6:11)
- o I am dead to the old man; consequently my flesh is powerless.
  (Romans 6:6)
- o I am yielded to God. All my rights and expectations are His.

(Romans 6:13)
- I am free from condemnation and the vicious cycle of sin and death.
(Romans 8:1-2)
- I am following after the Holy Spirit which leads to life and peace.
(Romans 8:6)
- I am a recipient of eternal life through Jesus Christ.
(Romans 6:23)
- I am a son of God; consequently, I am led by the Spirit of God.
(Romans 8:14)
- I am confident that all things work together for good, and I am being conformed to the image of Christ.
(Romans 8:28-29)
- I have been given all things. I am protected—Who can come against me?
(Romans 8:31-32)
- I am a son of God and co-heir with Christ, sharing all His treasure.
(Romans 8:17)
- I am inseparable from God's love.
(Romans 8:35)
- I am more than a conqueror through Christ.
(Romans 8:37)
- I am established to the end.
(1 Corinthians 1:8)
- I am a recipient of things too wonderful even to imagine.
(1 Corinthians 2:9)
- I am God's temple, indwelt by the Holy Spirit.
(1 Corinthians 3:16-17)
- I am infused with Jesus, made acceptable to God, pure, and holy.
(1 Corinthians 1:30)
- I am already full, rich, and I reign as a king.

(1 Corinthians 4:8)
- o   I am of one spirit with God.
    (1 Corinthians 6:17)
- o   I have been bought with a price.
    (1 Corinthians 6:20)
- o   I am washed, sanctified, and justified in Jesus.
    (1 Corinthians 6:11)
- o   I am in the image and glory of God.
    (1 Corinthians 11:7)
- o   I am always led in triumph in Christ. I am a sweet aroma manifesting the presence of God wherever I go.
    (2 Corinthians 2:14)
- o   I am a new creation, the old is passed; all things have become new.
    (2 Corinthians 5:17)
- o   I am adequate for anything because my adequacy comes from God.
    (2 Corinthians 3:5)
- o   I am Christ's ambassador.
    (2 Corinthians 5:20)
- o   I am strongest when I am weakest.
    (2 Corinthians 12:10)
- o   I am crucified and the life I now live is not mine but Christ's.
    (Galatians 2:20)
- o   I am strongest when I am weakest.
    (2 Corinthians 12:10)
- o   I am redeemed from the curse of the law.
    (Galatians 3:13)

As previously highlighted, James 4:8 gives this additional promise regarding our prayer lives: "**Draw near to God and He will draw near to you**" (NKJV). It may be awkward at first, but PULL (Pray Until Love Leads). Job 33:14 assures that God WILL speak to you however He chooses (NLT). He might speak to you through His Holy Spirit per John 14:26 (NIV), through nature per Psalm 19:1-2 (ESV), through a gifted believer per Romans 12:6-8 (NIV), through difficulties per Psalm 119:67-68 (NLT), through music per Psalm 98:4 (ESV), through repeated instances per Isaiah 46:9-11 (NIV), through dreams and visions per Job 33:15-18 (NLT), through an audible voice per Deuteronomy 4:36 (NIV), through peace per John 14:27 NIV), through supernatural manifestations per Exodus 13:21 (NIV), through your inward witness AKA your conscience per Romans 8:16 (NLT), and lastly, but most important of all, through Scripture per Jeremiah 15:16 (NLT).

2 Timothy 3:16-17 elucidates that "All Scripture is God-breathed and is useful for teaching, rebuking, correcting and training in righteousness, so that the servant of God may be thoroughly equipped for every good work" (NIV). Just remember, God is a God of order, never confusion. Do not allow yourself to be confused in His presence. Our human nature makes it so easy for us to overcomplicate God's ways but John 10:10 gives us the simple understanding: all good comes from God and all bad comes from the enemy. Period. Full stop. Let me elaborate:

God's voice:	Satan's voice:
Leads you	Pushes you
Stills you	Rushes you

Reassures you	Frightens you
Encourages you	Discourages you
Enlightens you	Confuses you
Calms you	Worries you
Comforts you	Obsesses you
Convicts you	Condemns you

If you can only remember two of these, remember that <u>God convicts, and the devil condemns</u>. I know how easy it is to think God judges us like we judge ourselves but that is contrary to His word! Romans 8:1 says "There is no condemnation for those who belong to Christ Jesus" (NLT). Maybe you'd tell me, "But what if I lied/stole/harmed/fornicated/cheated, etc., etc., etc.?" to which my response would be "BECAUSE GOD SAID SO." Or perhaps you'd ask "But what if I caused mess/confusion/disruption/chaos/pain, etc., etc., etc.?" to which I'd also reply, "BECAUSE GOD SAID SO! Either you're going to believe God's Word or you're not!

If I'm striking a nerve, and you've never read the fictional book *This Present Darkness* by Frank Peretti, give it a read. Peretti's remarkably visual writing will make you shockingly aware of the supernatural battle going on around you, that you may not know to take seriously.[14] Although Peretti construes his own depiction of angels and demons, God's Word is clear that spiritual warfare is REAL. This book reminded me that prayer is our best weapon against it!

Another excellent read if you want to learn to pray without

ceasing and engage in an ongoing conversation with God instead of being trapped by structured discipline, is *The Practice of the Presence of God* by Brother Lawrence (born Nicolas Herman).[15] This read will encourage you to go to God for all things in your calendar (and more)! But I particularly love that it inspired me to set prayer reminders through the calendar app I use on my phone. From family members' work presentations to birthdays of friends to recalling deceased loved ones' last day on earth, to dance recitals and sports tournaments, I pray over it all. I also make sure when God places someone, anyone, on my mind, I drop whatever I am doing to say a quick popcorn prayer over them.

No matter how God speaks to you, He will never give a word contrary to His Holy Bible. God is never early and He's never late. He's always right on time and His plans for you, NO MATTER WHAT YOU'VE DONE, are good. God is a God of LOVE and order. If the voice you are hearing doesn't sound like those things, then it is not from Him. Envelop your whole life with prayer and watch the blessings pour down! God wants to spend time with you! Genuine, unrehearsed time!

Matthew 6:7 says "But when ye pray, use not vain repetitions, as the heathen do: for they think that they shall be heard for their much speaking" (NKJV). If you don't have a prayer journal, get one! A 99 cent notebook will do the trick. Or even a journal with prayer prompts. The only word of caution I would give you is to be careful about resources that restrict you. Pre-written prayers may provide you with ideas, but the temptation to read them without the words being from your heart is too great. Since variety keeps your prayer life fresh, on the pages that follow, **I'll share 65 types of prayer that have brought my family and I closest to the Lord during this waiting season**. Whenever you try one, I strongly urge you to WRITE YOUR EXPERIENCES DOWN. If you're like me, you may automatically think there isn't much point to this because of your propensity to lose it, but I assure you there is!

We all have busy brains that get sidetracked by a million things while praying. You know, thoughts of food we forgot to put away, or a loved one we were supposed to call. There are so many interruptions that can make us forget what we were even praying about! Writing, unlike thinking, requires greater focus, so writing prayers helps one harness a wandering brain and helps one to better listen to God.[48] Plus, *just in case I don't lose whatever I'm keeping notes on,* writing my experiences gives me a record of what I was praying about so I can look back and be amazed by the moves of God in my life.

1. **Study the Lord's Prayer.** Stop using the Lord's Prayer like a ritual. You are God's child, not a beggar! Don't plead for Him to move. Know He already did! Act like He unconditionally loves you until you believe that with all that you are! Rather than ritualistically using the Lord's Prayer, read it, meditate on it, and tell God the wisdom you're drawing from it, which you'll apply to

your life. For example, since the Lord's Prayer was written before Christ's resurrection, you can rest assured that God will NOT "lead [you] into temptation" as mentioned in the thirteenth verse. As another example, I gleaned from the eleventh verse ("Give us this day our daily bread") to pray with intrepidity instead of "if's." I learned to say "God, I'm taking your abundant provision that's already mine according to Psalms 132:15" (NIV) instead of praying something like "God I know I'm not worthy or deserving, but if you would be so gracious, I would love for you to provide for my family and I." I learned in Hebrews 4:16 that God wants us to be so familiar with His love that we approach Him boldly (NLT). So instead of approaching Him like my judge or disappointed boss, I'm learning to approach Him like my loving Daddy God. Growing up, I heard the Lord's Prayer so often when I attended Catholic mass with my dad that I honestly didn't know it came from Matthew 6:9-13. It is actually the prayer that Jesus used to model to His disciples the correct posture of your heart when talking to God. Jesus did not say, "Here is an idea for prayer for you to repeat over and over throughout your life" but rather, "When you pray, pray this way!" As I noted earlier, Matthew 6:7 tells us we're not to make "vain repetitions expecting that we will be heard for our many repetitive words" (NIV). Furthermore, in John 14:13-14 Jesus tells us "Whatever you ask in My name, that will I do, so that the Father may be glorified in the Son" (NLT). Notice that the Lord's Prayer is not prayed in the name of Jesus. Therefore, it technically does not qualify as a new covenant prayer that we should be repeatedly reciting since we've been instructed to pray in the name of Jesus. Hence, my recommendation is not to copy its words, but rather its intentions. There is so much insight to be uncovered in those 72 words in the Lord's prayer! As you study them, tell the Lord about your refreshed understanding of them.

2. **Good 'ol ACTS.** Since the ACTS prayer method is based on the Lord's Prayer, I also used to think it was reserved for Catholics. How wrong I was! The four types of prayer that go by these names are found in many places in the Bible! The ACTS prayer model can help any believer focus on who God is and what He has done before laying desires before Him so He'll reveal His continued work. It's as simple as this:
1. Adoration (praise) "Lord, you are…"
2. Confession (let something go) "Lord, I receive your forgiveness for…"
3. Thanksgiving (thank you) "Lord, thank you for…"
4. Supplication (please - praying for needs of others and self) "Lord show me…" and "Lord, I am declaring"

3. **Five Rs Examen Prayer.** Yep, you guessed it. The Examen Prayer is another prayer method I learned in Catholic church growing up. It's a prayer that was developed by St. Ignatius Loyola in the 16th century that helps one to review their day with Jesus, examine where one shined His light in the world, and where one fell short, that way Jesus can highlight where one needs work, rather than letting those areas rear their ugly heads over and over on future days without correction. Here's what you discuss with the Lord in this prayer:

    1. RECOGNIZE your blessings
    2. REQUEST for the Holy Spirit to show you what you need to see
    3. REPLAY your day
    4. REPENT for where you fell short
    5. RESOLVE to do better tomorrow

4. **Five Finger Prayer.** I learned this in Awana as a kid: Thumb- pray for those closest to you (family and friends), Pointer- pray for those who lead and guide (mentors, teachers, colleagues, pastors, police, etc.), Middle- pray for those in authority (city, nation, and world leaders), Ring- the weakest finger reminds us to pray for those who are overwhelmed (by sickness, sadness, loneliness, etc.), Pinky- this smallest finger reminds us to pray for ourselves last (our requests, needs, desires, etc.)

5. **No More Loopholes Prayer.** Read 2 Chronicles 7:14 and believe that IF you humble yourself and pray and seek God's face and turn from your wicked ways, you will hear from heaven and God will forgive your sins and restore your land! Receive God's forgiveness for thinking your wrongs are not *that* bad. Turn away from your sin! Don't entertain it! Turn away from it! Dedicate yourself to constantly placing yourself under God's Word and staying in your spirit instead of your flesh! Say "God, You set me free! What You have is so much greater than what I think is great!"

6. **Thanks, Take, Love Prayer.** "Father, thank You! I take my _______ (insert any character trait such as faith, confidence, worth, etc. the enemy has tried to steal) back. I love You, Father!"

7. **Position in Christ Prayer.** Declare aloud: "I am worthy. I am helped. I am loveable."

8. **Lack Nothing Prayer.** "Father, thank You that You have already provided everything I need. You never deny me anything good!"

9. **Staying Thankful.** Name aloud as many reasons as you can think of to bless God's name! Make this simple prayer about HIM and not about you!

10. **TTYL Prayer.** Draw four boxes and answer the following questions.

Thought	True?
(Tell God about the negative thought that is stealing your mood.)	(Is it true or false? Have God help you to see things not as they seem to be but as they are.)
Yahweh	Lighten
(Yahweh=eternal I am; Share with God aloud what Scripture says.)	(CHOOSE to give this heavy load to God. When the thought tries to return, tell it NO!)

11. **Love Simile Prayer.** Simply say "God, your love for me is like …." and you fill in the blank with any comforting comparison that comes to mind. I appreciate that this forces us to pray with more periods than question marks. Remind yourself God is not mad at you! You can approach Him without any fear! He took ALL of His anger out on His own son over two thousand years ago on the cross.

Remember in John 19:30 Jesus proclaimed, "It is finished" (NIV). BELIEVE those words! Does God have to send Jesus to be crucified again in order to convince you of this truth?! It's done. His wrath is gone. Poof. The end. When we pray timidly believing as if He is mad or disappointed, we're almost embarrassing God's reputation. When others hear us pray from a heart of defeat instead of from a heart of triumph, they probably think of us like an abused animal and God like a careless owner. How sad! Focus on His love, instead of your inadequacy!

12. **Plain Hamburger Prayer.** Bun (praise), patty (petition), bun (praise). That's it! This will prevent you from fixating on and thus intensifying your fears by making a fuss about everything that is going wrong in your life. Here is what that sounds like in prayer: "Oh God, I am so scared of ______ and ____ is so bad!" Even if faced with a hard blow at word or a hard medical diagnosis, pray more like this: "Father, thank You that Your name is above every name. Cancer has a name. Layoffs have a name. Co-workers' complaints have a name. AIDS has a name. These things the doctor told me are in my body have names. You are above them all! Thank You that You are greater, stronger, and more powerful than all of this!" It's that simple! Here's another: "Father, this is so small in comparison to what You're able to do. I don't receive the commentary my co-worker shared with me today. You have the final Word! You're a good father!"

13. **Getting Jiggy with Philippians.** Read Philippians 2:5-11 aloud as a song or rap: "Consider the example that the anointed One has set before us. Let His mindset become our motivation. He existed in the form of God, yet He gave no thought to seizing equality with God as His supreme prize. Instead, He emptied Himself of His outward glory by reducing Himself to the form of a lowly servant (yes sir).

He became human. He humbled Himself in obedience to God and died a criminal's death on a cross. Therefore, God exalted Him to the highest place and gave him a name that's above every name. That at the name of Jesus every knee should bow in Heaven and on earth and under the earth and every tongue acknowledge that Jesus Christ is Lord to the glory of God the Father" (Amp, NLT, ASV). Now, based on Christ's example, declare in the name of Jesus one thing from this list that you are embracing and one opposite thing that you're forgetting:

- In the name of Jesus, I am embracing humility, not pridefulness.
- In the name of Jesus, I am embracing silence, not noise.
- In the name of Jesus, I am embracing connection, not isolation.
- In the name of Jesus, I am embracing trust, not anxious thoughts.
- In the name of Jesus, I am embracing gratefulness, not self-focus.
- In the name of Jesus, I am embracing delight, not assumptions.
- In the name of Jesus, I am embracing intentionality, not passivity.

14. **Because God Prayer.** Commit to God that you are finished wondering all of the "What if's" and acknowledge that every "What if" is from the enemy. Follow this up with the words BECAUSE GOD and then a Scripture that slays the thought. (Example: God I acknowledge that the thought "What if I don't keep my job?" is from the enemy. BECAUSE GOD 1 Corinthians 14–16 says You are not the author of confusion, but of peace" (NKJV).

15. **Make a Discovery.** Study a new idea or fact to thank God for something you didn't even know existed. Check out a library book on gardening or animal science or watch a few YouTube videos about Hawaiian culture or Persian recipes. There is SO MUCH we don't know! Researching pickleball or astronomy or the endocrine system in the human body increases our understanding of the enormity of God's work, reminding us just how huge He is. In light of His vastness, nothing we deal with is really *that* big of a problem.

16. **Zooming Out Prayer.** Calm Down. Keep your eyes shut for 30 seconds and ask yourself these 4 questions: 1. If I get this, am I happy? 2. Who is my source? 3. If Jesus comes back today, does this really matter? 4. Am I believing in the almighty God posited in Job 38:25-27 when Job asks, "Who has cleft a channel for the torrents of rain and a way for the thunderbolt, to bring rain on a land where no man is, on the desert in which there is no man, to satisfy the waste and desolate land, and to make the ground sprout with grass" (ESV)? Declare Jesus, portrayed in John 16:33 as the overcomer of the whole world, as your problem solver instead of yourself (NLT).

17. **Breathing Prayer.** Thank God for the breath in your lungs and exercise it in 3, 2, 1! Try each of these exercises 8 times:
3. Two quick, short inhales, one regular exhale (all with your nose)
2. Breath in and out of your nose. When you exhale, hum with your mouth shut.
1. Use your fingers to direct your breath; Inhale through your left nostril and exhale through your right nostril. (Hold whatever nostril you're not using. Then switch.)

18. **Revelation Prayer.** Quit fearing the silent treatment and dare to trust God. Ask Jehovah Rohi (our shepherd as

David uses in Psalm 23) for revelation! Ask Him where you are in this process you're enduring, ask for your next steps, ask what you need to do to move this forward, and most importantly, thank Him for answering you and allowing you access to His throne room! Take comfort in knowing Jehovah Rohi knows and sees all. In Jeremiah 33:3, He says "Call to me and I will answer you. I'll tell you marvelous and wondrous things that you could never figure out on your own" (MSG).

19. **Pass the Oil!** James 5:14-15 says "Is any one of you sick? He should call the elders of the church to pray over him and anoint him with oil in the name of the Lord. And the prayer offered in faith will make the sick person well; the Lord will raise him up. If he has sinned, he will be forgiven" (NIV). In case you didn't know it, the same authority Jesus has to heal the sick, cast out demons, break strongholds, and raise the dead resides in YOU as long as you believe Jesus to be your Lord and savior! Think about the penitent thief who died on a cross next to Jesus. We learn from his deathbed request for Jesus to remember him in the Gospel of Luke that **simple faith** in who Jesus is and what He can deliver brings salvation, even in one's final moments of life. All the thief had to do was believe Jesus was a Savior King able to take him to His real heavenly kingdom. If you're overcomplicating this, stop! Ask your closest loved one(s): "In what areas of my life do you see me needing to mature?" This is scary, yet insightful at the same time. Based on their answer, have them select three Scriptures to declare aloud over you. (If they think you struggle with impatience, for example, all they have to do is Google three Scriptures that specifically address overcoming impatience.)

20. **21 Gifts.** Read about the 21 gifts God freely gives to all of His believers so you can tap into them for yourself! Nine of

them are presented in 1 Corinthians 12, seven of them in Romans 12, and five of them in Ephesians 4. Study one gift per day until you've learned about them all. As you pray and internalize them, claim them as your own! For example, "God, I know the gift of healing is mine and I'm taking it in the name of Jesus!"

21. **Planting Seeds.** Get a dollar pack of seeds or beans. Every time you pray over your current situation (like me with wanting to know where I will work tomorrow), place a seed into a jar. As they increase in number, the visual of all these seeds planted in the spirit will reassure you of your consistent pursuit of the Lord. Know that He does hear you and honors your pursuit!

22. **7 Types of Prayer from the Bible.** A strong prayer life incorporates various prayer types; it doesn't robotically stick to the same kinds of prayer over and over. Take a week studying Scripture and examples of the following seven types of prayer from the Word of God:
    1. Adoration
    2. Lament
    3. Thanksgiving
    4. Petition
    5. Deliverance
    6. Contrition
    7. Guidance

23. **Calendar Prayers.** Get a calendar and mark every day for the upcoming month with different prayer requests, preferably for a different person or family each day of the month. As each day comes, reap accountability from your calendar and follow through with praying over the requests you listed.

24. **Driving Prayer.** Maybe this is the only time you're alone with God. Take advantage! Pray aloud and worship without any distractions! Shout, scream, and yell if you want to! No one can stop you!

25. **Snail Mail Prayers.** Buy postcards and stamps. Get addresses of friends and family members (yes, even if they live in the same city as you) and ask for their top prayer requests so you can send them a handwritten prayer for that request on a postcard. Try to write one a day for a whole month and mail them all out when the month's over.

26. **PRAY.** This is an easy one. P stands for *praise*. R stands for *repent*. A stands for *ask*. Y stands for *yield*.

27. **JOY.** Another easy one, both in memorization and execution. J stands for *Jesus* and represents a time to express your love and gratitude toward Him. O stands for *others*, representing placing the needs of someone else above our own. And Y stands for *yourself*. Simply say, "God, show me how much you love me today."

28. **Whole Wide World.** Buy a map and pray over one country each day until you've prayed for the salvation of people in every country in the whole wild world.

29. **Siren Prayer.** When you hear the siren of an ambulance, fire truck, or police car, offer a prayer for comfort and protection of the driver, the person needing help, and their families.

30. **Prayer Closet Prayer.** Find a space in your house where you can pray in absolute silence. Do not resist the quiet. The enemy wants you to get busy doing just about anything else. OVERCOME THE PLOYS OF THE ENEMY. CHOOSE JESUS!

31. **Body Prayer.** Draw an invisible line from one ear to the other, representing the horizontal line of the cross, and declare aloud "I am listening for your voice God, and my ears are open to hearing your Word all the day long." Then begin drawing an invisible line from your face down to your feet as you pray declarations over your other body parts, one at a time. As you touch your eyes, say "God I see your glory in all of my life." Touch your mouth and say, "God I am unashamed to say the name of Christ and speak of you to others." Touch your heart and say, "I am loved by you God and I belong to you." Touch each of your hands and say, "God equip my hands to show who You are to others through my work and deeds." Touch your feet and say, "I seek only to follow you God, and to walk in your ways."

32. **Interactive Gratitude Journaling.** Healing is found not in the absence of pain, but in the presence of Jesus. Do you know the name Jesus means "God saves"? You're made perfect in His presence. Simply grab a fresh page in a journal and draw a horizontal line dividing it in half. On the top, write "Dear God" and start sharing with Him from your heart what you are grateful for. Then, take a moment to listen to God's response, and on the bottom, write "Dear Child of Mine," followed by your impression of how God's responding to you.

33. **Nature Prayer.** Go outside and lay on the grass. Bask in God's goodness. Ask for His help to use your five senses through your spirit instead of your flesh so you can see as He sees, hear as He hears, taste as He tastes, smell as He smells, and touch as He touches.

34. **Prayer with Others.** Prayer shouldn't be focused solely on ourselves. In fact, Jesus encouraged us to gather together in

prayer. He promised to be in our midst wherever two or more are gathered in his name. Praying with others increases our faith and stamina. Plus, we get encouraged when others intercede on our behalf. We also get practice praying aloud for others. With that said, the remaining prayer types on this list should involve those closest to you.

35. **Listening prayer.** I love to take my family to pray outside amid God's creation with a journal and a pen. I tell them God gave us two ears so we will listen twice as much as we speak. I set a timer for 10-15 minutes and we all sit in silence, listening, and doodling in our journals whatever God drops into our spirits whether it's a certain word or phrase, a Bible verse, lyrics to a song, or an image for us to draw, etc. After this we each share what we got and it always fits perfectly together as if we each had a piece of a puzzle that God used to project one cohesive message for that day.

36. **Balloon Prayer.** Write down something you need God's help with on a balloon. Blow it up, but don't tie it. Instead, you and your loved ones all let your balloons go after the count of 3! Grab the balloon that lands nearest to you and pray out loud over that person's need.

37. **Candy Prayer.** Pass a bag of colored sweets around as you and your loved ones each pick a sweet. Each person will pray a short prayer about the category linked to that color. Here are some category ideas:
    Red: family
    Pink: friends
    Green: animals/environment
    Yellow: work/school
    Orange: other countries/missionaries
    Purple: church

38. **Spaghetti Praise Prayer.** Read some Bible verses about God's character. Take turns saying words to describe God. Then give everyone some cooked spaghetti and encourage them to make one of the words that describe God. When done, each of you will pray using that word.

39. **Family Prayer Journal.** Dedicate a notebook as your family's prayer journal to track prayer joys and concerns. Pass it around at dinner time so everyone gets a chance to write in it.

40. **Letter to Self Prayer.** Choose a promise from the Bible to declare over yourself and write a letter telling yourself ways you need to see yourself more like God sees you. Say all the things you wish a Godfather or mother would say, both corrective and motivational. When done, have your spouse or a close loved one read it aloud to you and then have them pray that the encouragement you gave yourself be deeply received and applied.

41. **Baking Prayer.** Bake something with a surprise element inside, like brownies with nuts, cake with peanut butter chips, cookies with chocolate chips, etc. As each person gets a dessert treat, for every surprise element inside, they must pray to God about one thing they are grateful for. What a great way to earn your dessert calories!

42. **Double Cover Prayer Chains.** Cut small rectangular strips of paper and write a prayer on each. Link them together and do this for as long as you'd like--a week, a month, whatever. When you decide you're done, you can work backwards, praying each prayer again, as you unlink papers one by one. Talk about changes you observed from the time the prayers were initially written to the time you prayed them again.

43. **Prayer Walk.** Walk outside together praying aloud or quietly. As you walk by others' homes, pray for the health and salvation of the people living in them. Do the same for those in any cars passing by.

44. **ABC Prayer.** Take turns offering a caring prayer about something beginning with each letter of the alphabet.

45. **Power Prayer.** Get something noisy with a power plug like a blender, hair trimmer, electric hair dryer, etc. Ask your loved ones to describe its purpose and discuss your amazement at what it can do. Point out that without electricity (power), this tool won't work. Compare the power that prayer can bring to your lives to the power that electricity brings to the tool you have. When we serve God and converse with Him through prayer, He gives us power to do amazing things.

46. **Tasks Prayer.** Chores are such a chore, or are they? Life's all about perspective. Instead of dreading chores, I encourage you and your loved ones to embrace your chores as a gift! As you and your family take time to wash clothes, clean the dishes, tidy the house, etc. say a prayer of thanksgiving to God for blessing you with clothes, food, your home, etc. Remind your family it is better to have what you have, chores and all, than to lack and have no chores at all.

47. **Hand Squeeze Prayer.** Gather as a family in a circle. Hold hands and close your eyes. Choose someone to say a prayer of petition for spiritual or physical goods for the family. When they are done, they squeeze the hand of the person to their right and that person squeezes the hand of the person on their right, so on and so forth until the first person who prayed squeezes the hand of the person to their right for a second time, at which point they shout "Time!" (Time this

to see how long it takes you to squeeze hands around the circle.) You'll repeat this in between prayers until everyone in the circle has prayed. Try to get faster and faster, beating your best times! It's a fun way to stay fully attentive while praying!

48. **Family Tree Prayer.** Each loved one shares a memory of someone in the extended family. As you finish talking about the person, spend time in prayer thanking God for them and their influence on the family.

49. **Candle Prayer.** Let each person light a real or fake candle as they intercede on behalf of someone else's request. When done, sing "This Little Light of Mine" together.

50. **Headline Prayer.** Lay out a real newspaper (usually found at gas stations and grocery stores) and let each loved one choose a story to pray about.

51. **Bubble Gum Prayer.** Give each family member a colored gum ball and ask them to pray for the first thing that comes to mind when they saw the color of their gum ball. Close by seeing who can blow the biggest bubble!

52. **Hat Prayer.** Each loved one writes a prayer of praise or concern on a small slip of paper. All the prayers are tossed into a hat. Every person draws out a slip of paper (except their own) and prays for that request. If you don't have a hat, a bowl or cup works just as well.

53. **Bonfire Prayer.** Each loved one holds a stick, twig, or small piece of wood and says a prayer aloud declaring something they're letting go of, then tosses their stick in the fire, symbolizing the end of whatever the stronghold was and the beginning of their full surrender to God.

54. **Peacemaking Prayer.** Use this prayer when two loved ones are disagreeing. Grab any object (stick, remote, cup, you name it) and tell them the first person holding the object needs to confess their part in the disagreement in wording like "When I _____, I'm sure you felt _____." Then they pass the object to the other person who will confess their part in the disagreement using the same wording. Then the object will get passed again as the two take turns praying aloud to God to ask for forgiveness for not showing love to their loved one. We all need to remember that a sin against a person is ultimately a sin against God, whose greatest commandment is for us to love one another.

55. **Ball Toss Prayer.** Have your loved ones stand in a circle. One person begins by holding a soft ball (or water balloon if you'll do this outside)! The person holding the object offers a prayer acknowledging their dependence on God like "I need God because…" and then tosses the ball/balloon to someone else, who prays the same, and tosses to someone else. Continue until everyone has had the chance to pray.

56. **Paper Airplane Prayer.** Each loved one writes on a full sheet of paper a simple prayer for something they desire or something they need help with. Then each person folds the paper into their best paper airplane. Before flying them, write GOD on a large sheet of paper or a white board and place it in the middle of the floor. Ask everyone to throw their paper airplanes to land on the GOD sign. Let them have as many attempts as they need. Emphasize to your family that just like our planes take time to hit the mark, the same is true with our prayers, which God answers in HIS perfect timing.

57. **Cube Prayer.** On a wooden block, dry erase block, or small square cardboard box, draw a different symbol or

write a different name on each of the six sides. Have each loved one roll the cube like dice, then offer a prayer of intercession in accordance with the symbol or name they land on.

58. **Location prayer.** Go to a location and pray over your petitions regarding that location in person. Pray for favor, blessings, intervention, or whatever outcome you are asking for at that location. Remember no door opens or shuts without God's orders!

59. **Flashlight Prayer.** Wait for nighttime and turn out the lights. Give each of your loved ones a flashlight. This is extra fun when the flashlight is covered with different colors of tissue paper. Each person only turns their light on when it is their turn to pray a prayer of praise, expressing their love for a blessing God bestowed upon them in the past. (It's storytelling time!)

60. **Paper Towel Prayer.** Take a roll of paper towels OR toilet paper and spend some time writing short, encouraging Scriptures on as many sheets as you and your loved ones can. Re-roll them when done. When a person comes across the Scriptures, tell them to declare them aloud in prayer! This will edify and uplift them!

61. **Prayer of Special Blessing.** Ask one loved one for their prayer requests and have that loved one kneel in the center as all others gather around to lay their hands on the person's shoulders/head/arms/heart, or wherever the Holy Spirit leads them to lay their hands. Offer prayers of comfort, thanksgiving, healing, transformation, or whatever is needed. Do this for a different loved one each day until everyone has had a turn. Repeat as often as you enjoy.

62. **Washed Away Prayer.** Give each loved one a washable marker to write on their palm one sin they want washed away. Take turns praying aloud a prayer of confession. Bring out a bowl of water, soap, and a washcloth/towel. Have each person wash their own hand OR another person's (especially if this is a sin this person has held onto for a while) and hold it up to God once it's clean, thanking God that because of Jesus' death on the cross, our sins are forgiven!

63. **Parachute Prayer.** Secretly assign each family member one of these five main forms of prayer: Blessing and Adoration (acknowledging our dependence on God), Petition (asking God to grant a desire of our hearts), Intercession (praying for the requests of others), Thanksgiving (thanking God for all He does for us), or Praise (expressing our love for God). Form a circle around a large sheet, with each loved one holding onto its edges. Each time a prayer is offered, those who didn't pray guess what kind of prayer it was. If they answer correctly, everyone gets to raise the sheet high, then lower it slowly. If they answer incorrectly, everyone shakes the sheet left and right, left and right.

64. **Faith works prayer.** Write the word "faith" on a poster. Have each family member add post-it notes to the poster containing examples of prayers that God has answered. The prayer can be from a situation in the Bible, from their own experiences, or from someone else's experiences. Tell God you recognize that answered prayers encourage people's faith. Seeing how God came through in the past gives us faith for the future.

65. **Hand stack prayer.** Everyone takes turns saying single sentence gratitude prayers on the same subject, like favorite memories from the day or favorite character traits in each

other. As each person takes their turn to pray, they add their hand on top of someone else's. The one who starts (and therefore has their hand on the bottom), decides when to stop the prayer by lifting everyone's hands up, just like sports teams do before a big game.

I've saved my best faith boosting suggestion for last: **pray in tongues for ten minutes a day!** PLEASE DON'T STOP READING HERE.

If you haven't prayed in tongues before, my suggestion to do so may be EXTREMELY off putting. I get it. I was there! But have you ever thought that it might be controversial for a REASON? As in because it's a secret prayer language that the devil can't understand? Believe me. If the enemy can pervert our view of this weapon, he will. I know this takes faith to even read because you've probably at least heard someone pray in tongues before and your natural mind convinced you that it's a bunch of bobdily gook. It's not! Let's let the Word of God introduce the topic. Romans 8:24-27 says this:

> "For in this hope we were saved. But hope that is seen is no hope at all. Who hopes for what they already have? But if we hope for what we do not yet have, we wait for it patiently. In the same way, the Spirit helps us in our weakness. We do not know what we ought to pray for, but the Spirit himself intercedes for us through wordless groans. And he who searches our hearts knows the mind of the Spirit, because the Spirit intercedes for God's people in accordance with the will of God" (NLT).

"Wordless groans" help you abide in the will of God. Reading this for the first time helped me to feel less unqualified. Sometimes even the word tongues is intimidating. If it is, call it spirit taught words instead. They don't have to make sense to you, and they may make you feel foolish at first, but surrendering yourself fully to this prayer process without being blocked by embarrassment or doubt will enable the Holy Spirit to intercede for you. Let Him carry the burdens you don't have words for! It's a total game changer!

Once I got this right, everything else that was right followed. I stopped praying the same scripted prayers every day and allowed myself to be a human, not a robot, before God. Can you imagine how dead and boring any friendship of yours would be if the only words you spoke to that friend were the same exact words you recited the day before that and the day before that and the day before that? One simply can't have a robotic prayer life like that and wonder why they're not feeling anything when they pray.

For me, the key to unlock my boring prayer life was to start devoting ten minutes a day to praying in tongues. Just ten out of 1,440 minutes we get each day is certainly doable. I look up ten minutes worth of worship music on Spotify and play it so loud that I can't hear my doubts! This is important because I used to be especially skeptical about praying in tongues. It seems like an off-limits taboo topic, but I'm sure I'm not alone. Most born-again Bible believing Christians I've known think praying in tongues is fake. If the devil can keep you from trying it, he can keep you from reaping from it!

Let me put the devil on blast. Yes, tongues is for anyone. 1 Corinthians 14:1 says, "Follow the way of love and eagerly desire spiritual gifts…For anyone who speaks in a tongue does not speak to men but to God. Indeed, no one understands him; he utters mysteries with his spirit." (NLT) Speaking in tongues aids personal growth and trust in the Lord. Paul asserts in verse four that "He who speaks in a tongue edifies himself" (NLT). Speaking in tongues can help the Lord draw emotions out of your spirit which you cannot express with words.

The first time I was invited to an altar call where people were praying in tongues, I remember being wrought with disappointment. I held my hands open to the Lord, dropped my jaw, and cried as nothing came out. I thought praying in tongues meant some sort of superhero wind would enter my body through my mouth like you'd see in a movie, and I would start to speak a magical foreign language. That sure isn't what happened! I recall a sister in Christ telling me to get out of my head, that all I was doing was making noises unto the Lord and trusting Him to make sense of them. She even told me to start and stop several times to show me no pixie dust was involved. I was the one making these sounds and believing in faith that God would use them to do work in me that I didn't know needed to be done.

Most people begin with tiny little sounds akin to baby

babble: a, ba, sa, ta, sha, etc. The sounds you make do start to change after a while, as God orchestrates, but He places no time limit on it. It's not comparable to exercising or going on a diet that guarantees a certain change by day 33, though I can guarantee it does produce change in everyone who utilizes it. What happens neurologically—as we'll explore further in the next stride—when one prays in tongues makes fighting past the awkwardness so very worth it. And for busy minds like mine, I sure appreciate that it prevents my thoughts from wandering since it occupies my voice and mind simultaneously.

If you want new results in your prayer life, please hear me out. You won't get new results with old actions. I promise you that. Praying in tongues can help you break pattern emotional states that dominate you in the midst of hardship (ie. anxiety, worry, fear of failure, fear of death, etc.).

Life Application Challenge 5*: Pray in tongues for ten minutes a day! As culled from Isaiah 28:11, allow the Holy Spirit to elicit His hidden wisdom from your "stammering lips" (NIV). The Bible says when you are praying in tongues, it is your spirit that is praying. Then it gives you this command in 1 Corinthians 14:13: "If you speak in tongues, pray also that you may interpret," (NLT). Keep a pen and notebook with you so you can write down revelations you receive!*

Lyrics to Adam's Pick: "Reason to Praise" by Bethel Music and Cory Asbury

After this stride, I thought I'd suggest reading the lyrics to Prayer Warrior, sung by Heirloom, because it reminds me that regardless of my job description, I can stand in the gap for others and reach Heaven. I can be a prayer warrior! My firstborn son Adam's pick, which he was introduced to by Journey Church in McAllen, Texas, does the same, times ten. When I'm at my end, I look at Adam and I remember his name means "new beginnings." Each of us are always just one right choice away from a new beginning. "Reason to Praise" dares Adam to praise God for not ignoring his prayers or withdrawing His love from him, as promised in Psalm 66:20 (NIV). We all know to praise God for blessings we have now or

had in the past, but if we want to take our faith to the next level, we'll praise Him for unrealized blessings! The ones we have yet to see with our natural eyes!

When I'm at my end,
You're just getting started
When I hit a wall,
You just walk through
When I face a mountain,
You are the Maker
So it's gotta move

When I'm out of faith
and You are still faithful
When I'm at my worst
and You are still good
In all of my questions,
You are the answer
It all points to You

'Cause You're the God
of the breakthrough
When I'm breaking down
You'll be working a way
through
When there's no way out
This one thing I know,
You're still on Your throne
So whatever I'm feeling
I've still got a reason to

Praise, praise

I've still got a reason to praise
Praise, praise

'Cause You're the God of the
breakthrough
When I'm breaking down
You'll be working a way
through
When there's no way out
This one thing I know,
You're still on Your throne
So whatever I'm feeling
I've still got a reason to praise
Help me say
Praise, praise, yeah

Out of our wrongs, You write
our story
And out of the cross come
rivers of grace
And out of the grave bursts a
revival
No tomb can contain

Praise, praise
I've still got a reason to praise
Come on, sing this with me
(2X)

You keep moving, You keep
working
So I've still got it
I've still got a reason to praise
You keep moving, You keep

I've still got a reason to praise

When You come around
Dry bones come to life
Deserts to paradise
Stones just start rollin' away
When You come around
My heart starts to beat again
Lungs stretch to breathe You in
Souls just erupt into praise (2X)

'Cause You're the God
of the breakthrough
When I'm breaking down
You'll be working a way
through
When there's no way out
This one thing I know,
You're still on Your throne
So whatever I'm feeling
I've still got a reason to praise
Praise, praise, yeah

I've still got a reason to praise

working
So I've still got it
I've still got a reason to praise
You keep moving, You keep
working
So I've still got it
I've still got a reason to praise
You keep speaking, You keep
acting
I've still got it
I've still got a reason to praise

Praise, praise
I've still got a reason to praise
Praise, praise
I've still got a reason to praise
Praise, praise
I've still got a reason to praise
Praise, praise (still got it)
I've still got a reason to praise
Praise (praise God), praise
(from whom all blessings
flow)
I've still got a reason to praise
Praise, praise
I've still got a reason

To praise

<u>Stride 6: Internalize</u>

2 Kings 5:11-14

Naaman is Healed of Leprosy

Elisha [whose name means "God is salvation," was the prophet successor of Elijah] sent a messenger [to Damascus, Syria, to be exact, which happens to be the oldest continuously inhabited city in the world] to say to Naaman [commander of the Syrian Army who struggled with pride], "Go, wash yourself seven times in the Jordan, and your flesh will be restored and you will be cleansed."

But Naaman went away angry and said, "I thought that he would surely come out to me and stand and call on the name of the LORD his God, wave his hand over the spot and cure me of my leprosy.

Are not Abana and Pharpar, the rivers of Damascus, better than any of the waters of Israel? Couldn't I wash in them and be cleansed?" So he turned and went off in a rage.

Naaman's servants went to him and said, "My father, if the prophet had told you to do some great thing, would you not have done it? How much more, then, when he tells you, 'Wash and be cleansed!'"

So he went down and dipped himself in the Jordan seven times, as the man of God had told him, and his flesh was restored and became clean like that of a young boy (NLT).

Naaman thought he was a pretty big deal, and in the eyes of man, he was, but earthly successes matter not to God. What we think will directly become who we are. Naaman thought he was above average society and acted as such.

When he caught wind that the prophet Elisha—who had healed a great number of ills—was coming to his land, he practically demanded preferential treatment from Elisha, and as someone with such a high social rank, he was appalled when Elisha told him to go wash himself in the Jordan River, where commoners bathed. But this was for a purpose. Naaman's pride was killing his conscience and his potential. He needed to humble himself and yep, take a bath, seven times. Perhaps each dip was to shed a different flaw standing between him and God—once for stubbornness, once for arrogance, once for cynicism, etc. etc. I wonder how many dips Elisha would say that you or I nccd and for what.

I know one of my dips would be for not forgetting after forgiving. As Jennie Allen attests in *Get Out of Your Head*[56], I have to become great at forgetting. I can't say I'm a new creation, with a new identity, and a new drive, if I am still convinced that Jesus needs me to help him remember my own or others' track records. Like Naaman, I need to forget that my past is filled with how incredible I am, and that I've built my identity upon praises of others and my abilities, yet I've wondered why before this wait, I wouldn't feel like I needed God or why I didn't want to grow in spiritual maturity.

Maybe you need to forget because you built your identity on the opposite—your lack of amazingness—and you can't seem to find your worth, let alone be bold enough to sow seeds of life into another person. Or maybe you just need to forget the past. Maybe your thoughts are consumed with your fear that if people knew about the shameful things in your past, they'd want nothing to do with you. This, too, is a form of pride. Remember I is in the center of this word: prIde. Whether constantly thinking highly or lowly of oneself, the heart issue is the same: pride.

Through Naaman's seven dips, we learn an important lesson on respecting how the Lord plans to heal us internally, instead of how we envision the healing should go. Changing circumstances are inevitable for all of us, but whether we grow through them is optional. Daily we can choose to increase our faith or increase our fear. It's one or the other.

Amid the bubonic plague in 1910, so many people were dying that the American government began paying people large sums of money to bury bodies in mass graves without fearing they'd get sick and die, too. Canadian-American missionary John G. Lake was up for the challenge. As a matter of fact, he would help carry and bury loads of dead bodies without any payment in return. He chose faith over fear. As documented by Andrew Wommack in *The Power of Imagination*, once a doctor directly asked Lake, "What have you been doing to protect yourself?" to which Lake replied, "I believe that as long as I keep my soul in contact with the living God so that His Spirit is flowing into my soul and body, that no germ will ever attach itself to me, for the Spirit of God will kill it."[16]

Lake believed this so wholeheartedly that he challenged the doctor to prove his belief with science. He had the doctor take foam from the lungs of a dead plague victim to examine under a microscope so they could see masses of living germs and then Lake told the doctor to put the deadly foam on his hand and to watch what would happen under the microscope. To the doctor's amazement, each of the germs died instantly upon contact with Lake's skin. Lake told the doctor, "That is the law of the Spirit of Life in Christ Jesus… When a man's spirit and body are filled with the presence of God, it oozes out of the flesh and the pores and it kills the germs."[16]

Tell me. When was the last time you were attacked by something of smaller magnitude, yet you accepted it? For example, think of a time when someone in your family caught a cold and you expected to inevitably get it? Or a time when an unexpected bill came in and you assumed you wouldn't be able to make it through the month? What if in those types of scenarios you chose to internalize your faith and forced your fears to starve to death? Consider trials practice. If you master activating your faith to overcome small challenges, you're much more likely to activate your faith to overcome big challenges, too.

To change results, you have to change behavior, but to change behavior, you have to change the emotional state you're in and that takes more than saying "Lord, help me feel better." It also requires a change of focus. To maximize your experiences of praying in tongues, as we discussed in the stride before this, pick any one Scripture of the week to stand on beforehand. There's plenty of material to choose from. I began with James 1:2-4 and prior to praying in tongues, said aloud: "I will be full of joy, even in my troubles, for I know that these difficulties will develop my character, strengthen my patience, and give me hope" (NIV).

Take advice from Bernard Baruch who attests that "it takes seven repetitions for the human brain to learn anything."[49] Following this line of logic, pick a Scripture of the week to meditate on. I encourage you to download the free app called Shut Up, Devil. (It's red.) It is like a dictionary of common issues along with Scripture declarations to silence evidence of those issues in your life. You'll say your Scripture declaration seven times throughout the day. I have seven alarms titled "Declaration Time" in my phone to remind me to do so. I set them two hours apart from 7am to 7pm so they go off at 7am, 9am, 11am, 1pm, 3pm, 5pm, and 7pm. You'll do this for seven to fourteen days straight—or longer if you don't have the Scripture down yet. I prefer a full fourteen days because then it stays with me for life! So every two weeks, I work on a new Scripture declaration. And no, this is not hard to do while working because saying the declaration takes less than ten seconds. Say it under your breath if ever you have to but really *try* to speak it. There is so much power in your tongue! And you're likely to believe it quicker if you hear yourself speaking it! Your brain favors your voice!

Memory work like this, along with mental gymnastics activities like painting, drawing, crafting, solving math problems, or solving puzzles, actually keep your brain younger, longer! As does good mental health, restful sleep, and a healthy diet.[17] To aid the memorization process even further, I often follow a classical approach, singing the words of a Scripture to a tune I am familiar with—usually a nursery rhyme, rap, or chant, but it can be anything.

You can tell me you're too busy, but I'll tell you eternity is on the line! Just do it! I used to avoid carving time out for this because I was "too busy" too but honestly, I didn't actually want to. I was stretched thin as it was and I didn't want to assign brain waves to anything else. I just didn't have the nerve to say that. Sometimes changing our prayer life is like starting to force ourselves to go to Bible study, or to eat healthier, or to work out. We drag our feet getting there but once we make it, we are glad we went.

Consider Scripture to be your bullets and prayer to be your spiritual gun. When trials come, you want your spiritual gun loaded! And this is an easy way to load it one week at a time! If you are left alone to your own devices, your thoughts are likely to be negative. In fact, out of the average 50,000 thoughts produced per day in your mind, 70% to 80% of those are negative! That's an average of 35 to 40,000 negative thoughts each day![18] It's no wonder why we need to be more intentional about our input! Garbage in, garbage out. But if you put the Word in, voila, when you need it, the Word comes out! No matter where you are or what you're doing.

Contrarily, the world will tell you an easy fix to your problems is simply saying positive affirmations over and over like "I am awesome, hear me roar! I'm mighty, I'm bold, I'm strong…" In my experience, that gets me fired up for a minute, but does not stay with me throughout the day or make any necessary changes to my heart.

Learning Scripture heightens my experience while praying in tongues because it helps me fixate my thoughts on the Lord. While praying in tongues for ten minutes a day, I deeply inhale the presence of God and exhale praises to Him. I also make a radical change to my physiology. I lay a blanket on the floor and kneel. My head rests in my hands on the floor as a sign of surrender to God's plan instead of my own. This is paramount. Science has long demonstrated that how you position your body fires off a different biochemistry in you. Male or female, a 2010 study conducted by the Harvard School of Business shows that positioning matters so much that just by making a noticeable difference to our typical posture (like kneeling instead of slouching), our testosterone levels increase by 20%, we decrease our cortisol (the stress hormone) by 22%, and we're 33% more likely to take action where we wouldn't have before because fear would have stopped us.[19] Isn't that incredible!

Christian neuroscientist Dr. Caroline Leaf, who has devoted her life to studying the inner-workings of the brain, has discovered that when we pray in the Spirit (tongues), our brains go into the highest intellectual state possible. She further shares:

> "I know for myself that when I pray in tongues, lots of ideas and creative thoughts come to my mind. I am in a place of receptivity that makes it easy to remember all kinds of things that are important to my vision, goals, and strategies. So as I pray in tongues I am writing down lots of really great ideas and thoughts that help me plan out my future goals."[2]

Likewise, Pastor Peter Pilt of Nowra Church of Christ in Australia, who is respected as one of the most creative preachers on the planet, has credited his daily time spent praying in tongues for easily half of all his creative ideas. Thus, he encourages other followers not to feel witless if they begin making the same sounds over and over when praying in tongues. That's normal. This is all about FAITH. A friend told me that for the whole first year after welcoming the Holy Spirit to fill her while praying in tongues, she only said a few short words repeatedly. But she was persistent regardless and one day, the dam broke, and she broke out in a flood of supernatural tongues—meaning she made many other sounds that were all new to her! Praise God!

Praying in tongues has been scientifically proven to make a

person healthier! In an article she penned on tongues, Sharon Hardy Knotts shared that brain surgeons at Oral Roberts University did a study of what happens in the brain when people pray in tongues. They determined participants secreted two chemicals that can boost the immune system by 35-40%! She spurs readers to think about the effects this can have on opportunistic diseases such as cancer, while explaining that "God created the immune system to be our defense against harmful invaders: bacterial, viral, fungal, parasitic, and even malignant."[57]

It is when the immune system is weakened that such pathogens can attack and overwhelm our bodies. We all know that keeping our immune system strong is vital to warding off diseases, and that it's salient for us to eat a healthy diet void of foods that are heavily processed."[57] Likewise, proper exercise and sleep are needed to keep our immune system strong, because God has designed our bodies to recuperate and repair themselves during sleep."[51]

Knotts adds that researchers from the University of Pennsylvania Healthcare System discovered that when one is speaking in tongues, there is decreased activity in the frontal lobes of the brain, which is the area associated with being in control of oneself! She explained that "they measured regional cerebral blood flow by special imaging machines, while the subjects were speaking in tongues; [this] showed that they were not in control of the brain's usual language centers during this activity. This was consistent with the participants' claims of a lack of intentional control while speaking in tongues and reflected a complex pattern of changes in brain activity."[50]

At the end of my ten minutes in tongues, I'll often lift my head/chin up, push my shoulders down, straighten my spine as I sit down on my couch, and kick my feet up to take stress of my heart as more of my blood gets to circulate back to my heart without fighting gravity. I place both of my hands behind my head as if I'm relaxing on a lounge chair at the beach while still maintaining my best possible back posture. I sit breathing deeply in this position for a brief moment, and I tell the Lord I am resting in Him. I thank Him for embracing me. As Sarah Mackenzie says in Teaching From Rest, "Rest, then, is not the absence of work or toil. It is the absence of anxiety or frenzy."[58] It's knowing God's got this. I can mess up every single day and He's STILL got this. He's got my husband, our children, our finances, our future. Everything. And I can trust Him more than my ability to make everything work out fine.

After decluttering so I could summon weekly meetings with roof busters, plus forming the daily habit of exercising and reading the Bible, I would say internalizing God's peace by learning Scriptures and praying in tongues is the most significant tool God has been using for my revival throughout this cherished waiting season. Praying in tongues has set me free from the mundane. It has shifted my perspective of God from being just another subject to study in my homeschool schedule to being my everything and anything. Because of the chains broken by praying in tongues, I find myself now talking freely to God all throughout the day and even at night if I wake up with attacking thoughts. Praying in tongues has helped me to better understand those attacking thoughts. Although they may not completely disappear, I've learned I can gain power over them.

Only God has access to our thoughts. The devil does not have access to our thoughts. But the devil does have access to whatever we speak into existence so the moment something negative goes from a thought to a word, or a sentence, or a proclamation, we are giving Satan a foothold. Knowing this, I measure my words so much more carefully now, and I finally understand why other Christians do too. I used to be the girl who would judge other Christians for being too giddy because that wasn't comparable to my life, but now I see them using the joy of the Lord as their strength and it doesn't mean that they don't go through their own mental battles because I'm sure they do, but they leave them inside for God to handle and don't allow Satan to use them to create more strife. I cannot say enough how sweet this newfound freedom is in my prayer life. Thanks to praying in tongues.

Before I started doing this, I'm sure my brain must have looked like a hoarder's house because I never turned it off. I was always thinking, thinking. thinking. My wheels were always spinning, spinning, spinning. Tongues for me has been much like cleaning the entire house that is in my brain and when I come out of just ten minutes of doing it, I feel new and refreshed. I feel calm. I feel ready to take on any conversation, any task, any chore. And I enjoy my obligations so much more after internalizing God's peace through Word memorization and praying in tongues. The littlest things like getting to serve my husband by preparing a meal for him produces more joy, than dread, in me. Washing the dishes and serving my kids by not asking them to do the dishes brings me so much joy too.

After praying in tongues, serving in any capacity for my family, or for others, brings me so much more joy, whereas amid the loudness of my busy life before, any of those things would have easily been the straw that broke the camel's back. My life was so unnecessarily full that I could not enjoy any moments—big or small. I give all praise and glory to God for this fresh chance to know Him in life, and to ensure my family knows Him as well, and that I get to leave a legacy behind of constantly pursuing Him, not just seeking him for one minute in the morning, before dinner, or before bed. I'm so thankful that the Lord planted the seed of want in me as soon as I asked for it—that seed has made me hunger for more of His presence in every moment of every day. I've seen Him come down and flood every place I enter, changing the atmosphere upon my entering. He's taken me up higher to His mountains of love and glory! The higher I get, the further I am from life's problems. As demonstrated in Matthew 6:33, I am learning to seek first the kingdom of God, and His righteousness; and trust that all my needs are met (KJV).

Prayer of any kind is like turning a faucet knob to get the living water (Jesus) to flow in and through you. But I find that communication with the Holy Spirit is quickened when I pray to Him in tongues. When I pray in my known language, the water still flows, just slower like when we try to prevent our pipes from freezing as cold weather comes, whereas when I pray in tongues, the faucet opens to its max and I can drink more of the living water in a shorter amount of time because I am being filled with the Holy Spirit! If you've never asked to be filled with the Holy Spirit, you should! I didn't ask until this beautiful season of waiting came because I was finally free from distractions and desperate enough, to seek it. It's like I went from accessing a glass of water to accessing the entire pacific ocean!

If you aren't disturbed by how little you can accomplish in your own strength, you won't be desperate enough to ask God for His. The bigger your pride and control, the less room you have for the Holy Spirit in your life. In the words of Wayne Grudem, when we altruistically pursue the Lord, we undergo "an event subsequent to conversion in which a believer experiences a fresh infilling with the Holy Spirit that may result in a variety of consequences, including greater love for God, greater victory over sin, greater power for ministry, and sometimes the receiving of new spiritual gifts."[21]

Matthew 3:11 records that Jesus Christ would baptize those first baptized by water "with the Holy Ghost, and with fire." This is why many people say a "fresh infilling" can feel like heat all over their body, shocks of electricity, a raised heartbeat, faster breathing, even falling to the ground. I haven't had one of these experiences yet but I am excited to. For me, infilling typically consists of feeling overwhelmed with emotion and moved to tears. I've also experienced an incessant quivering and tingling of my lips. Like 1 Corinthians 4:20 says "The kingdom of God does not consist in talk but in power." I have felt that power, but only because I finally got off my high horse where I was in control. I stopped allowing my talk to pass for my walk and I finally acknowledged what little spiritual fruit I was actually bearing. This made me distressed enough to finally die to self and be filled with the Holy Spirit.

Just like changing from one set of computer software to another, Joyce Meyer attests to anyone's ability to reprogram a "worldly" mind to think as God almighty thinks. Meyer encourages her readers' ongoing internalization of a new mindset by having them picture a baby who is learning to walk. The baby falls many times, and often cries while doing so, but the baby is persistent and gets right back up to try again and again. Meyer explains that learning to change our thinking is just like that. There will be perfect days and there will be far from perfect days where our thinking is completely negative, but the point is not to give up. If you had to eat an elephant, you would only be able to eat it one bite at a time. If you want to think like God, you will only be able to engage in transformation, one day at a time, or sometimes, more realistically, one hour at a time, one minute at a time, or one moment at a time.

Some stinkin' thinkin' is deeper seated in our minds and takes more than just desire to uproot. Exposing the beautiful interconnectedness of Scripture and science, in her bestselling book *Switch on Your Brain*, Dr. Leaf teaches a five step process which, if used in a 21 day detox cycle, actually eliminates a toxic thought you have and replaces it with a new neural network in your brain. I like to call her process my daily Neurogenesis brain breakfast.

Every day through what scientists term Neurogenesis, your brain births new nerve cells that are ready to receive whatever information and thoughts your mind will feed it. Obviously to improve your thinking, you must learn to feed it God's truth about you instead of Satan's lies. But be prepared: like people say about diets, this is more of a lifestyle change than a temporary fix. If you are looking for instant gratification, you won't find it. This is WORK, but it's necessary work! Your future and your legacy are on the line. Do you want the little ones who look up to you to struggle with the same toxicity? Of course not!

For starters, there are some ground rules. You need to know and believe that your brain is plastic! I find learning about neuroplasticity—the brain's malleability or ability to change in response to intrinsic or extrinsic stimuli by reorganizing its structure, functions, or connections—to be empowering! Our minds have the power to change patterns of our physiology and those patterns can change our brains.

Here are some examples. You might be surprised to know that when you are feeling lonely, your brain will unconsciously associate physical warmth with social warmth if you take a hot bath. When you're trying to cut back on your food intake, spending just one minute imagining that you are already full will help your brain select a smaller portion of food. When stress has you feeling you need more control in your life but the thought of cleaning your home is equally stressful, all you need to do is begin in the farthest corner of one single room, look at your feet, pick up whatever is right in front of you, and put it away.

Once you've put a single something away, force yourself to return to the same corner and do it again. Don't allow yourself to reach past what is in front of you for an easier, random task. Stay focused on what's in front of you and move clockwise from there. One section at a time. Returning to the same sections again and again will bring your brain delight as you notice the path behind being cleared. This visible result of your actions in real-time will motivate you to continue cleaning. Whereas when picking up randomly, there is no visual cue sent to your brain that you're making any progress, and you perceive the whole place to be just as messy as when you started.

When you want to find pleasure in the hard things you must do, all you have to do is give it a compound purpose by associating a hard thing with something you enjoy. For example, if you dread running on the treadmill but you love competitive baking shows, allow yourself to watch competitive baking shows while running on the treadmill! When you're doubting your productivity, keeping a to-do list or an agenda can encourage you to accomplish more.

Much like seeing yourself clear one piece of a room at a time, the visible action of marking something off your list or placing an 'X' on your agenda for the day actually releases a flood of dopamine in your brain that will propel you forward to completing more tasks. Dopamine is one of the four feel good hormones. (Serotonin, endorphins, and oxytocin are the other three). Dopamine is the neurotransmitter released in the brain that makes you feel pleasure as a part of your brain's reward system. It also plays an important role in helping nerve cells to send messages to each other so without enough of it, you lag and are more likely to suffer from mental disorders like depression, schizophrenia, and attention deficit hyperactivity disorder (ADHD), amid a myriad of medical conditions like Parkinson's, restless legs syndrome, and chronic muscle pain.

In addition to acknowledging your brain's plasticity, another ground rule is knowing and believing that you are not a victim of your biology and you are not predispositioned to be a bad person. Your future needs you! Your past doesn't! You must understand that your mind and your brain are not the same thing. Your mind is the thoughts you conjure, whether healthy or toxic. Your brain is the organ within your skull that provides the rest of your body with instructions. Though different, they are thoroughly connected. Your thoughts cause your brain to release neurotransmitters, chemical messengers that allow it to communicate with parts of itself and your nervous system. These neurotransmitters control practically all of your body's functions, from hormones to digestion to feeling sad, happy, stressed, or mad.

Each of the 50,000-70,000 thoughts you will think on average in a given day has a real and direct biological effect on 75 to 100 trillion cells in your body.[18] Simply put, your mind is controlling your brain, and your brain is controlling your life and future. Hopefully this excites you more than it scares you, because this means if you, as the landlord of your mind, evict the toxic thoughts that most prevalently attack you, you can actually change the landscape in your brain and in turn, your whole life! As pointed out by Shawn Achor in *The Happiness Advantage*, the goal here is to learn to consume enough healthy thoughts that they eventually become a part of automatization, meaning they become habitual enough to reach the non-conscious metacognitive level within your brain.

Around 95% of everything we do—our routines and patterns, automatic body function, emotion, personality, creativity, values and beliefs, cognitive biases, and long-term memory—stems from this non-conscious part of our brain.[22] It's no wonder why becoming positive is not as simple as flipping on a light switch!

Think of how you learned how to drive a car. At first you got around slowly and probably nervously, thinking about every movement of your hands on the wheel and your foot on the pedals. Accelerate, slow down, stop. Until over time, the skill of driving a car became so rooted in your brain that you could drive and not even think about it. Why? Because it moved from the conscious mind to the nonconscious mind. This is precisely how Dr. Leaf's detox works. It takes one of her twenty-one-day detox cycles to remove a weed (a toxic thought) and plant a seed for a flower (a new healthy thought). Then it takes two more twenty-one-day cycles for the flower to sprout and bloom—meaning for the new thought to automatize, or to take root, in our non-conscious brains.

Yep, you read right: this process takes 63 days (three cycles of 21 days)—one cycle nurtures the thought enough to join our long term memory and the next two cycles turn the new thought into instinct/a habit. You don't forget to take your vitamins since you know they produce a positive effect in your body, right? The same principle applies here. Your thoughts are as real as vitamins and if you commit to this process, it's important for you not to skip any days. Your new flower has to be watered daily in order to grow and thrive.

Dr. Leaf's brain detox consists of the following five steps: gather, focused reflection, write, revisit, and active reach.[2] Below I've outlined my adaptation of this process. In italics, I have provided my own examples. Just keep in mind that only the third step requires writing. The rest can be kept in your mind. I have typed a peek into my mind while completing each step only so you have an idea of how to do it yourself.

Ground Zero: Bible and Prayer in Tongues (11-15 minutes; again, this is my adaptation)

Foundational verse=Romans 10:17: "So then faith comes by hearing, and hearing by the word of God" (NKJV).

When we read the Bible, we converse with God. We make the important switch from talking about Him to talking with Him. The more we read, the more real He becomes. The more we read, the more we love Him. The more we read, the more we trust Him.

Likewise, as we abandon Christianese to freely release speech-like syllables instead of words as we pray in tongues, we experience a direct prayer language between our spirit and God's. The resulting feeling of "self-edification" is both Biblical and scientific. The human body produces adrenaline and endorphins when it experiences something new, emotional, exciting, and/or disconnected from rational thought.[60]

Step 1: Gather (1-2 minutes)

Foundational verse=2 Corinthians 10:5: "We take captive every thought to make it obedient to Christ" (NLT).

Many people do not think very often about what they think about. They just let their thoughts live inside their head, without observing or questioning them.[59] Bring to the forefront of your mind the toxic word or phrase that needs slaying. What feelings and emotions does this thought generate in your mind and in your body? Ask why. Why do you think this? When/where did it originate? Like David asking God to search his heart, ask God to search yours. Is there someone you've tried over and over to forgive but still have unforgiveness for? Is your worth dependent on your profession or how successful you are? Do you find yourself constantly saying you're stressed or overwhelmed? Are you fearful of an outcome of a certain medical condition? Now's your chance for victory, friend!

Let it out. Don't be afraid.

My example—My toxic thought running continuously in my mind is that people think I'm a loser and not enough. My mind is tormented by everyone else's reaction to me. My self-worth is entangled with my performance instead of my identity in Christ. My body freezes at times and shakes from stress. What I perceive to be God's disappointment in me frightens me. I worry about other professionals thinking I'm less intelligent than them. They don't come from where I come from. I fear failing my husband. His faith is more admirable than mine. Not being the wife he deserves or the mom my kids deserve also scares me. I think this because I don't want to misalign my priorities as my single mom did when I was growing up. I don't want a broken relationship with my family. And since I was fourteen, I have been trying to prove to people that despite getting pregnant, I do matter. I've buried past regrets with degrees and accomplishments to prevent people from seeing my insides. I want people to be proud of me.

Step 2: Focused Reflection (1-2 minutes)

Foundational verse=Philippians 4:8-9 - "Finally brothers, whatever is true, noble, right, pure, lovely, admirable, if anything is excellent or praiseworthy – think about such things" (NLT).

Let the deconstruction begin. No more dwelling on the

negatives! It's time to focus on what you will replace the toxic thought with. Describe a new thought aloud. Keep it as brief as you need but ground it in God's Word. I STRONGLY recommend finding a Scripture-based declaration in the free app called "Shut Up, Devil." That's what I do. I repeat this declaration again and again. Name the feelings and emotions that you want to experience in your mind and body in association with this new, healthier thought. Then close your eyes and imagine your free future. What can happen in your life, faith, relationships, career, etc. when the toxic thought dies?

*My example: In the fear section of the "Shut Up, Devil!" app, I read 1 John 4:18 which says, "Where God's love is, there is no fear, because God's perfect love drives out fear." And I read Isaiah 41:10 which says "Do not fear, for I am with you, do not be afraid, for I am your God. I will strengthen you, I will help you, I will uphold you with my victorious right hand." My **new thought** is a combination of these two verses: <u>"God loves me and His love for me drives out all fear from my life. He strengthens, helps, and upholds me with His victorious right hand."</u> This new thought makes me feel peace, joy, happiness, and eagerness to keep striving forward, not to become stagnant. My body feels lighter and younger. My head is high, my posture is straight, and my shoulders are down/back. My future is full of smiles and hope! I see myself sitting in the palm of God's mighty right hand! My husband is sitting with* *me, and all five of our children too. We are all laughing and enjoying one another's company. We don't contemplate yesterday or tomorrow. We are living in the present with hearts full of gratitude.*

Step 3: Write (2-3 minutes)

Foundational verse: Psalm 103:2: "Bless the LORD, O my soul, and forget not all His benefits" (ESV).

Feed your faith and your fears will starve! Journaling about God's provision in your life will help you "forget not" His goodness. Begin watering your new thought flower by writing down anything that you find encouraging, be it something funny your kids did, or your spouse said, a quote, a phrase, or Scripture you admire, or you can even spend this time drawing something that inspires you. When performance is measured, performance improves, so draw or write anything reflecting your progress toward positivity. When you can see progress before your eyes, the Holy Spirit can begin to bring revelation and healing where you need it.

My example: I want to journal about what a beautiful morning I had yesterday. Almost all of my family has been fighting a cold, and my oldest son pulled a muscle in his back, so I took him to get x-rays. The hospital I brought him to is huge and had recently reconfigured due to post-covid-19 staff shortages. I tried not to show any frustration in my face, but every time I had to take my newborn, who is also combating a cold, in and out of the car in the cold weather, I was feeling my joy slip away. Then, amid my anxious thoughts, the Lord suddenly laid it on my heart to get some red roses for my mother-in-law and my sister-in-law, who are always so good to me. "Done. I can do that," I thought.

I dropped my son off to run some of his own errands while I went to the grocery store to get a curbside order. My newborn fell asleep during the drive, so as you can imagine I didn't want to wake her by carting her into the store to get flowers. God knew and paved a way. His Word says He rewards obedience with more grace! What a Savior! This is good news because Jesus' love and presence fuels our Christian life! We experience abounding joy in His presence, which gives us power and strength, as recited in Psalm 16:11; Nehemiah 8:10; Isaiah 41:10 (NIV).

While I was in the parking lot, I saw a woman was selling something and my knee-jerk reaction was to find a different parking spot because I didn't want to be bothered but thank God I picked up my head and saw that in this woman's hands were some beautiful red roses, just as I had envisioned getting for my mother and my sister-in-law. And I wouldn't even have to get out of my car! That was so God!

I pulled over to purchase the flowers from the woman, and

she began speaking life into me and telling me to thank God for my treasures (my children), for they are His richest blessings bestowed upon my husband and I. I have been so aware of what a blessing they are throughout this season of waiting, and her words were a comforting confirmation to my soul that I am doing exactly what God wants me to do—rearing them well. I ugly cried as she began praying for me. In prayer, she told me the only instruction book I need for raising God's arrows is the Bible. She said that all the truth that I need and they need is found there and she said God is turning my tears into joy! I smiled and asked if I could pray for her in return and I prayed the blessing from Numbers over her. She cried and said that she needed that blessing too. Moments like this didn't happen to me when my life was full of noise. Now here in the quiet, I am able to be touched by God so much more and I'm SO GRATEFUL!

Step 4: Revisit (1-2 minutes)

Foundational verse=Isaiah 55:8: "For my thoughts are not your thoughts, nor are your ways my ways," declares the LORD (NLT).

You're again inviting the Holy Spirit to help you rewire your thoughts to be like His thoughts. The easiest form of learning is repetition, right? Repeat your new thought again and again along with a simple hand or body gesture (again so your brain *sees* your progress) that takes no longer than ten seconds (usually five seconds or less). I tend to keep the same gesture throughout the detox, but you could also change it up weekly, semi-weekly, each cycle, etc. You do you!

Some simple examples are saying your new thought aloud while stomping your feet four times as if you're clobbering the toxic thought, manually pushing your shoulders down and your chin up, gently tapping your heart or your head three times, pulling out a pocket mirror to see yourself, or closing your hand in a fist near your skull like you are grabbing an old thought from your head and then opening your hand like you're throwing it away, or making a gun with three fingers while only bending your ring and pinky fingers as if you're shooting your old thought. Reflexologists believe one small change in your physiology like this actually makes you hyper aware of your activities by calming your nervous system and making you breathe deeper.[54]

My example: While drawing an invisible heart in the air and then flexing my right arm, I'm repeating my new thought over and over:

God loves me and His love for me drives out all fear from my life. He strengthens, helps, and upholds me with His victorious right hand. God loves me and His love for me drives out all fear from my life. He strengthens, helps, and upholds me with His victorious right hand. God loves me and His love for me drives out all fear from my life. He strengthens, helps, and upholds me with His victorious right hand. God loves me and His love for me drives out all fear from my life. He strengthens, helps, and upholds me with His victorious right hand. God loves me and His love for me drives out all fear from my life. He strengthens, helps, and upholds me with His victorious right hand. God loves me and His love for me drives out all fear from my life. He strengthens, helps, and upholds me with His victorious right hand. God loves me and His love for me drives out all fear from my life. He strengthens, helps, and upholds me with His victorious right hand.

Step 5: Active Reach (7x throughout the day + whenever the toxic thought surfaces)

Foundational verse=Luke 21:19: "By your endurance, you will gain your life" (ESV).

This is when you actively reach for your own freedom from bondage! I told you this would take effort. You have to work hard at work worth doing! You need to repeat your new thought and gesture from Step 4 a minimum of seven times a day. Because forgetting is all too easy, I strongly recommend setting seven reminder timers in your phone two to three hours apart to make sure you accomplish this daily. Alternatively, you might track your progress by simply keeping a notebook with you throughout the day and using it to record check marks or tallies each time you recite your new thought with your hand gesture. But this requires extra diligence. You must also be prepared to repeat your new thought and gesture each time the negative thought comes up. When it comes, STOP IT IN ITS TRACKS AND REPEAT YOUR NEW THOUGHT AND HAND GESTURE! Each time you do this, you are feeding the new thought and simultaneously starving the toxic thought.

My example: I like for the new thought and gesture to be the first thing on my mind when I wake up and the last thing on my mind before I fall asleep so that's already two usages. I have daily timers set in my phone titled "Water the flower!" that go off at 7am, 10am, 1pm, 4pm, and 7pm for the remaining five usages. If I am somewhere quiet, I simply place my phone on vibrate. The notebook doesn't work for me because I get too busy to remember to use it. But of course, if at any time I'm randomly attacked by a toxic thought, I don't allow myself to be too busy to once again recite my new thought and gesture. I'm devoted to this. Without labor, nothing prospers!

It may seem like a lot but I assure you you'll get this process down within the first week that you faithfully use it. As a matter of fact, my husband and I are going through a brain detox together right now and it takes us five minutes each morning. This is what it looks like: We spend ground zero apart (we read the Word and pray in tongues solo with God) and then we follow Dr. Leaf's five step brain detox together, like so:

1. (Silently in mind:) Here's my hard thought and how it makes me feel (1 minute)

2. (Silently in mind:) Here's my new thought (from Scripture) and how it makes me feel (1 minute)

3. Write down a happy memory (2 minutes)

4. (Silently in mind:) Here's my new thought (from Scripture) again with hand gestures and my prayerful invitation for the Holy Spirit to help me rewire my thoughts.

5. We double check that our alarms are set on our phones to remind us to recite our new thoughts with hand gestures five more times throughout the day before reciting it a final time before bed.

Don't limit this process to negative thoughts. You can also use Dr. Leaf's brain detox to be cured of an often-overlooked prayer blocker: unforgiveness. It's overlooked because it's easy to think we're over an offense that we swept under a rug to avoid thinking about it. If you're not sure if unforgiveness is in your heart, ask someone in close relation with you if they believe you are still holding onto any hurt or trauma from your past. This is SO important!

Mark 11:22-26 clearly teaches us that unforgiveness hinders

our faith from working. The Father can't forgive our sins if we don't forgive other people of theirs. Maybe you're the kind of person who can forgive in an instant and move on. If you are, I applaud you. I tend to take longer than I'd like to get over things. For most of my life, I carried soul wounds related to my mom. I pretended to be healed by avoiding her and any thoughts about the situations that perpetuated my wounds, until I learned from Dr. Leaf that I can take an active role in my forgiveness journey. When you follow Dr. Leaf's process, the new neural pathways you form (series of connected neurons that send signals from one part of the brain to another) are detectable in brain scans, as is evidence of the no longer detectable neural pathways that you destroy! This is hard, necessary work.

Life Application Challenge 6: In 1 Timothy 4:13, Jesus commands, "Until I come, devote yourself to the public reading of Scripture, to exhortation, to teaching" (NLT). Pick a Scripture to internalize this week by reciting it seven times a day consecutively or every two-three hours throughout the day when your alarms go off. If you want to heal your deeper thoughts, work through Dr. Leaf's five step brain detox once per day!

<u>Lyrics to Hannah's Pick: "Million Little Miracles"</u>
<u>by Elevation Worship and Maverick City Music</u>

This one is my firstborn daughter Hannah's favorite worship songs and it suits her. Hannah, whose name means graceful and favored by God, epitomizes contentment in the Lord. Daily she teaches our family to realize the truth of 1 Timothy 6:8: God has provided everything we need for our present happiness (NIV). I love living in the moment with Hannah. Whether it's packing a diaper bag for her younger siblings without being asked, or making a detailed drawing while praying without seeking any recognition or praise, Hannah's generous spirit keeps our whole family humble. She helps us remember that when we magnify God, we realize how insignificant our problems really are.

Dr. Amanda Kay Cruz

All my life,
I've been carried by grace
Don't ask me how
'cause I can't explain
It's nothing short of a miracle
I'm here

I've got some blessings
that I don't deserve
I've got some scars,
but that's how you learn
It's nothing short of a miracle
I'm here

I think it over and it doesn't add
up
I know it comes from above

I've got miracles on miracles
A million little miracles
Miracles on miracles
Count your miracles
One, two, three, four,
I can't even count 'em all

You held me steady
so I wouldn't give up
You opened doors
that nobody could shut
I hope I never get over
what You've done

I wanna live with an open heart
I wanna live like

I've got miracles on miracles
A million little miracles
Miracles on miracles
Count your miracles
One, two, three, four,
I can't even count 'em all

Miracles on miracles
A million little miracles
Miracles on miracles
Count your miracles
One, two, three, four,
I can't even count 'em all

I can't even, I can't even count
'em all
I can't even, I can't even count
'em all
I can't even, I can't even count
'em all
One, two, three, four,
I can't even count 'em all

Yeah, I can't even count 'em
all (2X)
I try and I can't keep up (2X)
Yeah, I can't even count 'em
all (2X)
Count 'em (2X

Like when You healed my
mother
When You redeemed my
father

Peace before Increase

I know who You are
I hope I never get over
what You've done
It's not coincidence and it's not
luck
I know it comes from above

You kept my mind, Lord

You healed my body, Jesus
Oh, I can't even count 'em all
I try and I can't keep up
'Cause every day there's a new
miracle

I got breath in my lungs
I got clothes on my back
My mother would say,
I got food on my table
Lord, I know that You're able

Say, I can't even
I can't even
I can't even
Too many to count

I've got miracles on miracles
A million little miracles
Miracles on miracles
Count your miracles
One, two, three, four,
I can't even count 'em all

Miracles on miracles
A million little miracles
Thank you Jesus

Even in the death of my
brother
You were closer than no other

Oh, You broke my chains
You saved my life
You set me free
You gave me victory
Oh, I can't even count 'em all

for the miracles on miracles
Count your miracles

One, two, three, four,
I can't even count 'em all
One, two, three, four,
I can't even count 'em all (4X)

<u>Stride 7: Raisin Cakes</u>

Hosea 1:2, and 3:1-5

Hosea and Gomer

This was the Lord's first message to Hosea [a prophet who preached in the northern kingdom and prophesied just before the destruction of Israel in 722 BC]. The LORD said, "Go, marry a prostitute who has had children as a result of her prostitution. Do this because the people in this country have acted like prostitutes—they have been unfaithful to the LORD [and Hosea did just that, and with Gomer went on to welcome to the world three children—only one begotten by Hosea as evidenced by the words "she bore him a son" in Hosea 1:3 as opposed to Hosea 1:6 and 1:8 which say only that Gomer "bore a" daughter and then another son. The children's names symbolized God's judgements against the unfaithful, idol worshiping nation of Israel. Like us when we stray away from God, Gomer strays away from Hosea and commits adultery, ultimately landing herself in slavery, stripped of everything she once valued more than God, but eventually her husband retrieves her, taking her back into his home and forgiving her, just as the Lord God did for His people.]

Hosea Buys Gomer Back from Slavery

Then the LORD said to me again, "Gomer has many lovers, but you must continue loving her. Do this because it is an example of the LORD's love for Israel. He continues to love them, but they continue to turn to other gods, and they love to eat those raisin cakes" [which were intended to be worship offerings for the false god Asherah (SEC)].

So I bought Gomer back for fifteen shekels of silver, and one and one-half homers of barley [just over forty gallons of barley is worth another fifteen shekels of silver, and thirty shekels of silver is equivalent to six months of wages at the time—the same amount Judas was paid to betray Jesus (SEC)]! Then I told her, "You must stay at home with me for many days. You will not be like a prostitute. You will not have sexual relations with another man. I will be your husband."

In the same way the people of Israel will continue many days without a king or a leader. They will be without a sacrifice or a memorial stone. They will be without an ephod or a household god. After this, the people of Israel will come back and look for the LORD their God and for David their king. In the last days, they will come to honor the LORD and his goodness (NIV).

Want to know how to fixate more on God than on your problems? You fixate on God more than your problems. You force yourself to stop paying mind to whatever attention-stealing raisin cakes or "other lovers" that are exciting you more than the Lord. In Hosea's day, raison cakes were likely eaten as part of sacrificial feasts in the temples of idols, so they symbolize prioritizing other gods/distractions over the one true God.[52] Whereas Gomer completely failed to lead a God-centered life, Hosea epitomized one. They're both proof that one's relationship with God is mirrored in one's relationship with others, particularly with one's spouse.

Hosea doesn't stand out because he works on his works. He stands out because he works on his faith. He loves the Lord so much that he longs to please him by obeying him. As 1 John 2:3 contends,

"We can be sure that we know God if we obey His commandments" (NLT). When you spend time with God, truly getting to know Him, you will obey His commandments. You can't get there if focus solely on obeying. If you're failing in the area of obedience, it's not an obedience problem, it's a knowing God problem. The more God-focused you are, the better your life will be. Don't get overwhelmed by your to-do list. Get overwhelmed by the love of God. The better you get to know Him, the more your actions change.

I cannot imagine how difficult it must have been for Hosea to continue opening his heart to his unfaithful spouse again and again, ultimately giving EVERYTHING he had to save her from the consequences of her own actions! Why did he do it? Because he knew and loved the Lord! He didn't give up on Gomer so God could show us a portrayal of His love for us!

No sin we commit is too immense to stop God from coming after us with His perfect, everlasting love. Read 1 Corinthians 13:8 which says, "Love never fails" and then 1 John 4:16 which says, "God is love." Translation: if God is love and love never fails, then GOD NEVER FAILS! Proverbs 3:5-6 deepens this truth by telling us, "Trust in the LORD with all your heart. Never rely on what you think you know. Remember the LORD in everything you do, and he will show you the right way" (GNT).

Raisin Cake 1: Money

Hosea let nothing get in the way of his obedience to God. Not even money—the #1 reason for divorce in America. Throughout our marriage, money has been the biggest raisin cake for Husseim and I. From the weight of excessive debt, to accusations of one-sided spending, to living with more month than money despite both of us working full-time, Husseim and I used to spend a lot more time talking about money than about our faith. Before the wait it had gotten so bad that every time I walked into the same room as Husseim, he would ask, "What are you trying to buy now?"

Believe me when I say I sucked with money all my married life. Mega sucked. I won't pretend to have it all together now, but I am growing, daily, in my understanding and in my gratitude for having a teammate to budget with. Husseim knows that the first ten percent of all income we or our kids receive goes to the Lord's church. Husseim knows when the Lord has your money, He has your heart. Many financial hardships have not knocked us down because of my husband's mature understanding of money and its role in extending God's Kingdom. We have seeds in the ground and can declare tithing rights over our circumstances. If not for this incorruptible hope, I'm certain our relationship would have collapsed long ago. In the spiritual walk, money tends to be the last thing people give up and the first thing they take back when times get rough. It's the last to come and the first to go, as church elders say.

Peace before Increase

As soon as this beloved restoration period began, I studied financial solutions like a student studying for an exam. It dawned on me that in order to get better at anything in life, you have to put some skin in the game and practice, not just sit idly by hoping change will come.

Through my absorption of best money saving practices, the Lord opened my eyes to better spending habits for the FIRST time ever! I canceled trips, I changed to a most basic gym membership, I cancelled my satellite television package, my hair appointments, and all of the kids' activities, playdates, and homeschool field trips that weren't going to help them get to Heaven. I even ordered one month worth of groceries (breakfast, lunch, and dinner) for $400! For our family of seven! HALLELUJAH! I know you want to know how; it's simple. I served fruit bars—which I bought in bulk—or one easy breakfast bread per week cut into squares for breakfast. I prepared various easy egg recipes for lunch—egg and cheese, egg and chorizo, French toast, cheesy egg on toast, ham and egg, bean and egg, pepperoni and egg, hot dog and egg, you get the idea. Meanwhile, I spent as little time in a store or curbside as possible. The key is to buy your groceries for the month instead of each week and plan the same seven days of meals to be repeated in a pattern for four weeks; for example, the next four Mondays we're having beeftato casserole, the next four Tuesdays we're having beef and broccoli, so on and so forth. Since we live in a time that meat is more expensive than ever before, the more one buys at once, the more money is saved. We bought four ten-pound logs of ground beef and have been going through one log per week. Okay, that's it. I'm stepping down from that soap box but one day, I'd love to write more about our grocery wins.

Other small victories to celebrate: I started rewarding kids with visits to the library instead of Barnes and Noble, I bought a year-long membership to our local museum instead of paying weekly for visits to the movies/trampoline park/arcade/etc., I started packing our lunches whenever we were away from home, I learned the art of couponing, I stopped having my debit card on me (I don't have a credit card and never have) whenever I needed to drive somewhere so could I focus only on the task at hand without making any unnecessary purchases. I deleted the Amazon and eBay apps from my phone and committed to the Lord not to peruse them through Safari. I've even stopped taking any trips to Five Below or Dollar Tree. Showing my kids my love by buying unnecessary things was something I'd become skilled at; now I'm giving them my undivided time and they love it SO MUCH MORE.

Frankly, I am floored by all of these changes. When I first learned of the gift of this waiting season, I feared the worst case scenario. I thought surely a door is closing and my family will go hungry. Even since realizing I wouldn't stop being paid—as God would have it—throughout this wait, I have still renewed my mind financially. Over the years, the Lord and my husband both tried to show me better ways to use money, but trying to get me to buy into changing anything that felt comfortable was like attempting to remove a brick wall with your bare hands. It wasn't happening.

Husseim has wanted me to stop spending frivolously on the kids for so many years and I resisted, resisted, resisted. Now, I feel empowered! Sad of course, too, that it took all of this to transform my heart and break the stronghold of entitlement off of my life, however here I am! I praise God! I am dancing with this beautiful family of mine! Finally, I see my love of material things and activities was higher ranking than my love of the Lord. I also see now that work can't be the star of my life! Jesus's heart and my heart is for my marriage and our arrows! No more putting them aside!

Raisin Cake 2: My Phone

As I awoke to the imbalance of my own self vs. God thoughts early on in this wait, something else God revealed to me personally was what a raisin cake my phone was. It was the #1 reason I didn't obey commandment #1 as recorded in Exodus 20:3: "Thou shall have no other Gods before me." My phone was a god. I was bowing down to something I can hold in my hands. Maybe you can relate. Maybe you, too, often look down at your phone. Maybe you need to look up more, and notice the clouds, the trees, the wind! Notice God's majesty! Can you imagine what your emotional and physical posture must be like from looking down at your phone all the time?

Michael Winnick, CEO and founder of dscout.com, found that people touch their cell phones 2,617 times a day and that most people, on average, spend three hours and fifteen minutes on their phones each day. He further states that half of all phone pickups happen within three minutes of a previous one! Eric Owens adds these harmful effects phone overuse has on our lives and health:

- Low-quality conversations
- Poor sleep
- Adversely impacts problem solving and short term memory
- Obesity
- Loneliness
- Poor academic performance
- Anxiety
- Poor relationships
- Unhappiness
- Triggers negativity, distress, and less emotional recovery
- And the correlation between smartphone addiction and depression is alarming[55]

So, while the quickest fix is a thirty-day cold turkey reset where you can only use your phone to text or call for thirty days (no apps allowed whatsoever), here are the regular and ongoing practices I've put in place to break my own phone obsession:

1. 24 Hour Break: I fast from my phone one day a week, usually Saturday or Sunday so I don't worry my loved ones who reach out to check on me.

2. Keeping Night for Sleep: I use a real alarm clock and do not charge my phone in my bedroom.

3. Making Access Difficult: To avoid mindlessly checking my phone every 3 minutes, I make it hard for me to get to throughout the day, by keeping it far away or by placing a rubber band or hair tie on it so I have to actually pause to think before unlocking it. If you add a little bit of deterrence or friction to anything, our human nature makes us less likely to be tempted. Knowing this, I've been keeping my phone upstairs most days or at least in another room and I only check my email, calls, and messages during a set block of time daily (for me between 9pm and 10pm). This has redeemed my perspective of my phone. It is my last priority now and I am no longer a slave to it! If you have to have yours during the day for work purposes, then try putting it away (in your kitchen cabinet, for instance) as soon as you get home. Wall Street Tech columnist Christopher Mims says, "The more you physically remove the phone, the more you can build a habit of having some ability to ignore it when it's on your person."[55]

4. Using Less Tempting Devices: I move over to other devices

(iPad or laptop) when I need to use a certain app or website for professional or homeschool purposes. The more I can avoid holding or touching my phone, the easier it is for me to stay in control. Just like a recovering alcoholic avoids going to a bar to make sobriety easier.

5. Choosing my People over my Phone: how often do you check your phone only to realize there was nothing worth checking? I had to get over my FOMO (fear of missing out) by telling myself it's better to prioritize relationships over acquisitions. I assure myself that quality relationships trump quantity of experiences and possessions every time. Am I saying in-person communication with those we love matters more than chasing trip, activity, or purchase plans?! YES! And this is coming from the mom who once thought she was a failure if she didn't take her kids to a different activity or at least buy them one new treat each day! Relational investments and cultivating the skills that they require, inevitably leads to levels of fulfillment far greater than one could receive from a phone, a new pair of shoes, or some new club membership.

The busier we get and the more we become set in our ways, the easier it is to rely on our own experiences instead of the simple truths of God's Word. Question yourself: when a hard decision needs to be made, are you quicker to relate it to a personal story or a Bible story? If our lives are filled with I, I, I, I, I, we're limiting our outcomes to our own devices instead of opening our outcomes to God, who knows exactly what life is throwing at us AND how to turn it around for our good!

If ever you can't get yourself to soak in the Word, reach out to a fellow believer who knows the Word well. Proverbs 11:14 asserts, "Without good direction, people lose their way; the more wise counsel you follow, the better your chances" (MSG). Wise counsel can raise options to consider that you hadn't. Most importantly, spiritually minded people will give you Biblical input, rather than just practical life advice. If you can't think of a person in your world who would do this for you, go to church. There are lots of them there.

Raisin Cake 3: Negative Thinking

Yet another raisin cake I had to learn to let go of is a negative self-view, especially as a wife. For most of my marriage, I placed my husband on a pedestal and myself in the sewer. I thought he had a depth of faith that someone like me could never acquire. Often this negative perspective led me to distance myself from him out of pity for him. Until this wait. The Lord has been teaching me that I have a huge role to play as my husband's helper. The word wife in Hebrew is "ezer" meaning "helper." First God creates man: "Then the Lord God formed a man from the dust of the ground and breathed into his nostrils the breath of life, and the man became a living being" and then Genesis 2:17-18 adds: "The Lord God said, 'It is not good for the man to be alone. I will make a helper suitable for him" (NLT).

This isn't exactly a bumper sticker Scripture. My guess is it's challenging for a lot of women to stomach. The very thought of being "a man's helper" used to make me nauseous, for I never imagined myself as a housewife. Cue I-n-d-e-p-e-n-d-e-n-t woman by Fifth Harmony. Know anyone who can relate? I'll be the first to admit that my role as a wife used to be influenced more by the world than by the Word. I was constantly aiming to prove that career-focused women don't need to fit in old fashioned molds. I thought only those who stay at home have time to be authentically supportive wives. I could barely maintain my many responsibilities, let alone be desirable as a mate. I couldn't have been more wrong.

In the Old Testament of the Bible, the word Ezer is used 21 times, almost always referring to God.[51] It is His name. The Lord God Almighty is called our "helper." Here are a few examples from the New Living Translation (NLT):

- o The Lord is with me; he is my helper (Psalms 118:7)
- o Our soul waits for the Lord. He is our help and our shield

(Psalms 33:20)

- o My father's God was my helper

(Exodus 18:4)

- o You [God] are the helper of the fatherless

(Psalms 10:14)

Wow. Moses himself recognized the true meaning of ezer when he named one of his sons Eliezer in Exodus 18:4: "The other [son] was named Eliezer [My God is Helper], for he [Moses] said, "The God of my father was my helper, and delivered me from the sword of Pharaoh" (ESV). Women are created to reflect God's own image as ezers. What value He gives all females! How precious we are in His eyes! God is not a personal assistant or apprentice. He's not a doormat for people to stomp on. He renders aid and strength to His people so they can complete what He calls them to do.

Just as God purposefully enhanced the garden with a woman, He enhances all the places women frequent, with our presence! We are people's ezers—the ones they can turn to in times of need or support. Isn't that beautiful? Now I love encouraging wives to consider refreshed ways they can help their husbands. Ephesians 5:22-24 tells us "Wives, submit to your own husbands, as to the Lord. For the husband is the head of the wife even as Christ is the head of the church, his body, and is himself its Savior. Now as the church submits to Christ, so also wives should submit in everything to their husbands" (NIV).

Being a better teammate for my husband financially was the beginning of submission for me. I had to relinquish defining submitting as my becoming lesser than, inferior, or inadequate, for none of those thoughts concur with the Word of God. I had to learn that Jesus has a heart specifically for women. If God valued men and not women, why did He create a woman in the first place?

Every woman should know she is God's idea, and He holds her dear to His heart! Even in Biblical times during which many women were not valued as they should have been, Jesus consistently showed women their worth. Never did one find him calling women "slaves" or "property." No, oppression did not and does not parallel with the character of God. Think about it. When Jesus reigned on the Earth, many men, even fathers, saw their daughters as bargaining chips. Not Jesus. He showed his care for women. Look up His talk with the Samaritan woman at the well in the fourth chapter of John or the description of a woman in adultery who He spoke to freely in the eighth chapter of John.

Women like Mary, Anna, and Elizabeth knew Jesus was the Messiah before the men in their lives ever did and after His resurrection, who is the first person he revealed Himself to? Mary Magdalene—a woman once possessed by seven demons who ultimately became one of the Lord's disciples! This was at a time that a woman could not be considered a credible witness in court according to rules set by men. But those rules were not established by God, who I presume intentionally wanted to show women that they hold a special place in His heart.

Jesus inspired many of the Biblical writers like Paul to draw attention to strong Godly women. Paul speaks about women like Lydia, the first European convert he'd seen, and Priscilla, a female missionary completely dependent on the Lord. In both the Old and New Testament, several women are blessed with a unique gift of prophecy and even awarded places of power contrary to the social norm which only placed men in power positions.

Whether you're male or female, I encourage you to ask the Lord to plant the seed of inquisition within you as you research some galvanizing women of authority in the Bible like Deborah, Yael, Miriam, Huldah, Naomi, Ruth, and Anna, just to name a handful. Let us not forget that the genealogy of Jesus Himself cannot be traced just to a man but to a man and a woman. The women who were part of Christ's lineage were each picked for a specific purpose. They were bold, courageous, and often rebellious. They were willing to do what they believed was right no matter what. Even if that meant grave sacrifices had to be made.

Think of Rahab who was a prostitute willing to give up her life just to help save Israelite spies. Think of Tamar who Judah wanted to outcast because he believed she was to blame for the deaths of two of his sons—her husbands—so she disguised herself as a prostitute to seduce Judah (her deceased husbands' father) and got pregnant by him, securing her place in the family. Think of Ruth, who was a Moabite widow so faithful to her mother-in-law Naomi that she heeded Naomi's guidance to marry Jewish kinsmen Boaz despite the approval of societal expectations.

Do you know what I love even more than the fact that Jesus made sure to include and love women in all aspects of his ministry? I absolutely relish that none of the women were strangers to trials. Esther went from orphan to queen, Gomer went from prostitute to faithful wife, Mary went from an unwed teenager to the mother of our savior, Abigail went from a miserable wife to a hero, Miriam went from a worrier to a wise connector, Martha went from preoccupied to understanding, Elizabeth went from disgraced to favored, Jochebed went from desperate to grateful, and so on. Their testimonies taught me to stop assuming everyone else's faith is bigger than mine and to start building my own faith up. In 2 Corinthians 12:9, Jesus says "My grace is sufficient for you, for my power is made perfect in weakness" (NIV).

Have you ever noticed how God's specialty is using the most unlikely of people to accomplish the greatest of tasks? I have come to believe that as ezers, women must be the first to recognize that when life hits hard, we need to take it slow. I was never going to be receptive to slowing down on my own. I'm glad I've been broken through this unexpected semester off from work because it has brought me to better understanding who I am in Christ! My growth has been in the breaking, not the blessings.

The Lord relentlessly shows me how much better I can be at my primary roles of Christ follower, wife, and mother, when I'm not overextended. I'm seeing that my professional role was truly the king of my life, and everyone and thing else was taking a backseat. Am I saying that women shouldn't be in the workplace? No, but I finally understand most men's God-given need to be providers for their families is Scripturally sound. Let's go back to the beginning of time, right after the Fall, when God evinced consequences to man and woman for their sins. Here is the consequence he gave the man in Genesis 3:17,19, & 16:

> "Thou shalt not eat of it: cursed is the ground for thy sake; in sorrow shalt thou eat of it all the days of thy life; In the sweat of thy face shalt thou eat bread, till thou return unto the ground; for out of it wast thou taken: for dust thou art, and unto dust shalt thou return." [And to the woman, God said,] "I will greatly multiply thy sorrow and thy conception; in sorrow thou shalt bring forth children; and thy desire shall be to thy husband, and he shall rule over thee" (NKJV).

Perspicuously, God's expectation is for the man to be the provider, toiling in the soil, while the woman's life is to revolve around her children and husband, as she was created to be his helpmate. *His Needs Her Needs* author and licensed clinical psychologist Dr. Willard F. Harley, Jr. writes about the revolution that has occurred in the workforce over the past fifty years. Unlike fifty years ago when men dominated the workforce and the divorce rate in America was under twenty percent, today women dominate the workforce in most careers and almost fifty percent of all marriages today are ending in divorce or separation.

Dr. Harley estimates that forty one percent of all first marriages now end in divorce in the U.S. Of course, the connection drawn here is my own and I cannot tell you definitively that overextended working women are the cause of the increase in divorces we have seen in America. I simply am awakening to the toll my working has had on my own marriage and I do suspect it rears its stressful head in other marriages, too. I'm not alone in my thinking. Dr. Harley adds:

> You might think that the cultural shift toward women in the workplace would change a woman's need for financial support. That's not necessarily the case. As a test of whether women still marry for money, I will sometimes ask an audience of young couples a question. 'If just before your wedding your spouse had announced that you should not expect him or her to earn much of an income, would you have tied the knot? Raise your hand if you would have gone through with the wedding knowing that you alone would have to support your spouse financially.' While almost all the men raise their hands, hardly a single woman's hand joins them.
>
> In truth, most women do marry a man expecting his partnership in financial support. They want their husbands to partner with them in supporting their family together and managing their finances together. Most men do not have that same need.[23]

Dr. Harley goes on to explain that whether they vocalize it or not, most wives expect their husbands not only to be employed but also to earn enough to support their family. Sure, many of them want to work too, but they do not want to *have* to work. Without the choice of whether to work or not, they grow resentful. And when that resentment grows, I suspect most women won't talk about it perhaps because they haven't pinpointed it as the issue or perhaps, because they don't know if others will accept the reason for their resentment.

The culture I grew up in featured strong women eager to combat thousands of years of slavery, oppression, and warmongering. Throughout movements like women empowerment and #metoo, women have been saluted for being bosses, for taking charge, for running the show, and for proudly proclaiming they don't need a man to take care of them. So it may not go over well if a wife tries to confess to her friends that she wants her husband to be the financial breadwinner. As influential as mainstream culture is, it doesn't always change the innermost desires women hold for their life partners. This applies to men too. They tend to have counter-cultural needs that may be left unsaid. Dr. Harley further finds that:

> Unmet emotional needs often trigger fantasies, and the need for domestic support is no exception. Let's say the fantasy of a stereotypical man goes something like this: His home life is free of stress and worry. After work each day, his wife

greets him lovingly and their well-behaved children are also glad to see him. He enters the comfort of a well-maintained home as his wife urges him to relax before having dinner, the aroma of which he can already smell wafting from the kitchen. Conversation at dinner is enjoyable and free of conflict. Later the family goes out together for an early evening stroll, and he returns to put the children to bed with no hassle or fuss. Then he and his wife relax and talk together, watch a little television, and, at a reasonable hour, go to bed to make love.

Some wives may have laughed (or become enraged) as they read the above scenario, but I assure you that a revolution in male attitudes toward housework that was supposed to have taken place with men pitching in to take an equal share of the household chores has not necessarily changed their emotional needs. Many of the men I counsel still tell me in private that they need domestic support as much as ever.[23]

This key question emerges from the two aforementioned unspoken needs of husbands and wives: how can a wife provide her husband with the domestic support that he needs and also receive from her husband the financial support that she needs? As a former admitted workaholic, I find it comical that God has me, of all people, addressing this question. I am the perfectly unlikeliest person for God to use for this platform. As such, I won't tell you that women shouldn't work, but what I am convicted of is this: wives must be ever so careful with what we allow on our plates. If working is one of the things on the plate, I believe we should make sure its portion is not bigger than the portion allotted to caring for our faith, our husbands, our children, and their home environment. I know this is a Word from the Lord for someone else. Not just me.

God gave women different gifts than the gifts He gave to men. Not so women would be of any lesser value than men, but so that in relation with one another, we could supremely complement each other. Matthew 19:4 affirms that "He who created them from the beginning made them male and female" (NIV).

In *Love & Respect*, Dr. Emerson Eggerichs skillfully explains that God made us pink and blue on purpose. We're not wrong, just different. Eggerichs assures us, "When you put pink and blue together, you get purple, the color of royalty; the color of God. Together, a husband and wife reflect God's image."[62] The key word here is *together*. A husband alone does not have all the ingredients to reflect God's image, nor does a wife. The goal of marriage is not to think alike, but to think together. When that happens, you can achieve so much more than you ever would've been able to achieve on your own.

Genesis 1:27 gives the following explanation: "God created man in His own image, in the image of God He created him; male and female He created them" (MSG). There are going to be moments of disagreement, but God has designed that! In Ephesians 5:33, Paul declares, "Each one of you must also love his wife as he loves himself, and the wife must respect her husband" (NIV).

Dr. Eggerichs adds this note from his research: "We asked

seven thousand people, 'When you're in a conflict with your spouse or significant other, do you feel unloved in that moment or disrespected?' 83% of the men said they feel disrespected. 72% of the women said they feel unloved."[62] What has helped me to eliminate the negative self-view raisin cake from my life is a newfound belief that women need to embrace our femininity and teach our daughters to do the same.

The ramifications of the actions of generations that have rejected said femininity in an attempt to position women as better than men have yet to be fully seen. Sure, men have abused power, especially physical power that the Lord has bestowed upon them, but women have also abused emotional power bestowed upon them. It's crucial for men and women to acknowledge the different gifts they possess. These gifts can be used to influence others positively or negatively. We must be careful. Here are different gifts God gave men and women:

Physical Strength // Tenderness

God gave men the gift of physical strength. In Matthew 11:29, Jesus said, "Take my yoke upon you and learn from me, for I am gentle and lowly in heart, and you will find rest for your souls" (NLT). Often men carry groceries, open jars, lift little ones, move machinery, etc. God has created men with the capacity to be physically stronger than women. A man's leg and arm bones are designed differently than that of a woman and can sustain denser, longer, and greater muscle mass.

God called men such as Adam, Noah, Abraham, Moses, David, and Jesus to serve as the focal points of His covenants with mankind. As noted by the Scott La Pierre Ministries, there were patriarchs instead of matriarchs, the tribes of Israel were named after men, the only legitimate mediators between people and God were men (i.e., priests instead of priestesses), God appointed kings as opposed to queens, the twelve disciples Jesus chose were men, the seventy evangelists who were sent out after the twelve in Luke 10:1 were all men, and the seven deacons in Acts 6 were all men.[63] With Christ as their model, all men should harness their strength gently.

//

1 Peter 3:3-4 says of women, "Don't let your beauty consist of outward things like elaborate hairstyles and wearing gold jewelry, but rather what is inside the heart—the imperishable quality of a gentle and quiet spirit, which is of great worth in God's sight" (NIV). The gentle touch of women is a gift from God that brings great comfort to this harsh world. Society often degrades women for being too emotional or sensitive, leading us to hide how we're actually feeling behind a tough exterior. In truth, women are invariably more concerned about others' perceptions than men are.

Granted there is definitely such a thing as being overly

sensitive, or not sensitive enough, but when properly harnessed, women's emotional tenderness can gift ease to burdened minds, joy to hardened hearts, and rest to troubled souls. This beautiful gift reminds me again of how we are viewed in the eyes of the Lord because lost people pursue him for all of these same helps! What an honor it is to be entrusted by God to be in touch with all sorts of emotions.

God's own character as portrayed in the Bible perfectly exemplifies the importance of feelings. To name a handful of His own emotions from the New Living Translation (NLT) of the Bible: God laughs (Psalm 37:12-13), God mourns (John 11:35), God hates (Proverbs 6:16-19), God loves (John 3:16), God rejoices (Psalm 104:31), God's pleased (1 Kings 3:10), God's displeased (Numbers 11:1), God's angered (Exodus 4:14), God's jealous (Exodus 34:14), and God's compassionate (Matthew 14:14). And yet, no one dares calling the Lord a basket case or a loose cannon! I believe the people who call women such derogatory names completely misunderstand the power of their sensitivity.

Leadership // Wisdom

God intends for men to lead. If a man becomes a husband, he is responsible for his wife's well-being in a way she is not responsible for his. That sums up Biblical male headship. It falls on men to take initiative in ensuring that their wives have adequate opportunity to spend time in Scripture and prayer. It falls upon the men to uphold peaceful living with their wives so that men's prayers (not women's prayers) are not hindered by any discord between them, as is discussed in 1 Peter 3:7 (NLT). As leaders, men bear the greater responsibility and the greater burden. They lead and provide. Men are the security-makers and women are the culture-makers.

Put simply, if women marry, most do not desire to work a 60-hour job. They want to provide for their number one companion on earth—for their husband. As previously mentioned, two-job families often do not allow for this. This feverish pace of life takes its tolls on relationships, on families, and on our spiritual lives.

Unlike men, women can innately grasp the obscure. God gives us no less intelligence than He does men. We're blessed with wisdom to see what's not evident to the average mind and can do so with exquisite accuracy when we're walking with the Lord. When we're not, our reading of others' character or motives may instead be fueled by our assumptions. Like the precious gift, the ability to discern can be misused but when leveraged for the good of the kingdom, it is more precious than gold. Charles Spurgeon once said: "Discernment is not knowing the difference between right and wrong but knowing the difference between right and almost right."

Call it a gut instinct or intuition if you prefer, but God gave women the powerful ability to emotionally and spiritually discern when something is wrong with another person. For example, if one of my children is asked how they're doing, a brisk "fine" in response may satisfy my husband, but not me. I'm more likely to probe further until I get to the truth. This gift is also why God drops certain individuals into our mind throughout the day. When God gives a woman a name drop, she better not waste it. She should do something about it! Whether it's praying for them, or reaching out to them, or offering them help, if you discern something about someone in your spirit, God is trusting you to carry out His love like a sponge expelling His Holy water. Don't seek only to absorb convictions. Like a sponge absorbing too much water, it isn't good for you or your faith. Active faith requires intention *and* action.

James 2:17 says, "Faith by itself, if it is not accompanied by action, is dead." In this same vein, Philippians 1:9-11 says, "It is my prayer that your love may abound more and more, with knowledge and all discernment, so that you may approve what is excellent, and so be pure and blameless for the day of Christ, filled with the fruit of righteousness that comes through Jesus Christ, to the glory and praise of God" (NLT).

Spiritual Stewardship // Resilience

Men are called to steward the spiritual wellbeing of their children and wives. They are to oversee their wives' ministry. 1 Peter 4:10 says, "As each has received a gift, use it to serve one another, as good stewards of God's varied grace" (MSG). A husband looking out for both for his wife and for the church will make sure his wife is giving her time to areas of ministry (in the home or outside of it) where she is called, serving according to her God-given gifts, and not overextending herself or ministering at the expense of her family. Being a supportive spiritual steward entails a husband encouraging his wife as she realizes and exercises her spiritual gifts.

Do you remember the Vicks DayQuil commercials that show a mom coming down with a cold but continuing to support her family anyway? The advertisement proclaims that "Moms don't get sick days" and we don't! The Lord grants women a divine deposit of resilience every. single. day. We don't have the same physical strength as men but they don't have the same fortitude strength as us. Because remember, we were made to complement one another! We're strong where men are not and men are strong where we are not. It's time to stop rejecting the differences between men and women and embrace them for how beautifully interwoven God made these differences to be!

If a trial comes, as women, we have God given pliability to push through and pull our whole family, husbands included, right along with us. When given a task, we model completing it with excellence. When a door closes, we remind our family that another will open. When hard news is given, we're the cheerleaders who boost the spirits of the whole family. Our lives are inspired by our

God pursuit, not our patterns.

One late night, our local Christian radio station shared a story about a woman who would always cut the head and tail off of a fish when she cooked it for her family. She passed this tradition onto her daughter, who one day ends up asking her mother: "Why do we cut off so much of the fish, Mom?" The mom didn't know exactly why; that's just how she always saw her mom do it, so she went and asked the girl's grandmother, "Why do you always cut the head and tail off of the fish in the pan?" The grandmother answered matter-of-factly: "because we never had a pan big enough to fit the whole fish." Now her daughter and granddaughter did have a pan big enough for any fish, but old habits were passed from one generation to another. Now they were sacrificing unnecessary fish meat.

Women ought to analyze their own lives and see if there are any areas where they are copying family-learned behaviors that aren't adding any inches to their height. These habits can get in the way of us being as resilient as God designed us to be. When we say something like "This just runs in my family" or "I get that from my mom," what we're really saying is we don't have hope that Jesus can change that area of our life. Proverbs 31:16-17 says of the Christian woman: "She surveys a field and acquires it; from her own resources, she plants a vineyard. She works energetically; her arms are powerful" (NLT). Veritably I tell you: if a woman sets her *open* mind on something, she will get it done—no matter what.

Assertiveness // Vulnerability

A man is created to be assertive in decision-making. Colossians 1:9-10 provides an inspiring example of how to pray for understanding and wisdom on behalf of another person. A Godly husband prays that his and his wife's decisions will honor God. He works fervently toward ambitious and noble goals and he helps ensure that the family's priorities aren't misplaced.

Life experiences may lead a lot of women to think the gift of vulnerability is one they wouldn't mind returning. There have probably been times that every woman's vulnerability has been exploited by people who she thought cared. She may have been told that she wears her heart on her sleeve and in relationships, exposing feelings is likely easier for her than men. Many—if not most—men are slow to name their feelings. This explains why women often say "I love you" first. God designed women to be more in touch with our emotions and therefore it is easier for us to be vulnerable than it is for men. Just like the Word of God says iron sharpens iron, I believe vulnerability sharpens vulnerability. As women, we teach those around us, including men, and yes, even including our own husbands, to be more authentic, more honest, and more willing to confess what they are going through.

It is a whole lot harder for a man to bear his heart, and

especially his struggles, than it is for a woman. The degree of difficulty a woman experiences when she has to admit something terribly wrong/sinful/embarrassing that she did gets multiplied by twenty for a man. Hiding imperfections comes more naturally for men than exposing them. So when a husband needs to share a hard truth with his wife, she should receive it with the utmost grace. When my husband and I need to share something that we know is going to be hard for the other person to stomach, we ask six intentional words to prepare the soil of one another's hearts for the discussion. Those words are: "Can you be Jesus to me?"

We use these extremely sparingly, mind you. Only for grim circumstances. We don't use them when we're about to reveal that we lost the remote control or that we left the garage door unlocked. We use them if we need to confess something serious like a wandering eye, or a breach of our integrity. Proverbs 31:30 says, "Charm is deceitful, and beauty is vain, but a woman who fears the Lord is to be praised" (ESV).

If you want to compare the marriage relationship to therapy, the wife's God-given vulnerability makes her much more comparable to a therapist and the husband to a question. Women have incredible powers to influence the mind and heart of not only their children, but their husbands as well. If a wife genuinely wants to score points with her husband, she must be his biggest cheerleader, emotionally and spiritually. She must speak life into him and compliment him on his efforts no matter how big or small they are. She must declare Scriptures over him out loud. Laying her hands on his head and praying for him each morning before he begins his day should be commonplace, setting a memorable example for the children to follow when they one day marry.

Confidence // Subtlety

Jeremiah 17:7 reminds men that strong confidence stems from trusting the Lord (NIV)! The deeper a man trusts the Lord, the easier it is for him to lead his wife and family with confidence. Of course, we live in a society that presents men as having no business taking charge. The dominant narrative advertises women carrying more authority than men. But the Godly husband listens to the Word above the world and leads his wife, confident that God calls him to do just this. He leads his wife with a humble confidence, even when he has to settle unpopular disputes. He reminds himself daily that God is willing and able to bless him for his obedience.

Women have the God-given ability to be subtle like the lady of Tekoa and bold like Deborah in the Bible. If you haven't read about Deborah, open your Bible to Judges four and five. Deborah is one of the most influential women in the whole Bible! Known for her courage and sagacity, she is the only woman of the Old Testament whose valiant faith actions are highlighted without her affiliation to a man, or relationship to a husband.

You should also read about the unnamed woman of Tekoa in 2 Samuel 14. After David's rebellious son Absalom was banished for murdering David's oldest son Amnon—killed in revenge for the rape of his full sister Tamar—Joab wants David to be reconciled to Absalom, so he tells David to go to Tekoa to find a "wise woman." Joab instructs the woman to pretend to be mourning, and she tells a story to David to gain his sympathy and favorable judgment. The woman explains to David that her son killed his brother, and now the rest of the family wants him killed. When David decides that her son's life should be spared, the Tekoite woman emboldens him to do the same for Absalom.

Can you relate to this? Has there been a time in your life where others entrusted you to have just the right words to say in just the right way? I know when my husband has a business inquiry or receives a call from an insurance company, he usually passes the phone to me and trusts that I'll know what to say, and how to say it.

If you knew me before I entered this waiting season, you'd know I have spent the last sixteen years of my life as a self-proclaimed workaholic, and I have fought many fights with my husband and even my children over things I did not want them to expect from me because of the priority I placed on my career. Often, I would tell them they couldn't expect me to go grocery shopping, go outside, relax, tidy up, read a book, etc. (some of the simplest things) just because of my work responsibilities.

Many times, I shared with my husband in private that I had a fear that the title of my life, if it were a book, would be "Hold on." Because when my husband needed something from me, that was the response: "Hold on." When my children needed something from me that was the response: "Hold on." Even when my extended family members needed something from me or my friends needed something from me or fellow church goers needed something from me, my response was often "Hold on." The truth is later never comes, and the Lord is teaching me in this season that the only way to be in his presence and ever present with those I love is to be so careful about what I allow to consume my time and my emotional bandwidth.

Maybe there are some jobs out there that allow you to show up, do the work you're asked to do, and when you leave, that work stays at work. Cherish that set-up if you have it. That's a beautiful concept to me because it helps prevent work from leaking into other more important areas of life.

Raisin Cake 4: Self Centeredness

A fourth and final raisin cake that steals my focus away from God is my self-centeredness. Thinking too much about whatever benefited me led to my inability to give my husband his rightful place as lead Christ follower, husband, and father. I have long had a strong tendency to be in charge. With that said, another lesson the

Lord has opened my eyes to in this precious wait is that this parenting thing is actually much simpler when I don't go at it alone. To silence the attacking thoughts from the enemy that would tell me we're not getting things right as parents, Husseim and I had to learn to act how we want our kids to act. If we want them to be prayer warriors, we have to be prayer warriors. If we want them to value going to church, we have to go to church without fail. If we want them to be patient, we have to be patient. If we want them to be polite, we have to be polite. Seeing the recurring image of wives submitting to their husbands in the Bible as I've begun studying it more and more has been integral to replacing me self-centeredness with humility. And it turns out my kids have also benefited from watching my transformation unfold.

Fierce Marriage founders Rick and Selena Frederick bring it home saying, "When you fight for the health of your marriage, you fight for the health of your kids. God's design for marriage is also his design for raising children."[24] Children need their mom and dad in the home. Lately, I've found it heart wrenching when people who are going through hardships in their marriage, decide it is inequitable to stay with their spouse just because of the children. If the children are the only reason for fighting for a marriage, I believe that to be a worthy reason. I'm sorry that I'm not sorry for saying that, given it is counter-cultural, and society praises individuals for their pursuit of happiness. What is happiness, anyway?

How can you compare superficial happiness to the deep happiness found when you go through hardships in life and overcome them together? The grass isn't always greener on the other side. Instead of looking for new grass, can't we water our own? Throughout this most glorious wait, the Lord has been showing me how vital it is to fight for one's marriage for the sake of their children. Of course, I am not advocating for anyone to stay in a dangerous or abusive situation. Please reach out for help for yourself and for your children if this is the case, but if it isn't, please receive with an open heart, the data I'm about to share with you. If it helped to chip away my own self-centeredness, odds are it can help chip away yours, too.

The United States has the highest rate of children living in single-parent households of any nation in the world.[25] Patrick Bet-David, father of two sons and two daughters, bestselling author, and founder and CEO of Valuetainment Media, delineates the following statistics:

> About 80% of single-parent homes are led by single mothers. At a rate of 23% of children living with one parent and no other adults, the United States stands over three times the world average of 7% of children raised by one parent. For reference, the number stands at 3% for China and 4% for India. This is not an area where we want to be competing with other countries for dominance. It may be two or three or four decades before we see the full side effects of this.

Even for children with their father present in the home, the average school age boy only spends about 30 minutes per week in one-on-one conversations with his father. For comparison, the same boy, on average, will spend 44 hours per week, watching television, playing video games, and surfing the Internet. 90% of all homeless and runaway children, 63% of teen suicides, and 85% of children and teens with behavior disorders come from fatherless homes. Fatherlessness, likewise, has a direct link to teen pregnancy and sexual activity. Roughly 70% of teenage pregnancies come from women who are raised in fatherless homes and these women have significantly higher abortion rates than women raised by a father and a mother.

Girls with no fathers have lower self-esteem. On the whole, fatherless kids are 20 times more likely to be incarcerated and 11 times more likely to exhibit violent behavior than children from two parent households. If a man and wife raise a child, they are less likely to end up in jail, but they have the same chance as children raised by just their fathers.[26]

Learning this information can enlarge an already problematic raisin cake like my previous tendency to control things as a parent, or it can disintegrate a raisin cake by inspiring a sense of empowerment in a parent. I'm hoping for the latter. We can lower crime, minimize mental health issues, help the economy, and decrease homelessness by bringing back the family nucleus. Perhaps like me, you were raised to thank those who served in the military for their service. The next time you see a father, who takes their job as a dad seriously, share some kind words with them too. They are making your life better and safer by remaining in their child's life.

According to LifeWay Research Group, Father's Day is the

holiday with the single lowest average church attendance–statistically lower than Labor Day, Memorial Day, and even the Fourth of July. This is mind boggling, especially when you consider that Mother's Day tends to be the day with the third highest church service attendance, after Easter and Christmas.[27]

According to data collected by Promise Keepers and Baptist Press, if a father does not go to church, even if his wife does, only 1 child in 50 will become a regular worshiper. If a father does go regularly to church, regardless of what the mother does, between two-thirds and three-quarters of their children will attend church as adults. If a father attends church irregularly, between half and two-thirds of their kids will attend church with some regularity as adults. If a mother does not go to church, but a father does, a minimum of two-thirds of their children will end up attending church. In contrast, if a father does not go to church, but the mother does, on average two-thirds of their children will not attend church.

When both parents attend Bible study in addition to the Sunday service, 72% of their children attend Sunday school when grown. When only the father attends Sunday school, 55% of the children attend when grown. When only the mother attends Sunday school, 15% of the children attend when grown. When neither parent attends Sunday school, only 6% of the children attend when grown. Now get ready for the kicker: if a child is the first person in a household to become a Christian, there is a 3.5% probability everyone else in the household will follow. If the mother is the first to become a Christian, there is a 17% probability everyone else in the household will follow. However, when the father is first, there is a 93% probability everyone else in the household will follow. Here's the point of all these statistics: Dad's impact on the kids' faith and practice is tremendous.[28]

I've learned in this adored wait that when it comes to raising our children, if Husseim wants to parent, I need to let him parent! As a perfect example, just yesterday, Husseim took our youngest son, who is three years old, to get a haircut for the first time. The experience rang alarm bells for me, because it showed me that I need to intentionally make more room for my husband to influence our children too. It's no secret that I carry a lot of the weight with the child rearing. So much so that when my husband took our son to get his haircut, I wasn't sure about letting him go without me. "Are you going to be okay?" I asked my husband as he scooped up our toddler, who was reaching for me and crying profusely. I never should ask questions like that. No wife should.

When a man steps up to do something with his kids, no one should get in his way. In fact, women should do everything we can to make his stepping up possible. We should ensure that life isn't so busy that there's no time for interactions between our children and their earthly father. The family legacy we're starting now will echo for generations to come.

Here is God's design: when a husband submits to the Lord, leading his wife and children with a servant's heart and nurturing their God-given talents, his wife can confidently submit to him—lean on him and trust his covering. I know this isn't easily digested by capable, independent women who hate the idea of submission. Some people at your church may have even said submission isn't relevant anymore, but let us not forget the apostle Paul's comparison of marriage to the connection between Christ and the Church. The relationship isn't of master to servant; it's of lover and beloved. Does a me-focused Western culture trump what the Word of God says?

As Lord of the Church, Jesus has given up His life in exchange for the life of His Bride. Whose His Bride? We are! This is what inspires Paul in Ephesians 5:23 to write, "For the husband is the head of the wife even as Christ is the head of the church, his body, and is himself its Savior" (ESV). A Focus on the Family article titled "Developing Shared Spiritual Intimacy" further elaborates:

> The union represented [in marriage] may be one of the greatest miracles in all of creation. But it's also something more. For in addition to everything else marriage means for a man and a woman, it has a deep spiritual significance — an eternal and cosmic significance… At the very highest level, it functions as an unparalleled working image of the seeking and saving Love of our Creator and Savior — the Love that compels Him to unite Himself to His people in a

mystical bond of eternal fellowship and never-ending interpersonal give and take.[29]

Submission in faith and in marriage, builds mutual trust. To experience true freedom, every believer has to experience full surrender. They must completely give the reins to God. Likewise, I'm beginning to grasp that God wants women to learn to surrender the reins to our husbands, not as punishment for being women, or as some unfair consequence for being inferior, but as a gift to women. What a gift it is not to have to wear the pants all the time and make all the decisions. I know I am not alone when I say running a household can be exhausting and overwhelming. I believe the Lord's call for me to give a final say on decisions to my husband is His way of caring for and protecting me.

My afflictions as a parent now feel so much lighter because I am sharing them with my husband and asking him to make final decisions. I used to go back-and-forth in a spiritual and mental tug-of-war when major decisions regarding the kids needed to be made. Now it feels refreshing to have a husband who wants to carry that burden. I'm reminded I'm not alone. It also feels good to have renewed confidence in my husband. How can I say I trust him fully if I won't let him make decisions in my or my children's best interest? Looking back at all the times that I ignored his thoughts or opinions, because mine were better, I realize what a disservice I did to our relationship because each time I ignored my husband, I taught my heart to be more callous and less trusting of him and I taught his heart to be more callous and less trusting of me.

As a woman welcomes her husband's parental involvement and decision-making, his influence can positively change her, and her influence can positively change him. Remember, marriage is about unity, not individuality. If you were capable of creating your best version of yourself alone, you could have stayed single. But if you're married, you've been given an incredible blessing. An opportunity to have your character, your heart, your mind, your soul, your whole being molded into a better you. How effortless it is for us to hear advice from paid professionals, like counselors, therapists, life coaches, and so on. It shouldn't be easier for us to put our confidence in those complete strangers than it is for us to put our confidence in the person we chose to be our number one ally in this life.

Each time a wife asks her husband for a greenlight or advice, she should heed his feedback. No matter what a husband says, a Godly wife can take it in without getting mad at him for his insight. Again this reminds me of Christ's relationship with man because I'm sure there's been times God has given you an answer too that you didn't want or like, yet came around to accepting. Women can show Christ their growth by coming around to accepting their husband's leadership and wisdom quicker.

Heated fellowship cools down so much faster if wives agree to husbands' proposed solutions. I know that's not always easy, but when I look back on all the years of my marriage, and think about some of the worst fights we've had, they weren't over huge decisions, like whether or not to buy a house or whether or not to take a job. They were almost always over trivial things like if I should take the kids on a movie playdate four consecutive weeks in a row or if we should make sure the kids stay for at least three hours at a family function. With each fight, I would dig my heels in until I got my way. Or if I did try to submit to my husband's way, I would have a really hard time committing to the submission. I would wear a bad attitude that you could see all across my face and in my actions. I would sulk. I was pretty pathetic now that I think about it. Self-centeredness got the best of me time after time. And for what? None of those wins gained me any points in Heaven. None of those wins gained me any points with Father God. None of those wins won me any points in my husband's heart. None of those wins won me any points in my children's hearts. If they won me anything at all, they won Satan's satisfaction because I succumbed to being yet another disrespectful wife. Remember this: Satan cannot do anything to you without your consent or cooperation.

Not every relationship is the same, but most of the time, men have a desire to provide, to lead, and to protect and women have a desire to care, nurture, and support. Try we might to deny these instinctive desires, because much of today's society doesn't value them, but their presence cannot be ignored. It seems quite obvious to me that those desires were planted in us by God Himself to make marriage possible. In 1 Corinthians 7:28, Paul says that if we marry, we have not sinned, but we will have "trouble" (NLT). I believe that trouble would be so much less complicated if we stuck to the simplicity of the marital relationship that God designed.

Like a ying and a yang, the husband and wife have different strengths. If we would use those strengths to complement one another, instead of fighting one another for the right to use strengths that God didn't intend for us to use, agreement would be easier to reach.

How would I tell a pants-wearing wife to let her husband man the ship? I would tell her to take a long hard look at why she wears the pants. Such a wife would probably be tempted to tell me that she tried giving authority to her husband in the past, and he would never make up his mind or he would never speak up/say anything, but that's not grounds not to try again to let his voice be heard. I'd also ask her this: do you want to show your children that you have such little trust in the man you chose to be their father that you don't ask him to carry the weight of the family or make decisions for the family? Or do you want your children to build trust just like you in their father that he is a good-willed, God-fearing man? Again, giving husbands the final say is to be thought of as a gift to women, less pressure on them, not a curse or a punishment.

Certainly, if something comes up that a husband denies or disagrees with, and it dearly matters to the wife, she should sit and thoroughly explain to him why it matters and he should hear her and consider changing his position but nine times out of ten, he is going to steer his wife the right way. He did not marry his wife to hurt her or to upset her. He married her to do life with her in unity like iron sharpening iron. There is power in spouses making each other better.

The Lord's been showing me that husbands and wives should decide nothing alone. I should ask my husband for his opinion even on the smallest decisions, like choosing the groceries or picking out what I should wear for a night at the movies. When I make these decisions by myself, I'm likely to make assumptions and assumptions rarely turn out to have truth. I've learned I should show my husband that he matters by asking for his input even when choosing activities for the kids. In this gift of waiting, I had to learn to stop avoiding bringing up certain entertainment ideas for the kids just because I was so sure my husband would say they don't need to do anything or go anywhere. I realize there are a lot of decisions I used to make on my own without asking my husband because I felt so sure that he would say no and I wanted to 100% guarantee that what I desired to happen, would happen.

That secrecy not only bred distrust in my heart for my

husband, but it also bred disloyalty in his heart for me. He felt betrayed when he would find out after the fact about decisions that I made because I didn't have the courtesy to consult him first. I'm sure he thought "If she wants to raise the kids by herself, why am I even here?" Of course, I never thought of it that way. I just couldn't see past my self-centeredness to involve him in the decisions that I would make, especially on behalf of the children. I never should have assumed that my husband doesn't care just because he is quiet, or responds with less emotion than I do. I have to remind myself, daily, that men and women are different. Individuals are different. Everyone has their own unique personality. So just because a husband doesn't respond the way a wife responds doesn't mean that he cares any less for the children than she does.

How I wish I'd learned sooner to die to self and put my husband's needs above my own. Here we go; another punch to the gut. Like some of you reading this, I spent most of my upbringing aspiring to be a strong, fierce woman. I never wanted to be told to put my husband's needs before my own. I'm not saying gals should put themselves down or leave their self-esteem in the gutter, but I am encouraging women to conform themselves in the image of Christ, who would always put his bride (you and me) before himself. Now, when I arise in the morning and seek the Lord, I ask Him to reveal where I can care for my husband. The littlest things like preparing him breakfast, or buying him a cup of coffee, or sitting and reading a devotional with him, or laying a hand on his head and praying for him, matter. Husbands are constantly told they need to treasure their wives, but should wives not do the same for their husbands?

Furthermore, the Lord has taught me to speak with my husband before turning to others. This is another exceptional way to build confidence and trust in a marital relationship. I'm now striving to show my husband that even when I disagree with him, I can withstand difficult conversations, rather than taking my concerns to a friend or family member. Talking behind my husband's back is not only dishonoring to him but it's terrible character formation for me. It teaches me to run away from resolving problems and to trust the advice of others over the advice of my husband. I have to remind myself constantly that my husband is a good-willed man. He did not marry me to ruin my life. He married me for the better life we could achieve together.

When my husband says something, I'm learning to value it as I would words spoken by the president, a pastor, or someone I look up to, not because he is above and I'm beneath but because I should admire the one I love! I can also value his words through action alone like the other day when I wanted to drive to the local heated pool for a swim, but my husband advised against it because it was under 55 degrees outside. The old Amanda would disrespectfully go anyway because she didn't want anyone, including her husband, telling her what to do. The restored Amanda stayed indoors, heeding her husband's advice.

Similarly, when a fellow homeschooling family invited us to meet up at a museum recently and my husband asked me to take our kids to a park instead to pinch pennies, the old Amanda would have found a way to get to the museum even if it meant covertly moving funds around to do so. Notwithstanding the chance to see some friends, the restored Amanda instead found reasons to agree instead of reasons to disagree and we still had a splendid time at the park. Afterward, I needed to run to the store for pasta sauce, but Husseim cautioned me not to get distracted—meaning not to buy the kids unnecessary drinks and snacks. The old Amanda would ignore his opinion and get the kids something to munch on as a diversion, assuming it to be unfair that he can make a harsh judgment call without understanding how challenging any trip to the store is, especially with little kids. The restored Amanda asked him if he could watch the kids while I go to the store solo, or if he could make the trip to the store for me. He gladly obliged with the latter.

As the Lord has been guiding me through fervid character training in this waiting season, not only has my parenting improved as a byproduct, but the intimacy in my marriage has as well. In every area I have sought the Lord for wisdom, He has delivered. With regard to intimacy, He has shown me that my husband needs sex like I need water. It's a deep physiological need in men that only a woman can fulfill. The more often my husband and I are intimate, the less it feels to me like another chore, so Husseim and I have begun aiming to be intimate at least every other day. With frequency like this, we've grown to expect sex just like we expect to have dinner. If we let too much time pass between though, I'll drag my feet getting there and my appalling energy will put the candle out, fast.

Every husband desires for his wife to want him like he wants her, albeit harder for them to admit because men try to do the honorable thing of covering up how they really feel for the sake of peace with their wives. To completely eliminate the raisin cake of self-centeredness in my life, I had to ask for my husband's forgiveness for past dishonoring behaviors and tell him about my intentions to be made new in Christ. I told Husseim that I'm still going to make mistakes, but that I am truly committed to my own restoration and to the restoration of our marriage.

Within the first week of this restoration, I found myself weeping at the feet of my husband. I bowed to him in respect and apologized to him with a sincere heart for all the times I dismissed his plans or leadership for my own. This probably sounds extraordinary to you, and it was especially out of character for me. I'm not saying that you have to do this to get in good graces with your spouse, but it's something that God convicted me to do for mine. I was so ashamed of all the times that I muted him for my own personal gain, and I wanted to show God, my husband, and my children that I was going to turn things around for the betterment of all.

Wives carry so much more weight than they may realize. Sure, it might be tempting to think it's the man's job to make sure the whole household is pursuing God, since they're supposed to be the spiritual leaders. It's easy enough to think, "If Dad goes to church, then we all go to church. If Dad prays, we all pray. If Dad worships, we all worship." But no, wives don't get a pass on this one. They don't get to say "Well we don't read our Bible enough because my husband never wants to" or "We don't get together to talk as a family because my husband doesn't like to." Women need to recognize the exceedingly influential role that we play as a wife and mother. Likewise, men and women alike need to realize the importance of a God-foundation for their family. Small dents in spiritual armor turn into major cracks over time, as exemplified in this scenario from Jim and Elizabeth George's workbook for *A Couple After God's Own Heart*:

> Daniel and Betty Sue had been "church hopping" for several months. They loved the Lord and were so thankful they were a Christian couple. Because they had both grown up in Christian homes, they had each known that's what they wanted in a marriage and family—that God would be first. Yet try as they had, something just wasn't quite right at the church they had been going to. Dissatisfied with the direction their church was heading, they talked and prayed, and they believed God was leading them to search for a new church. In God's timing they arrived at First Community

Church, and immediately they felt good about everything they saw and heard. The pastor was a solid Bible teacher, and they were quickly welcomed and absorbed into the life of the church. In no time, they felt right at home. This fresh, lively church experience went on for some time.

But then big changes took place. For starters, they gave birth to their first child. What joy! And what a thrill it was to take part in a baby dedication service for their precious one. However, with baby's and baby's parents' runny noses, sleepless nights, and changing routines, Daniel and Betty Sue didn't always make it to church. What's more, Betty Sue was afraid their little one might catch something from one of the other babies in the nursery. After all the colds and ear aches and fevers and doctor visits they'd been through over a period of months, they sure didn't want to bring home any new germs!

And of course, there was the ordeal of getting everyone ready for church and arriving on time. Eventually their church attendance became more sporadic. Then Daniel got a promotion at work, for which both he and Betty Sue were ecstatic. It was a terrific career advancement that came loaded with more money, stock options, a generous expense account, a company car--all the corporate trimmings. But the job had its downside: it was very demanding. Daniel had to go through some intensive training courses, and he also had to do a lot of travel. And when he wasn't on the road, he had to spend extra time at the office catching up with his workload.

With so many of their weeks spent apart, Daniel and Betty Sue decided their weekends needed to be more about them and their "precious." So they opted to try to attend the midweek couples Bible study... that is, if they could get a babysitter. So very subtly, their church attendance and involvement in ministry was sliding down their priority scale. But every time they felt a twinge of guilt, they reasoned that God would want them to work on their marriage and family first. And, hey, what better way to do that than to take a fun family camping trip this next weekend![64]

This scenario feels all too familiar. A little progress (good or bad) each day adds up to big results. From Daniel and Betty Sue's example we can all learn a critical lesson about consistency within our church community. Each day that we add to our marriages brings with it new layers of complexity. Being a part of a church body is necessary preparation for handling whatever comes with those layers.

Church should be a forethought, never an afterthought. Stay plugged in like your life depends on it, because it does! Eternity is on the line. If you stopped working tomorrow, how quickly would you be replaced and forgotten? Yet to your own family and your church family, you're irreplaceable. God instituted the church not for us to have a picture-perfect experience each week but so we'd never walk this difficult, sin-filled life alone. As Christ followers, we're meant to be evidence of God's redeeming grace in each other's lives, reminding us that our sin will never truly satisfy because Jesus is so much better. If no one gets to know you well enough to know what sins you're battling, then no one will be able to exhort, convict, and lead you back to Christ when you stray.

I've often heard people say the husband is the head, but the woman is the neck and lately I've been realizing how much truth there is to this. My own neck prior to this waiting season was constantly turning from the left to the right, even completely backwards, not set straight toward Jesus as it should've been. And since I've put my neck on straight and gotten my spiritual life back in order, making God my everything, the whole family has changed direction as well. My husband is following me and pursuing the Lord with refreshed vigor.

When my husband prays for me now, he thanks God for the amazing transformation He's done in me, He thanks God for the amazing wife that He has been blessed with, and He apologizes to God for times that he hasn't valued me. He has praised God for the encouragement that I give to him and he has said that the changes he sees in me have encouraged him to fix his own gaze on the Lord. He has been worshiping. He has been praying. He has been praising. He has been joining me and seeking fellowship with other believers. Our oldest son has followed suit as well. In the mornings, he gets up early with us, and he sits in the presence of the Lord with us, and with worship music on, he prays in tongues with us as we all pursue God's heart. Even our younger children are prioritizing God in their day and throughout their day. Why? Because that's what they see their mama doing. Let us not forget that parenting is more caught than taught. Before this waiting season, I was teaching my children about the Lord. Bible was a regular subject in the homeschool day. But I was not showing them the ways of the Lord. Growing quickly frustrated over lost items, releasing excessive anger over misbehavior of those I love most, being slow to forgive/give fresh chances. I had grown to believe that all of those flaws were inherited from my parents, and they were just there. If I could've changed them like turning off the lights, I would have done so years ago, but it wasn't that simple. Now that I'm all in with Jesus, I realize that those personality flaws were not truly me. They were symptoms of an exhausted me. They were the final straw in the life of a woman who was utterly overwhelmed.

Now that life has been stripped down to the simplest possible form to just being Amanda, the believer, the wife, the mom staying home most days with my kids schooling them, being wrapped up in the here and now, loving the Lord here, enjoying going outside here, enjoying each other's company here, not seeking entertainment elsewhere. Wow. This is where the real power is. Appreciating the smallest of things, is where the true transformation is. My former self-centeredness prevented me from cherishing the smallest of things before. I couldn't have even imagined my kids' life without piano or violin or dance lessons, or horseback riding or archery or the movies, or the trampoline park, or any of the many activities I got them involved in. Since I've taken them out and I've been more alert and attentive to them than ever before, do you know how many times they have asked me about returning to those activities? Not once.

Let me ask you something: what can you not imagine facing tomorrow without? Do you buy unnecessary things for your kids because it's easier or more convenient than going outside with them to play? Believe me when I say your kids will value your attention so much more than anything you ever buy them. The things you do buy them will just become lost most of the time anyways. *Yes Husseim, your wife just wrote that, and meant it.* Your kids certainly aren't likely to make it to adulthood with "things" but the memories of your presence will stay with them in their hearts for a lifetime. The ONLY place in your whole world where you are irreplaceable is in your home!

Except for your Bible, I'll bet none of your answers to my question about what you couldn't face tomorrow without are material things. Yet you're probably the proud owner of certain non-negotiables that you refuse to live without. You'll be glad to know I won't be proposing for you to sell everything and become a missionary. All I'm proposing is that you be daring enough to eliminate the raisin cakes in your own life by placing a one month pause on everything you can possibly pause. This is going to look different for each and every one of you because family values vary. Still, consider spending one full month cutting out as much noise as possible so your family can pursue the Lord and each other like never before.

Like me, the raisin cakes you're purging might be money,

coveting material possessions, your phone, your negative self-view, your self-centeredness, or maybe you have other raisin cakes stealing your gaze away from the Lord. Your raisin cake could be eating out and partaking in costly activities. What if like me, you told the kids, extracurricular coaches, mentors, and teachers, you were taking a one-month hiatus just to try a quieter life on for size. Consider what things you would be willing to cut if you your or your spouse's job situation suddenly changed. There's much power in you trying out major changes like this, without having to go through the pain of changing financial choices by force. Sleekest of all, if a big change ever does come your way, you'll be so much more prepared for it than I was.

Take a hard look at your habits. When you enter Heaven one day, and God asks you about how you spent your earthly time and money, will you be proud of your response? What changes can you make to better honor God and impress your spouse or closest teammate in life? Can you cook at home? Can you prepare tea or coffee at home? Can you do your own hair? Can you work out at home? Can you teach your kids skills at home instead of paying for them to learn skills somewhere else? I'm convinced we can learn practically anything for free on YouTube by the way; it just takes a little time and effort. I don't want you to be alone in this talk. Strategize with your roof busters and don't go too easy on each other. Don't allow each other to explain and justify all the reasons why you need this and why you need that.

Challenge each other to cut back on as many things as possible for the trial of one month to see how it feels. I suspect that after one month of trying this, many changes you make are going to stick because that's what God is starting to reveal to me in my own life. In every area I thought I would feel lack, I actually feel liberated!

If you're anything like my former self, you're probably not going to heed my advice, but I challenge you to be stronger than I was. Just changing your pursuit of the Lord is going to result in changes in your whole life. If you're married, it will also change your marriage and family for the better. Eliminate distracting raisin cakes and you'll hit the mega jackpot!

Life Application Challenge 7*: Stop eating raisin cakes that steal your affection for the Lord! Be daring enough to put a one month pause on everything you can possibly pause. Cut out as much noise as possible and enjoy pursuing the Lord and your family like never before. Ideas are not eating out, not participating in costly activities, not feeding negative thoughts, not prioritizing your desires over your family's. Take a one-month hiatus from the world, to try a quieter life on for size. In the quiet, you'll find your Lord and savior. In Jeremiah 29:13, God says that if you seek him with your whole heart, you will find him (NIV).*

<u>Lyrics to Emma's Pick: "I Thank God" by Maverick City Music and Upperroom</u>

None of us can stay stuck in a rut for long when my clever Emma's around. She can make marker or hardship disappear faster than Sonic the Hedgehog can run around the world and back! I believe laughter is her superpower. She's constantly making us laugh louder, smile bigger, and live better. We took her name from Emmanuel, meaning "God's with us" and she certainly reminds us of that. She epitomizes Philippians 4:4, rejoicing in the Lord always (NIV). Emma just loves to dance to this song.

Wandering into the night

Wanting a place to hide

I cannot deny what I see
Got no choice but to believe
My doubts are burning
Like ashes in the wind

This weary soul, this bag of
bones
And I tried with all my mind
And I just can't win the fight
I'm slowly drifting, oh
vagabond
And just when I ran out of road
I met a man I didn't know
And he told me
That I was not alone

He picked me up
He turned me around
He placed my feet on solid
ground
I thank the Master
I thank the Savior
Because He healed my heart
He changed my name
Forever free, I'm not the same
I thank the Master
I thank the Savior
I thank God

Hell lost another one
I am free, I am free, I am free
(x8)

He picked me up
He turned me around
He placed my feet on solid
ground
I thank the Master
I thank the Savior
Because He healed my heart

So, so long to my old friends
Burden and bitter night
You can't just keep them
moving
No, you ain't welcome here
From now 'til I walk
The streets of gold
I'll sing of how You saved
my soul
This wayward son
Has found his way back
home

He picked me up
Turned me around
Placed my feet on solid
ground
I thank the Master
I thank the Savior
Because He healed my heart
Changed my name
Forever free, I'm not the
same
I thank the Master
I thank the Savior
Oh, I thank God (x7)
That means what He did for
another
He can do it again
That means what He did for
another
He can do to us all
Get up, get up, get up
Get up out of that grave
(x13)

Peace before Increase

He changed my name
Forever free, I'm not the same
I thank the Master
I thank the Savior
I thank God

And if He did it for me,
He can do it for you (2X)

Get up, get up, get up
Get up out of that grave

Get up, get up, get up
Get up out of that grave (x11)

If He did it for me,
He can do it for you (x3)

The testimony of Jesus
Is the Spirit of Prophesy
That means what He did for another
He can do it again
That means what He did for another
He can do it again
The testimony of Jesus
Is the Spirit of Prophesy (x3)

He picked me up
Turned me around
Placed my feet on solid ground
I thank the Master
I thank the Savior
Because He healed my heart
He changed my name
Forever free, I'm not the same
I thank the Master
I thank the Savior
I thank God

<u>Stride 8: Search</u>

Matthew 20:1-16

The Parable of the Workers in the Vineyard

For the kingdom of heaven is like a landowner who went out early in the morning to hire workers for his vineyard. He agreed to pay them a denarius [the typical daily wage of a day laborer at the time] for the day and sent them into his vineyard.

About nine in the morning he went out and saw others standing in the marketplace doing nothing. He told them, "You also go and work in my vineyard, and I will pay you whatever is right." So they went.

He went out again about noon and about three in the afternoon and did the same thing. About five in the afternoon he went out and found still others standing around. He asked them, "Why have you been standing here all day long doing nothing?"

"Because no one has hired us," they answered.

He said to them, "You also go and work in my vineyard."

When evening came, the owner of the vineyard said to his foreman, "Call the workers and pay them their wages, beginning with the last ones hired and going on to the first.'

The workers who were hired about five in the afternoon came and each received a denarius. So when those came who were hired first, they expected to receive more. But each one of them also received a denarius. When they received it, they began to grumble against the landowner. "These who were hired last worked only one hour," they said, "and you have made them equal to us who have borne the burden of the work and the heat of the day."

But he answered one of them, "I am not being unfair to you, friend. Didn't you agree to work for a denarius? Take your pay and go. I want to give the one who was hired last the same as I gave you. Don't I have the right to do what I want with my own money? Or are you envious because I am generous?"

So the last will be first, and the first will be last (NIV).

The entire Gospel is encapsulated here. What an alluring illustration of our salvation. This parable hones in on the fact that we can't gain faith through work alone. Everyone is able to receive the same eternal reward, no matter when they accept Jesus as their Lord and Savior. This message is similar to the parable of the prodigal son as told in the gospel of Luke. Those who relate closest to the oldest brother of the prodigal son who was consistently faithful, yet went uncelebrated, may be tempted to think the longer they're faithful to God, the greater the prize they deserve, but that isn't so. God willingly and freely offers the same chance at salvation whether we're poor or wealthy, employed or unemployed, exuberant or sullen, loquacious or circumspect, saved as a youngin or saved on our deathbeds. By the grace of God through the ultimate sacrifice of His son, we are *all* given the opportunity to enter the vineyard (the kingdom of Heaven). As we saw with Naaman in the Jordan River, receiving that salvation takes a decrease of self and an increase of hope in things one cannot see!

When you're in need of hope, SEARCH for it! Don't lay in your bed expecting a dove to carry a letter of hope to you in its beak—not saying God can't and won't do that; I'm just saying to take an active role in your own transformation. If you're out in the middle of the ocean, you're absolutely going to pray to God to save you, but you are also going to do your part to kick your feet. If you, like me, are in a glorious waiting season, I encourage you to force yourself to kick your feet, every day! Expect that as the Lord uses this season to make something entirely new in you, you'll have some euphoric highs and some dispiriting lows. But keep moving toward Jesus, and away from the past. Some days you'll be sprinting to Him and on other days you might barely be crawling to Him. Either brings delight to the Father. He sees and is proud of your efforts.

Just two days after my sacred wait began, my husband ensured we got ourselves to a midweek church service. As soon as an altar call was announced, I beelined for the front. God embraced me that night through a powerful prayer partner who authoritatively shared these words with me: "The enemy is telling you that you'll be removed from your job but THAT IS NOT GOD. You're stressing and searching for jobs without remembering that God's in this. He's here. He's present." Those words have been branded on my heart, since.

As I've been strengthening my spiritual life throughout this golden waiting period, God has given me confidence to pursue the encouragement I need. He has grown my hope by blessing me with interactions with fellow believers, who have shared amazing testimonies with me of times in their own lives that they've chosen to follow Christ instead of others or themselves. Before this, I would rarely seek to begin conversations with others regarding faith, because I usually did a fine job of talking myself out of conversing with other Christians. I would think they were better than me. Their lives were better than mine. Their loads were lighter than mine. I was intimidated. However, the more people I talk to, the more I realize that everyone goes through junk. I'm not the only one. Thinking I'm the only one is believing a lie from the devil. Looking back, my avoidance of any conversations with fellow believers beyond "How are you?" was probably one of the devil's schemes too. He played me like a fiddle. He tried to eradicate my memory of Nehemiah 8:10 which encourages all believers to muzzle toxic thoughts by professing "the joy of the Lord is our strength" (NLT)!

Before I got the call from my work about taking a paid semester off from teaching—still in awe of God over this—a simple hug with a fellow homeschool mom who met up with me on her own volition inspired me to open like flower blooming after a long winter. With utmost compassion, this mom assured me that it's OKAY to lay my burdens down and let others help me to carry them. At that fragile point, I was already falling apart, and I hadn't even gotten the news yet about how drastically my world would soon change. This mom told me that she could empathize with me because she knows what it's like to work full-time while attempting to keep a marriage, home, and homeschool intact. She told me of her own past trials, like her and her husband's loss of a baby well into the second trimester of pregnancy, the loss of consistent income, the loss of a car, and even the loss of a literal roof over their head. Do you know what she told me she and her husband did once when their roof caved in on their house in the middle of pouring rain? They embraced one another, and danced. The joy of the Lord is their strength.

Another woman I heard about on our Christian Radio station shared that she royally upset her husband one morning when pancakes she left too long on the stove scented their whole house with a staggering burnt aroma. As she took the pancakes outside to the trash, her husband was so furious that he called her an explicative and locked her out of the house. Mind you she was barefoot and without water or keys in the 114-degree Texas sun. But she didn't retaliate in anger. Oh no. She simply walked around to a side door, let herself in, and gently said "Honey, just a head's up that I'm entering the side door." The grace of this woman astounds me. She is too close to God to allow petty behaviors of her husband to bring her down. The joy of the Lord is her strength.

During another instance of fellowship, I listened to tales of one mom's life before moving this far south—we live in the Rio Grande Valley, right on the Texas/Mexico border. She used to live further north in metropolitan middle-America where she thought she had it all. Granted, in order for her to stay home and homeschool her children, her husband had to work two jobs back-to-back and wasn't getting home until later and later each night. She thought they were making it. Sure, they were coasting along, but he was utterly exhausted. He was burning out. Until, one day the Lord allowed the rug to be ripped out from under them.

This mom's husband is from Mexico and did not have paperwork to legally reside here in the states. He was pulled over in a traffic stop that would eventually lead to his deportation from the country. This family ended up moving to a popular city in Mexico just across the border from deep south Texas, where I live. God eventually provided the wife with the best of both worlds. She received a job as a nurse where she would only have to work on weekends and could be present homeschooling her kids during the week and her husband? He became a full-time stay at home dad.

Both had their fears before settling into this new reality. The husband was not looking forward to 24/7 daddy duty and my friend was not looking forward to leaving everything she knew to now live in Mexico. In fact, she told me she fought God on this for a whole year before she finally started to accept glimpses of God's beautiful plan. He worked the bad out for good. Now she and her husband are both be equally active and present in the rearing of their children, and they lack for nothing. The joy of the Lord is their strength.

After a morning meeting in our homeschool community, about two weeks into this miraculous wait, I remember uncontrollably sobbing while singing the trinitarian doxology inspired by 2 Corinthians 13:14 (NKJV). The lyrics say: "Praise God, from Whom all blessings flow; Praise Him, all creatures here below; Praise Him above, ye heavenly host; Praise Father, Son, and Holy Ghost. Amen." From the depth of my soul, that day I declared Psalm 38:9 over my circumstances by voicing, "Lord, you know all my desires and deepest longings. My tears are liquid words and you can read them all" (TPT). In the same breath drawn to say this prayer, I received a text from a sister in Christ, telling me, "Girl, I could totally see you as an author." She was a bucket carrying His living water to me, right when I needed it most! The joy of the Lord is her strength!

That same day, a fellow homeschool dad told me he unexpectedly lost his job of many years and yet he, his wife, and their two beautiful daughters have never gone without. This dad was given a position of leadership in his church and takes it upon himself to sell baked goods and bracelets to support his family. It's hard labor and people can be ruthlessly mean, but the joy of the Lord is his strength.

Before a service our son invited us to, a pastoring couple currently ministering out of a borrowed church and seeking to open their own church, told me their family of five once made it on a mere

$15,000 a year. According to them, their cups were overflowing, not because of income, but because the favor of God was on their lives. They said to this day they have way more than should be possible on what they have earned as ministers. They are living proof that in times of economic or family difficulty, the Lord's blessings are promised to those who faithfully pay their tithe! The joy of the Lord is their strength!

Within the first week of this waiting season gifted to me by God, I had a dream of the face of a new woman who joined our homeschool community. I woke up knowing God wanted her to pray with me. The very next day when our community got together, I stayed for lunch, which was radical in and of itself because I typically avoid socializing. As a public school teacher, I tended to avoid the lunchroom out of fear that I'd get involved in gossip or friendships that could lead to disappointment. This tendency followed me into my role as a homeschool parent so even though I knew there was someone I hoped to see that day, I wasn't about to go looking for this woman who I hardly knew. As fellow homeschool families consumed their lunches, I awkwardly shuffled back-and-forth between inside and outside with my kids until finally I saw an empty seat on a bench next to a fellow mom near the playground. I asked her if she minded if I sat there. She didn't mind, and as God would have it, unbeknownst to me, this woman I sat with is close with the woman I saw in my dream so before I knew it, walking straight toward me was the woman who I knew needed to pray with me. I briefly explained my circumstance and asked if she could speak any hope into my life. She had just the story.

She said years before becoming a parent to her two adopted children, she and her husband had a beloved dog who they deeply cared for. She loved this dog so much, in fact, that she would take him everywhere with her. She bought a car with a special hatchback just for her dog. She took her dog to the park with her, to stores with her, everywhere, and one day she got devastating news that he had cancer and the veterinarian estimated he had six months left to live. She and her husband vowed to make it the best six months they could. Lamentably, things progressed from bad to worse quicker than expected. They had to take their dog in for a blood transfusion, and he died on the operating table. She was beside herself with grief. She knew she was losing him, but she didn't know he was going to die so soon, and she had secretly wished she could have preserved a stamp of his paw print as a memory of him. She didn't share this with anyone because it didn't matter anymore.

Now, her only idea of a memory of him might be his collar so she got in her car and started to drive to the veterinarian to see if maybe she could retrieve it, but her husband ultimately talked her out of it. He didn't want her emotions to dominate her, and it was quite possible that they didn't keep the collar, which would only heighten her disappointment. She listened to her husband and returned home to grieve with him until one day, in the mail came a package with a beautifully written note from the vet about the incredible qualities her dog had. Obedient, loyal, and patient were some of the words they used to describe her dog. Then, the letter said that they felt it in their hearts that they should send her the dog's collar *and* a stamp of his paw print—something that only God knew she longed for. She said in this moment, she learned that the God she grew up knowing, who loves His people and loves His church, also loved *her* individually, and wanted a personal intimate relationship with just her. The joy of the Lord is her strength!

After hearing this woman's testimony and praying with her, I was so excited to continue pressing into the Lord. Resembling Forrest Gump conversing with each passer-by on a park bench at this point, beside me next came another woman, whom I greatly admire. This woman told me not to forget that we make plans, but God directs our steps. She homeschools as well, and her husband works as a traveling doctor. It was looking like he was going to have to be gone for all of January to make ends meet until the Lord supplied him with an unexpected pay increase of an extra $400 per hour. PER hour! Because of that hug from God, he would start the new year with his family instead. The joy of the Lord is this family's strength.

A young girl I mentored from our church's youth service was terribly ashamed of her curves because other teens constantly reminded her that she wasn't slim like most other girls her age. To make things even worse, she loved hunting with her dad and often dressed in camouflage. She was teased for looking more like a boy than a girl. The bullying she experienced got bad enough that the only solution she could think of was to end her own life. Thankfully, she didn't follow through. One night, at about 2 in the morning, the Lord prompted me to text her a video of a Craig Groeschel sermon. She watched it, gave her life to the Lord, and asked to sign up to be baptized at our church the following week! And guess what?! Her parents and siblings were all so inspired by the changes they saw in her, that they wanted to get baptized too! So, the whole family was baptized together! The joy of the Lord is their strength!

A man from Western Australia came to speak at a church I visited. He lost his dad to a heart attack at the age of seven and was furious with God. He ended up joining a gang and at the age of seventeen, he and his gang went to see Billy Graham while on tour so they could kill him! But as God would have it, nine out of ten gang members accepted the Lord as their savior before that could happen! This man recalls God Himself asking Him, "Why are you really here?" And then assuring him, "I didn't take your dad away from you. I love you." Now the joy of the Lord is his strength!

When Husseim and I visited a healing conference at Charis Bible College in Woodland Park, Colorado, out of the hundreds of others in attendance, a prophet spoke a word specifically for

Husseim to expect double for our trouble in the coming year! While this was happening, I met a woman who God sent to the conference just for me! We met sitting across from one another on lobby couches. I'd excused myself from the conference to nurse my newborn daughter and was drawn to this woman's angelic glow. The God in her is so pronounced! We lightly discussed the message being shared before she began walking away. I felt an irrefragable tug in my soul to stop her so I could collect her contact information.

Once I stopped her, she said she was waiting for me to ask. She proceeded to inform me that she was in between assignments as a traveling nurse and was only in Colorado for that weekend. She wasn't even there to attend this conference. She was convicted to change her plans that night, and said with certainty that it was because God wanted to align her path with mine. She has been a devoted prayer partner of mine ever since. I cannot tell you how many times she has followed conviction from the Lord to check on me in the perfect moments, when I most need to be reminded of God's love for me. She is a God mother I have grown to deeply cherish!

A dear friend from my church once found herself in a loveless marriage. Married to a high school sweetheart since a young age, she and her husband shared two sons, but she often felt her husband only paid mind to his work, and his role as a provider, but not to his role as a friend or a confidant to his wife. Eventually, the missing pieces were fulfilled by another man whom she began an affair with. Ultimately, her husband found out and they divorced. Her husband would tell you he never lost hope of their reconciliation until she had to reveal to him something that he already knew deep in his spirit—she was pregnant by the other man. Remarkably, he still did not turn his back on her. He continued to pursue God and never abandoned his tutelage for his, by then, ex-wife. Throughout her pregnancy, he would check on her, bring her food, hold her stomach, and care for her, as if the baby was his.

As God would have it, immediately after the birth of what would be the first and only girl in their family, they reconciled against all odds. They remarried, added one more son to the kin, and now serve the Lord by helping other married couples stay married. They have seen and known that marriage is worth fighting for. The joy of the Lord is their strength!

Another woman we met through marriage ministry shared that she and her husband were brought together at a young age as well, but he was not ready to commit to the woman God chose for him. So he left her and began a "situationship" with another woman with whom he had two daughters. After much growth that needed to happen before he would be ready for the right one, God completely transformed him, and then he returned to the woman of his dreams. They married, and as God would have it, welcomed two sons together. They wouldn't tell you life is always a cakewalk because consequences of disobedience have left a residue to be dealt with, but their unshakable faith helps them persevere. The joy of the Lord is their strength.

This past Christmas I, along with some friends and family members, decided to look into sponsoring a child at an orphanage in Cozumel, Mexico that we had the privilege of visiting during a recent trip. After background checks and application materials were all vetted and accepted, the director emailed me a list of names and ages of the orphans who weren't fully supported yet. (It typically takes ten sponsors to financially cover all needs of one child.) My kids and I prayed about it and then my oldest son Adam said the Lord gave him a name: Jose. I hadn't shown Adam the list. It only had six or seven names total, and one of them was, indeed, Jose. He seemed like one less likely to be chosen by other sponsors because he was the oldest orphan on the list. He's already an adult, actually, and attending school to become a pastor. Not only that, but Jose's name was the only name typed in red. To this day, I still have no idea why, but when I showed Adam, every hair follicle on both of our bodies stood straight up! We were reminded of when Jesus speaks in the Bible, words directly from Him are written in red. And there's more. Jose's middle name is Rafa, reminding us of Jehovah Rapha, one of the seven names of God shared in the Old Testament. It means "The God that heals." Wow, what a hug from God. In the healing season we are in, that was so huge for us. The joy of the Lord is our strength!

Another constant reminder that God heals us is in the name of our newest daughter. While pregnant with her, we ran a blood test to find out her gender as we had with all of our other children without fail. This time, the 99.9% accurate blood gender test said we were having a boy, so after prayerful consideration as a whole family, we decided to name this baby Josiah, meaning "God supports and heals us." When we committed to this name, we had no idea how much it would impact us in the season to come. After ultrasound imaging toward the end of my pregnancy refuted the findings of the blood test, we didn't know what to believe and just left it in God's hands until delivery. I brought boy and girl clothes to the birth with me, just in case, and voila, we had a baby girl! We still loved the name God led us to so Josiah simply became Josie. (Shout out to her Godparents Lori & Ted Burns for aiding in that decision!) Josie is a beautiful, constant reminder that God is healing our whole family—and yes, in case you're wondering, the company who supplied the blood test sent us a full refund once we showed them her birth certificate.

That refund along with another unexpected refund came in clutch timing just recently when we woke up to a water heater mess. Our entire downstairs was flooded but the God who supports and heals knew this was coming and sent provision! Hallelujah! He even brought a surprise guest—a friend of a friend—to my women's Bible study that same day who was visiting from across the country but had a testimony of perseverance to share! She'd spent seven years moving from adjunct job to adjunct job before receiving the permanent role she now has in higher education. Seven years! Yet, she never missed a bill, even when she wasn't sure if she'd be teaching or not. I was taken aback by her steadfast dependence on the Lord. We know unquestionably when things like this happen, we are covered because of our tithe. Take care of the kingdom and the Lord will take care of you! The joy of the Lord is our strength!

In an unforgettable sermon, I heard the story of a pastor whose granddaughter's hair got caught in a filter, while swimming in a pool. By the time the other children noticed, it was already too late. They screamed for help, and her father jumped in, untangled her hair, and lifted her limp body onto the deck. 9-11 was called and EMTs came to work on her, but couldn't find a pulse. They were just about to call in a body that they'd be bringing dead on arrival when the father loudl—and probably crazily to the outside world— yelled "The Lord rebuke you, Satan! No, you cannot have my daughter! We claim tither's rights in the name of the God of Abraham, Isaac, and Jacob!" Just as soon as he let out this blood curdling yell from the depths of his soul, the little girl woke up and stood up. A true miracle. She did go for examination at the hospital, but no injuries were found. She was perfectly well. What a testament to the promise exhibited in Malachi 3:11! The joy of the Lord is that father's strength!

A preacher we received prayer from on a day that Husseim's head pain intensified told us about a time that he struck a deer while driving home from a revival. He was so full of the Holy Spirit at the time that immediately after the impact, he and his friend retrieved praise flags from the trunk and began dancing in the streets unto the Lord, right in front of his badly damaged vehicle. "Jesus is getting me a new car!" he proclaimed in faith. How I adored his zest. With all his heart, mind, and soul, He believed what he said. And sure enough, with a tax refund in the exact amount he'd need for a new car, Jesus delivered! I remember him saying he never once allowed himself to wonder, "Why did this have to happen to me?" Instead, He thanked God that it happened to him—the one getting a tax refund, as opposed to another driver who wouldn't have had the means to fix or purchase another vehicle.

A family from my former home church took a leap of faith after the pandemic and started their own business. Before their consignment shop ever opened, they gave their church ten percent tithe off of every means of income they had. As God would have it, during their opening month, the local newspaper asked to put their consignment shop on the front page free of charge. They knew that had to be God! After this front-page appearance, customers poured in and their sales have been higher than they could've ever imagined! The joy of the Lord is their strength!

A woman I met at a Christian concert found out she was laid

off from her job where she worked for fourteen years. Sure, fear crept into her thoughts, but she claimed her tither's rights aloud each day since learning this news and within a week, she received a 26-week severance—a package of additional pay for an employee's past work that is given at the end of the employee's employment—and a job offer for a new position, paying double what she made in the old position. The joy of the Lord is her strength!

I love how Pastor Bill Winston explains the correct perspective of tithing: "A tithe does not become a tithe when we give it. It becomes a tithe when we get it. The moment we receive a paycheck, it becomes a tithe—not when we bring it into the house of God." Those who tithe have seeds in the ground that those who don't tithe do not. Those seeds are called "tither's rights," and they're found in Malachi 3:10-12. Amid my blessed wait, the Lord led me to search for these verses in the Amplified Bible, Classic Edition (AMPC):

TITHER'S RIGHT No. 1: PROVISION

The Lord provides for tithers. Malachi 3:10 gives the following instructions: "'Bring all the tithes—the whole tenth of your income—into the storehouse, that there may be food in My house, and prove Me now by it,' says The LORD of hosts, 'if I will not open the windows of heaven for you and pour you out a blessing, that there shall not be room enough to receive it.'" In Hebrew, windows mean floodgates, thus indicating that when we give our tithes as the Lord has commanded, our biggest blessings of all will be bestowed upon us. Bigger blessings than we can fathom. I love in this verse, that Father God says "prove me" as if to challenge us to test him. Tithers get to experience supernatural increase and overflow known to no one else. Proverbs 3:9-10 instructs us: "Honor The LORD with your capital and sufficiency [from righteous labors] and with the first fruits of all your income; so shall your storage places be filled with plenty, and your vats shall be overflowing with new wine."

TITHER'S RIGHT No. 2: PROTECTION

The Lord protects tithers. Malachi 3:11 renders this assurance: "'And I will rebuke the devourer [insects and plagues] for your sakes and he shall not destroy the fruits of your ground, neither shall your vine drop its fruit before the time in the field,' says The LORD of hosts." With tithing comes shelter from the enemy, who is here to kill, steal, and destroy. When under attack, tithers get to proclaim this verse against the enemy rebuking him. When we give God what is rightly His, He protects every single thing that we do and own.

TITHER'S RIGHT No. 3: PROMOTION

The Lord promotes tithers. Malachi 3:12 confirms this, stating "'And all nations shall call you happy and blessed, for you shall be a land of delight,' says The LORD of hosts." This speaks to the grace and favor, given to tithers. The Lord creates a magnetic pull for tithers. Success gravitates toward them. They are destined for greatness. Other people and opportunities are attracted to them and find joy in their increase. Their happiness is attractive too because it's not external; it comes from within. Amid this valued wait, my family and I memorized an intrepid prayer from Pastor John Hagee that reminds us of rights to provision, protection, and promotion:

> Heavenly Father, God of Abraham, Isaac, and Jacob,
>
> I come before You today as Your child seeking Your divine favor. Lord God, Your favor surrounds the righteous. In faith believing, I receive the favor of God now in every dimension of my life. Let the favor of God rest upon every member of my family. Let Your favor rest upon our health, our finances, and our relationships.
>
> Lord God, from this day forward I am going to receive the limitless favor of God--supernatural increase, pro-motion, restoration, honor, spiritual victories, petitions granted, and battles won that I don't have to fight. The favor of God is upon me; it goes before me, and therefore, my life will never be the same.
>
> In Jesus' name, Amen![61]

Through a deep soul search, this prayer, in accompaniment with the countless testimonies shared with me from others throughout the wait, I've come to realize how irrational my worry about work has been. A job's a job. I can't take it with me. But I do take my soul. What about you? What blessings do you imagine God has for you on the other end of your perseverance?

Life Application Challenge 8: If your heart is set on becoming or remaining wealthy, it will keep you from following the Lord. Give God his ten percent off of every dollar you receive! Invite someone older and wiser in the Lord than you out for coffee and ask them to share stories with you of times the Lord brought them out of a wilderness. Be encouraged that if God did it for them, He can do it for you! Romans 12:4-5 says that's because we're better together than we are alone (NLT).

<u>Lyrics to Isaiah's Pick: "My Story, His Glory"</u>

<u>by Kids on the Move</u>

Sometimes the simplest lyrics provoke the biggest wake up calls. Every time my youngest son Isaiah tells me "Mommy play nah nah nah pweeeeee" I don't know who it's better for--him or me. It refreshes my soul to watch Isaiah become consumed by the peace of God as he stomps on Satan with his feet, like Romans 16:20 proclaims we should (NIV). Isaiah, whose name means "God's salvation and restoration" loves to dance, dance, dance for Jesus and stomp, stomp, stomp the devil. When Isaiah entered our world it had been nearly five years since we had a little one in the house. With him, came renewed faith and restored hope for the future. The joy of the Lord is his strength!

We all have a story
A purpose you deigned
Every day
Every page
Written for me
By the love of Jesus Christ
So listen up, listen up now.
We're shouting hey
Living every day
Living to praise your name
Jesus let my life
Be your story
I'm alive
To live a life that shines your
light!
So listen up, listen up now!
I'm living, I'm living out loud!
Jesus let my life be your story!
Yeah
You're the one
I want my life to celebrate
'Cause you gave life to me!

We're shouting hey
Living every day
Living to praise your name
Jesus let my life
Be your story (x2)

Let my life be your story
My future's bright
'Cause you want good things
for me (x2)

So bring on tomorrow, bring on
today,

I'm living, I'm living out
loud.
Jesus let my life
Be your story!
We're singing out, Yeah
You're the one I want
My life to celebrate
'Cause you gave life to me
We're shouting hey
Living every day
Living to praise your name
Jesus let my life
Be your story (x2)

Nah nah nah nah nah nah nah
HEY (x8)
HEY! HEY!

Peace before Increase

I aint afraid of what comes my
way
Let my story
Every page
Bring glory to
Jesus' name!

We're singing out
Yeah
You're the one I want my life to
celebrate
'Cause you gave life to me!

Stride 9: Fast

Esther 1-10

72 Hours that Saved the Jews

In accordance with the Contemporary English Version (CEV) of the Bible, the book of Esther recounts a story of dramatic reversal—a failed attempt to suppress Jews forever. At the center of this saga is a Jewish orphan, Esther, who was raised by her cousin Mordecai—a noble man who once prevented the king's assassination—since her father died during her mother's pregnancy and her mother died during her delivery. Against all odds, Esther weds King Xerxes, and succeeds the dethroned Vashti as Queen of the Persian Empire (modern day Iran). All ten chapters of her engrossing story can be heard in under thirty minutes on YouTube or viewed as a film—my favorite version of which is on Pureflix.

As the new, unpredicted queen, Esther faces grave danger when, in Esther 3:5-6, a power-hungry advisor to the king named Haman, becomes so enraged that Moredcai would not "bow or pay him homage," that he "sought to destroy all the Jews who were throughout the whole kingdom of Ahasuerus—the people of Mordecai." As a result, Mordecai pleads with Esther to help save the Jews. The thing is, Esther can't just text the king to ask him to spare her people. She would have to risk her life, for approaching the king without being summoned first, was punishable by death, per the law of the time. Adding further insult to injury, at that point, it had been THIRTY days since Esther was last summoned, implying that perhaps she'd lost the king's favor to the many concubines he likely kept on "standby" in his harem, so, in Esther 4:16, Esther calls a fast:

> Go, gather all the Jews who are present in Shushan, and fast for me; neither eat nor drink for three days, night or day. My maids and I will fast likewise. And so I will go to the king, which is against the law, and if I must die, I die.

Those 72 hours of fasting changed the history of the world. Esther receives ineffable favor for her people—in some funnier than Shakespearian ways, particularly when Haman suggests a parade assuming it will be for him, and the king follows his advice but in Mordecai's honor instead! Esther and her people went from hopeless to hopeFUL just like that! They gained honor and promotion. According to Esther 8:1-14, King Xerxes' response to Esther's request to prevent the annihilation of the Jews, is to give Esther the estate of the Jews' enemy, Haman. And that's not all. King Xerxes also gives Mordecai his signet ring, which once was Haman's—this change of hands signifying that Mordecai had replaced Haman's position in the kingdom. Esther appoints Mordecai over Haman's estate and again pleads with the king, falling at his feet and weeping. She begs him to put an end to the evil plan of Haman the Agagite, which he had devised against the

Jews. Then the king extends the gold scepter to Esther, and she arises before him to express these noteworthy words:

> 'If it pleases the king,' she said, 'and if he regards me with favor and thinks it the right thing to do, and if he is pleased with me, let an order be written overruling the dispatches that Haman son of Hammedatha, the Agagite, devised and wrote to destroy the Jews in all the king's provinces. For how can I bear to see disaster fall on my people? How can I bear to see the destruction of my family?'

> King Xerxes replied to Queen Esther and to Mordecai the Jew, 'Because Haman attacked the Jews, I have given his estate to Esther, and they have impaled him on the pole he set up. Now write another decree in the king's name on behalf of the Jews as seems best to you, and seal it with the king's signet ring—for no document written in the king's name and sealed with his ring can be revoked.'

> At once the royal secretaries were summoned—on the twenty-third day of the third month, the month of Sivan. They wrote out all Mordecai's orders to the Jews, and to the satraps, governors, and nobles of the 127 provinces stretching from India to Cush. These orders were written in the script of each province and the language of each people and also to the Jews in their own script and language.

> Mordecai wrote in the name of King Xerxes, sealed the dispatches with the king's signet ring, and sent them by mounted couriers, who rode fast horses especially bred for the king.

> The king's edict granted the Jews in every city the right to assemble and protect themselves; to destroy, kill and annihilate the armed men of any nationality or province who might attack them and their women and children, and to plunder the property of their enemies (ESV).

So, King Xerxes ends up ordering Haman to be impaled on the 50 meter high—that's taller than two school buses stacked vertically on top of each other—gallows that Haman had built for Mordecai to die on! After Haman dies instead, King Xerxes gives a second decree to preserve the Jews and grants them power to destroy all of their enemies within the kingdom! (Fun fact: the Feast of Purim, still celebrated by Jews to this day, was instituted to help the Jews remember their deliverance from Haman.) In addition to receiving the estate of his enemy Haman—whose ten sons were also hanged after they died in battle against the Jews—Mordecai was elevated to second-in-command in the kingdom! This reminds me of one of our family's favorite Bible verses from Psalm 57:6: "Whatever pit my enemies dig in my path—they fall into it themselves" (NIV).

Three days of fasting and prayer transformed Israel from a nation of defeat to a nation of favor. It's incredible to unpack Esther's and Mordecai's reliance on God for not only guidance, but for the anointing of their words. Never once did either of these Biblical heroes use their tongues to assault others.

If you can't control your mouth, you cannot control anything else. You think your misery is due to what is going on around you but it's actually due to what is going on inside you. Are you aware that griping is as bad as adultery in God's eyes? Try asking God for fire to reign on the messages you speak. Ask Him to anoint your words so they can help others and bring God glory!

The fact of the matter is complaining is more comfortable than changing. The Greek word translated from "complainer" means literally "one who is discontented with his lot in life."[65] Like the grinch who stole Christmas, it's easy to focus on the bad and see it get worse. Complaining is certainly not a reflection of Philippians 4:12 which reminds us to be content in the Lord instead of in what we have, nor is it a reflection of the fruits of the Spirit depicted in Galatians 5:22-23 (NIV).

Complaining robs our Spirit-deposited joy, peace, and patience by the heapful. Complaining not only deteriorates us inside but it also deteriorates the impression we give to others on the outside. It prevents us from remembering every person we get to be eyeball-to-eyeball with is someone who has value, someone who Jesus died for. It distracts us from being the only Jesus someone may ever get to interact with. What a shame it would be, if unbelievers were to connect our grumbling attitude with the walk of a Christ follower. Who would want that life?!

We can't change what we don't acknowledge. To boost self-awareness, try a gripe bracelet. Grab anything you can place on your wrist, be it a hair tie, a rubber band, or an actual bracelet, and each time you verbalize a complaint, move the bracelet to the opposite wrist. You'll be surprised by how many times it switches wrists throughout the day. According to Will Bowen, best-selling author of *A Complaint-Free World*, the average person complains between 15 to 30 times a day![65]

Frequently griping doesn't just suck the fun out of life, it is also dangerous for your health. A 1996 Stanford study proved that the more a person complains, the more s/he increases their levels of cortisol, also known as the stress hormone. Chronically high levels of cortisol can lead to a variety of health problems, including increased risk of depression, sleep issues, digestive problems, higher blood pressure, and even heart diseases. The Stanford study further demonstrates that complaining, or even being complained to, for 30 minutes or more can physically shrink the human brain! Researchers used high-resolution magnetic resonance imaging (MRI) scans to identify "links between long-term stressful life experiences, long-term exposure to hormones produced during stress, and the shrinking of the hippocampus."[30] (The hippocampus is the portion of the brain involved in the formation of new memories, emotions, and learning experiences.) So in other words, complaining for a half hour or more actually lessens your ability to acquire new experiences and knowledge. It makes you stuck in mud that gets deeper and deeper until soon enough, you can't take a step forward.

Once you're more cognizant of your typical perspective of life, up the ante. Start fasting to change your stinkin' thinkin'! I used to limit fasting to merely missing meals as a sacrifice to God. I thought it was easy because I would often get so busy that I'd miss meals anyway. And I certainly didn't mind shedding some weight as a result. Well, it turns out that's not fasting.

In her book *Fast Forward*, Lisa Bevere teaches us that the way we see is far more important than the way we look. I was treating fasting more like a diet which can change the way you look, but not the way you *see*. A diet, Bevere explains, can help us lose weight, but fasting helps us throw off the things weighing us down. When we fast, we channel wisdom learned by Clark Kent in *Man of Steel*. As a boy, Clark is overwhelmed by his surroundings and abilities. He laments that the world is just so big, to which his mother shrewdly replies, "then make it smaller." When we fast, it's not about being uncomfortable. It's about redirecting our gaze away from the things that consume most of our attention so we can be more aware of Jesus and the needs of others.[66] Hence, prefer to dub fasts interruptions. They interrupt and correct our focus![66]

When we fast, we are supposed to substitute the time that we would normally eat or look for something to eat with extra devotion to prayer, to reading God's Word, and to imploring (earnestly begging) God as we're taught in the book of Ezra. In this book, we read that after Israel spends decades in exile for disobeying God, His promise to restore them would finally be fulfilled. I'm sure it was hard for Israel, the tiny ethnic minority, totally obscure in the massive Persian empire, to believe this as they began the arduous journey back to their Promised Land. Hence Ezra "proclaimed a fast" seeking God's blessing on their trip, which was lengthy—four months to be exact—and dangerous. Ezra 8:23 chronicles Ezra confirming this when he states, "So we fasted and implored our God for this, and he listened to our entreaty."

In case you need more convincing, here are some Scriptures from the New Living Translation (NLT) of the Old Testament (OT) and the New Testament (NT) which exemplify the practice of fasting, for various reasons, that I encourage you to read and process with your roof busters:

OT:

- o In Esther 4:3—as we gathered in the introduction to this stride—after her Jewish cousin Mordecai won't bow down to the evil vizier Haman, he decides all Jews should be killed, so orphan-turned Persian Queen Esther asks the Jews to fast for her success in pleading with Persian King Xerxes I to spare their lives.
- o In Exodus 34:28, Moses fasts for forty days and forty nights without interruption while receiving the ten commandments from God.
- o In I Samuel 7:5, Judge and prophet Samuel gets the people of Israel to fast and confess their sins while they're being oppressed by the Philistines. He led the people of Israel from a system of judges to their first monarchy as they desired. Kings and queens were not God's design, but he granted the desires of their hearts to be like other nations.
- o In Nehemiah 1:4, after the power-seeking

Babylonians tore down the walls of Jerusalem and Solomon's temple in 2 Kings, in comes Nehemiah to help God's hand. Nehemiah prayed and fasted to God for four months before petitioning the Persian ruler to return to his home and reinforce Jerusalem's city walls.

- o In Psalms 35:13, 69:10, and 109:24, King David of Israel writes about his fasting. Most people imagine him as a muscular, mighty warrior, but Scripture reveals he was actually quite weak and thin physically—likely because he fasted so often.
- o In Joel 2:12, after a locust invasion leads to total devastation of the land in Israel, God uses His prophet Joel to command His people to turn their hearts back toward His through fasting.

NT:

- o In Luke 2:37, an entire life of fasting is depicted through the existence of prophetess Anna, who only had seven years of marriage with her husband and lived as a widow from sometime in her twenties until the age of eighty-four.
- o In Matthew 4:1-2, Jesus fasts for 40 days and 40 nights in the wilderness and then was tempted three times—physically, emotionally, and mentally in 4:3-4:10—by the devil. He resists, and tells the devil to get away!
- o In Matthew 6:16, as part of the Sermon on the Mount, Jesus commands His followers to fast but to not make it noticeable to others. He explains that whining so you'll get attention from others is not the point. The point is to draw strength from the Lord and to show this strength to others. A changed heart seeks validation from God, not others.
- o In Matthew 9:14, the disciples of John want to know why the disciples of Jesus weren't fasting like they

were but it was because Jesus was with them. After His ascension, the disciples of Jesus began to fast too.

- o In Acts 13:2, the church at Antioch fasted and prayed for Paul and Barnabas once God chose them to minister to non-Jews/gentiles.
- o In Acts 14:23, after praying and fasting, Paul and Barnabas keep God's command to start churches and appoint elders as church leaders in every city.

When I was younger, I was invited to go on a mission trip to Romania. I met with missionaries, filled out lots of paperwork, and learned all about the church building project I'd get to be a part of. Though my family couldn't afford for me to go, the seed to pray for others who could, had been planted, and I've not stopped praying for missionaries since. The memory of my involvement has withstood the test of time, as has a small bracelet I still have from one of the missionaries. Printed on it in cursive is an affable acronym for FAST: Focus, Abstain, Substitute, Taste. What pleasantly simple four step fasting instructions. Focus on God, Abstain from something that otherwise consumes a considerable amount of your focus, Substitute that something for more time reading God's Word and praying to Him, and Taste the Lord's remarkable goodness as directed in Psalm 34:8 (NIV). The welcomed standstill birthed by a fast will make you glad for even the most bitter moments in life that enable you to taste how sweet God truly is! There's a reason why the Bible doesn't say being happy is our strength. Happiness and joyfulness are not the same thing. The Bible says in Nehemiah 8:10 that "the joy of the Lord is [our] strength" (NLT). The joy of the Lord is a happiness that doesn't depend on what happens. It's a smile from the soul that emerges even when everything around you is crumbling because you know you have God, God is good, and that is enough.

Not sure what to fast? Assess your spiritual state first by asking yourself these questions, and then you'll know:

1. To what do I devote too little or much time?
2. What habits do I take part in that are damaging to my spiritual health?
3. What areas in my life are out of whack/unbalanced?
4. To what cuisine or material things am I too attached?

Carrying out a fast looks different for everyone. You might try eating only fruits or vegetables for 24 hours or you could go for a full-blown 21-day Daniel fast, devoid of all animal products and preservatives (no breads, meats, or sweets). You might take a weekend when you're off from work to engage in a three-day water only fast, or you might try a water only fast between 6am and 6pm for three days but allow yourself to eat supper for energy and watch your supper plate get smaller and smaller as your cravings for the Lord increase and your cravings for food decrease.

Fasting is excellent for your health too. It's a rare

opportunity for your body to rest and heal itself. Hence, many people make fasting a regular part of their health care in addition to their spiritual care. Fasting enables your gastrointestinal tract and metabolism to slow down, leading to natural healing as your body rids itself of the many toxins you consume in your food, especially if you enjoy tasty junk food—don't we all. In her research of the health benefits of fasting, Dr. Amy Richter adds that fasting extends longevity, promotes heart health and blood sugar control, fights inflammation, increases growth hormone secretion and muscle strength, aids in cancer prevention, reduces the progression of tumors, boosts metabolism and brain function, prevents neurodegenerative disorders, and improves blood pressure, triglycerides, and cholesterol levels.[32]

But it doesn't have to be food. As part of a sin offering for atonement, in the Old Testament, God's command for the Israelites to fast can be translated into the words "afflict yourself" as per Numbers 29:7 (NIV). Other ideas for such self-affliction are letting go of television, headphones, candy/sweets, snacks between meals, shopping, mirrors, gossiping, complaining, pride, worry, criticism, makeup, talking about yourself, interrupting people, checking your bank account or email (or only allowing one check per day at a predetermined time), skipping church, reading gossip/rumor sites, sleeping on a pillow, hot water when you shower, alcohol, coffee, and phone/social media, perhaps by using an app that restricts your access or by self-limiting your use to certain times in the day, or even simply giving up an extra hour of your time to spend with the Lord each day. A 24-hour fast each week has been greatly rewarding to our family. Right now, we fast from 8pm on Sundays to 8pm on Mondays to start our weeks right. In prayer over the weekend—usually during Sunday worship at church—we ask God to bring to our minds what we need to go without the following day and then whenever we think of missing that thing, we make extra effort to read the Word and pray.

In Psalm 63:1, King David writes "God, you are my God, earnestly I seek you; my soul thirsts for you, my body longs for you. And I am satisfied in you more than I am with the richest of foods" (NLT). Then in Psalm 69:10, King David pens, "I humble my soul with fasting" (ESV). Fasting boosts our reliance on God more fully for strength and can help us hear God quicker and clearer. Every time you're tempted to have what you're letting go of, or every time you feel a hunger pain, you should treat it like an alarm clock reminding you to pray to God so He can sustain you. You'll find yourself praying a lot more often than you normally do! You'll also build deeper gratitude for your blessings and deeper trust in the Lord as you allow Him to carry you through the experience.

Each time I pray while fasting, I am reminded what a gift it is to know Jesus deeply without a fleshly relationship with him. I'm inspired by the example of Paul, who only encountered Christ once in person while walking on the road to Damascus (in modern day Syria) with letters ordering synagogues to arrest all Christ followers and to bring them to trial before the Pharisees. Acts 9 records then-Saul being instantly blinded by a brilliant light, falling to the ground, and hearing a voice from heaven identified as the voice of resurrected Jesus asking, "Why are you using violence against me?" (NIV). Thus began the conversion of Saul, who will be named Paul, upon arriving at the truth of who Jesus is and what he should be doing with his life. He goes from ravaging the church and committing believers to prison and death as Saul to writing thirteen books of the Bible, making him one of the most read and quoted authors in the history of the world!

What most intrigues me about Paul's encounter with Jesus on the road to Damascus is that the rest of his relationship was with the spirit of God. And yet, Paul's faith was often more consistent than that of the twelve disciples who had three years in relationship with Jesus in the flesh. If you're anything like me, maybe you've wished before to sit next to Jesus and talk to him in person like his disciples. Maybe you've wished you could touch the holes in Jesus's hands like Thomas got to in order to believe. Or maybe not. In John 20:29, Jesus explains to Thomas that those who haven't seen him and yet believe, can go to a level that those relying on the flesh cannot go. He tells him "Blessed are those who have not seen and yet believe" (NLT). Jesus's explanation here helps us see why in 2

Peter 3:15-16, Peter, who was in Jesus's inner circle during his ministry here on earth, says "there are some things in [Paul's letters] that are hard to understand" as he grapples with comparing what Paul is saying to what he remembers about Jesus in the flesh.

Have any experiences you've had in the flesh ever been distorted over time? Think about all of the things that excited you about your favorite movie or video game when you were a child and then when you revisited that same film or game as an adult, you couldn't see what all of the fuss was about. It is our human nature to get over things in the flesh pretty quickly. When you get a phone call notifying you that you landed a job you interviewed for, you might be so thrilled that you jump up and down! That euphoric high might follow you into the first couple of weeks or maybe even the first month of work but then eventually it wears off. The same thing happens when you make an exhilarating purchase. Perhaps you buy some stylish shoes or tickets to see your favorite band in concert. These experiences are riveting, but your enthusiasm from them gradually wanes. Even after you drive a new car for a while, the novelty eventually wears off. I find it to be such good news that Jesus, the author and the finisher of our faith, knows this all too well about us.

Read and be moved by John 16 and 17. Then highlight John 16:7, in particular. Here, we read that it is to our advantage that Jesus goes away after His resurrection so we can have our own access to

God the Father through the Holy Spirit. Sure, walking the shores of Galilee with Jesus would be astounding. But if we could only get answers to our prayers in the flesh, that would mean booking a flight to Tel Aviv to line up with millions, if not billions, of others who also want to ask Jesus questions. It would also likely mean experiencing a brief burst of cheeriness and slowly but surely feeling that dwindle until the next time you can summon the funds to fly to Tel Aviv again. But this way you can talk to him wherever you are, whenever you want, and in *fellowship*, as recorded in 2 Corinthians 13:14—meaning consistently interacting with God as opposed to seeing Him once in a blue moon (ESV).

In 1 Corinthians 3, Paul says we are the Lord's temple, the intersection between heaven and earth (NIV). This means His spirit from above in heaven lives in us here on earth at all times! God doesn't do anything by accident. As John Bevere explains in *Holy Spirit: An Introduction*, God intended for us to have a long distance relationship with Him![33] If you've ever had a long distance romantic relationship, or if you and your spouse have ever had to spend time apart, you know all too well how much closer you get to someone when you're connecting on a soul and spiritual level, not a physical level. The physical relationship has the least depth since our flesh is unredeemed and gets tired of things ever so quickly. So, what a gift God gives us to not allow us to *only* know Him in the flesh. The only part of the GodHead with us here on earth is the Holy Spirit. The same spirit that descended upon Jesus *like a dove*. Not in the form of a dove of course, but as subtly and gently as one. He wants us to know Him better, and more intimately. He wants us to know His heart, His character, and His nature. We don't need an actual appearance of Jesus Himself to get close to Him. 1 Corinthians 2:11 proves we just need His spirit (NIV). Don't expect His spirit to share only with your eyes and your ears though. Even more so as Romans 8:16 says, His spirit speaks to us through an inner witness, which is an impression or perception on the inside of you (NLT).

You may have heard the inner witness renamed as a "gut instinct" or "intuition" by the world. The more time you spend in fellowship with the Lord, the more heightened your radar for this will become. Think about the murmurs toddlers make when they're first forming words. It takes time in fellowship with them before their parents can ascertain what they are saying and translate it for others. The same thing happens to us as we become increasingly familiar with God's voice, which feels uniquely different for each of us. Notice I said *feels* instead of *sounds*. While God can and does communicate using a clear, audible voice, He does so sparingly, or else we'd become tired of hearing it, like vexatious teenagers who craftily learn to drown out some of the things their parents tell them. Be it far from us to do that with God! I don't know about you, but I desire to be so attuned to God's holy spirit that I can decipher between Him and even an angel like Philip does in Acts 8:26. Every day I want to increase my capacity to receive what He has to say so I don't miss any miracles! In John 16:12, Jesus says "I have much more to say to you, more than you can now bear." If you've ever looked at other believers and wished you were as connected to the Holy Spirit as they are, remember you will get out of your relationship with Him what you put in. Do the work! Eternity's on the line!

Life Application Challenge 9: Stop your griping and start fasting! Plan and schedule a fast to get you out of spiritual bondage! It's time to turn your focus away from yourself, and unto Christ and others! The less you think of yourself, the happier you'll be! Fasting will boost your faith, as long as you keep it between you and God, respecting the guidance furnished in Matthew 6:16 which says, "When you fast, do not look somber as the hypocrites do, for they disfigure their faces to show others they are fasting" (NIV). Fasting will produce in you a greater life satisfaction, a deeper gratitude and desire for God, a higher sensitivity to God's voice, and a thorough cleansing of your soul.

Dr. Amanda Kay Cruz

<u>Lyrics to Josie's Pick: "Firm Foundation"</u>

<u>by Maverick City Music</u>

There's a peace about my Josie girl that all instantly detect when graced by her presence. She has a calming effect on people. Prior to her delivery, I was 2-3 centimeters dilated for about two weeks and yet, my thoughts rested completely undisturbed. I was uncertain about her estimated time of arrival and even her gender! Since we spent most of the pregnancy believing the blood test that concluded she was a he, we chose the name "Josiah" for her, meaning God supports and heals us. Josie's Godmother, Lori Burns, suggested we take Josie from Josiah and it stuck. How we adore her name now! Just as the meaning of her name expresses,

Peace before Increase

I'm reminded that life changes, but God doesn't. The presence of His Holy Spirit comforted me all the way to the delivery room where the song "Firm Foundation" was playing when I got to meet Josie Kay for the first time. Just two hours and two pushes after Dr. Wayne Wilson broke my water, Josie entered the world. As God would have it, she's my third vaginal birth after Cesarean (VBAC), my second drug-free birth, and at eight pounds, she's the biggest baby I've birthed! Her life encourages us all to believe Galatians 6:9 which states, "Let us not grow weary or become discouraged in doing good, for at the proper time, we will reap if we do not give in" (NIV).

Christ is my firm foundation
The rock on which I stand
When everything around me
is shaken
I've never been more glad
That I put my faith in Jesus
'Cause He's never let me down
He's faithful through
generations
So why would He fail now?
He won't (X8)
I've still got joy in chaos
I've got peace that makes no
sense
I won't be going under
I'm not held by my own
strength
'Cause I've built my life on
Jesus

He won't fail (2X)
He won't (4X)
Christ is my firm
foundation
The rock on which I stand
When everything around
me
is shaken
I've never been more glad
That I put my faith in Jesus
'Cause He's never let me
down
He's faithful through
generations
So why would He fail
now? He won't
Sing it out, sing
He won't
No, He won't, no, He

He's never let me down
He's faithful through every
season
So why would He fail now?
Can I sing my testimony?
Rain came, wind blew
But my house was built on
You
I'm safe with You
I'm gonna make it through
(I feel somebody's faith rising)
Rain came, wind blew
But my house was built on
You
I'm safe with You
I'm gonna make it through
Rain came, wind blew
My house was built on You
I'm safe with You
I'm gonna make it through
Yeah, I'm gonna make it
through
'Cause I'm standing strong on
You
Yeah, I'm gonna make it
through
'Cause my house is built on
You
Christ is my firm foundation
The rock on which I stand
When everything around me is
shaken
I've never been more glad
That I put my faith in Jesus
'Cause He's never let me down
He's faithful through

won't
He won't fail (2X)
He won't (2X)
He won't fail (2X)
He won't (2X)
I have a story to sing
This is my story, this is my
song
I have a testimony

I'm safe with You
I'm gonna make it through
Rain came, wind blew
My house was built on You
I'm safe with You
I'm gonna make it through
I'm gonna make it through
'Cause I'm standing strong
on you
I'm gonna make it through
'Cause my house is built on
You
I'm gonna make it through
'Cause I'm standing strong
on You
I'm gonna make it through
'Cause my house is built on
You

generations
So why would He fail now?
He won't (2X)
He won't fail (2X)
He won't (2X)
He won't fail (2X)
Never seen the righteous
forsaken
And He won't start now
Never seen the righteous
forsaken
And He won't start now
Rain came, wind blew
My house was built on You

Stride 10: Lighten Up

Eutychus Raised From the Dead at Troas

Acts 20:7-12

> On the first day of the week we came together to break bread. Paul spoke to the people and, because he intended to leave the next day, kept on talking until midnight. There were many lamps in the upstairs room where we were meeting. Seated in a window was a young man named Eutychus, who was sinking into a deep sleep as Paul talked on and on. When he was sound asleep, he fell to the ground from the third story and was picked up dead. Paul went down, threw himself on the young man and put his arms around him. "Don't be alarmed," he said. "He's alive!" Then he went upstairs again and broke bread and ate. After talking until daylight, he left. The people took the young man home alive and were greatly comforted (NLT).

This story of Eutychus dying from longitvis sermonitis cracks me up. I have been in similar shoes hearing someone who could talk the legs off a chair. You know, a person who you can ask for the time, and they'll tell you how to build a watch? Someone you'd change grocery aisles for to avoid bumping into their mouth that runs like an airport toilet?

Of course, this story wouldn't be as funny if Paul didn't find Eutychus and bring him back to life. It does not surprise me that he does. I expect nothing less from him after reading the short book of

Philippians and learning about Paul's relentless character as a believer despite many, MANY hardships. Once Paul brings Eutychus back in, the amusement continues. Paul simply picks up where he left off. He resumes his preaching until daybreak as if the window death and resurrection was no big deal! Sometimes asking a passionate preacher to say less is like asking a Ferrari to stay under the speed limit. Long winded preachers like Paul may be one of the reasons why pastors started doing sermon series, although I once heard by the time a man is wise enough to watch his step, he's too old to go anywhere. Ba dum tss!

In case you haven't caught my drift yet, this last stride is a reminder to lighten up! In the pages to come, we'll delve into the significance of **laughter, sacrifice, and intimacy**—all which I believe are key to the attainment of ZOE, a Greek word for life (ζωή) which occurs 135 times in the Greek New Testament. Specifically, it means eternal life or "The God-kind of life." It is the abundant, rich, divine nature of God; His fullness of joy, love, power, and ability. In John 1:4, we get a hint of what this life will do for us: "In him was life; and the life was the light of men" (NLT). Light stands for development. Read differently, this verse says, in Him was life; and the life was the development of men. Or, in Him was zoe, and zoe was the development of men.

Laughter

To relish in the God-kind of life, laugh more! Allow yourself to wonder why people park in a driveway but drive on a parkway? In similar fashion, why do we call it rush hour when nothing moves? Or why are there more plastic flamingos in America than real ones? Borrow some sagacity from the acutely wise King Solomon, son of King David, who propounds this in Ecclesiastes 8:15: "I recommend having fun because there is nothing better for people in this world than to eat, drink, and enjoy life. That way they will experience some happiness along with all the hard work God gives them under the sun" (NIV). Here are some of my other favorite Scriptures which remind God's people to laugh. All are from the New Living Translation (NLT) of the Bible:

- The one who rules in heaven laughs. (Psalm 2:4)
- You will laugh at destruction and famine, and need not fear the wild animals. (Job 5:22)
- He will yet fill your mouth with laughter and your lips with shouting. (Job 8:21)
- Shout to the Lord, all the earth; break out in praise and sing for joy! (Psalm 98:4)

- o A happy heart makes the face cheerful, but heartache crushes the spirit.

  (Proverbs 15:13)

- o Why am I discouraged? Why is my heart so sad? I will put my hope in God! I will praise him again.

  (Psalm 42:5)

- o All the days of the oppressed are wretched, but the cheerful heart has a continual feast.

  (Proverbs 15:15)

- o We were filled with laughter, and we sang for joy. And the other nations said, 'What amazing things the Lord has done for them.'

  (Psalm 126:2)

- o You have turned my mourning into joyful dancing. You have taken away my clothes of mourning and clothed me with joy.

  (Psalm 30:11)

- o God blesses you who weep now, for in due time you will laugh.

  (Luke 6:21)

According to the Mayo Clinic, some short-term health benefits of laughter include stress relief, enhancement of your intake of oxygen-rich air, stimulation of your heart, lungs and muscles, production of endorphins that are released by your brain, tension soothing, and the stimulation of circulation and muscle relaxation. Some long-term health benefits of laughter are the improvement of your immune system, pain relief, an increase in life satisfaction, and better moods. As a matter of fact, laugher is a prescription in Norway. There, doctors routinely inform their patients that people with a strong sense of humor outlive those who don't laugh as much.[35] The difference is particularly notable for those battling cancer, cardiovascular disease, and infection. More reasons for prioritizing laughter are listed in the figure below:

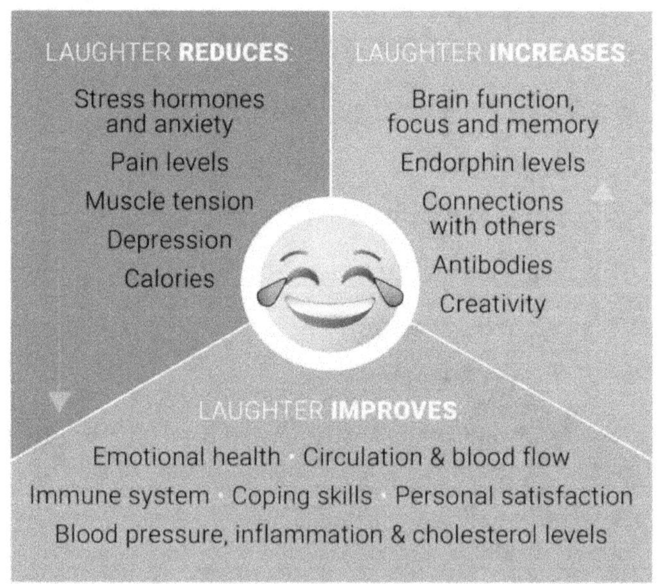

Source: Providence Health & Services. Blog.providence.org. 2022.

The nationwide Providence Seniors Health team concludes that 10–15 minutes of laughter burns about 40 calories, and our muscles stay relaxed for up to 45 minutes after a good laugh! Not only that, but the force that our arteries exert as our hearts pump—AKA our blood pressure—can drop as much as 5-7 millimeters of the mercury (mmHg) that we all have in our bodies, following extended laughter, and agitation levels can drop as much as 20 percent for those who laugh regularly.[36]

Laughter was renamed "internal jogging" by American psychologist William Fry, the father of gelotology. And for good reason. Multiple studies have proven that laughing has a similar impact as exercise on heart rate and heart rate variability.[67] In her study of nearly 21,000 older adults, Freda Gonot-Schoupinsky found that those who laughed every day were less likely to have heart disease, compared with those who never or almost never laughed. Similarly, in a close look at individuals with Type Two diabetes, the blood of those who watched a comedy film—instead of a boring lecture—had decreased levels of prorenin, a protein associated with the onset of diabetic complications. And laughing helps those in physical pain too: it has been proven to increase one's pain tolerance.[37] Here are the ways I've learned to laugh more, daily, amid this priceless waiting season the Lord has gifted me:

1. Keep a laughter journal! I force myself to jot down three funny things that happen per day! (I actually use a free speech to text site, speech.io, on my phone to document what happens, or I record a linked voice memo using

vocaroo.com, but writing these moments down is a quick option too.) My kids try to help get this job done as quickly as possible by being as hilarious as possible. They love competing to see who gets credit for getting me to laugh first.

2. Play a game with your friends or family! (Look up Jimmy Fallon games on YouTube for ideas!)

3. Eat a bag of Laffy Taffys and read the jokes in the wrappers.

4. Get a comic-strip subscription (online or in print).

5. Read about some autocorrect fails.

6. Tickle or get tickled. You're never too old!

7. Put an (unbreakable) glass of water near a cat or pull out a laser pointer.

8. Feed peanut butter to a dog.

9. Ask your dad or dad figure to tell you a joke.

10. Check out Bad Lip Reading or America's Funniest Home Videos on YouTube.

11. Listen to a (clean) comedy set or podcast.

12. Ask a preschooler to explain how something works (like trains or ovens or toilets, for example).

13. Check out your "memories" on social media or in your phone's camera roll.

14. Tell your favorite funny story and ask someone else for theirs.

15. Ask Siri if you're awesome, or to simply tell you a joke.

Peace before Increase

Laughter is a phenomenal barometer of your strength as a believer. If you're relaxed enough to laugh, you likely aren't turning people, places, or things into your source of life. In the words of radio preacher Chuck Swindoll, we should all laugh out loud more; it helps flush out the nervous system! Laughter is good medicine! It's the most beautiful and beneficial therapy God ever granted humanity. Laughter helps us cope, and it helps other medicine go down, like God's truth!

In *A Love that Laughs,* Ted Cunningham says "A human without laughter is like a wagon without springs, it is jolted by every pebble in the road!"[38] Good humor makes all things tolerable. It's free. When we laugh, Neuroscientist Sophie Scott vows that we exercise not only our minds but also our bodies. That's why we say things like "My face hurts or my side hurts" or why we leave completely exhausted from a comedy show.[38] Want even better news than that?! Your body can't tell the difference between real and fake laughter! So if wives aren't feeling "in the mood," we can fake it until we make it! We're good at that! ;-) Oops, I probably just sent your mind to the gutter faster than a rat dashes up a drainpipe. You know what it most likely means when we wives put on our sexy underwear, don't you? It means it's laundry day! :-P Har har. Humor grows two people closer together. It's more fun to laugh with others than alone! Tickle yourself to make yourself laugh; it won't work!

Laughter diffuses social tension and awkwardness. It makes

you more attractive. The mature laugh. My favorite high school English teacher, Mrs. Sorenson, would often say you grow up the day you have your first real laugh at yourself. Take God seriously, but not yourself. Take fun more seriously. Laughter pleases God! And it's the best way to cheer yourself and others up! It reminds us of the hope of heaven! As one the best-of-all-time spiritual mentors, Aiden Wilson Tozer, often expressed, the people of God should be the happiest people on earth! Each day, set a laughter alarm titled, "Have you laughed yet today?" And when it goes off, find a way to laugh or jot down a way you already laughed!

Sacrifice

Another way to lighten the mood, particularly for married folks, is for husbands to adore their wives and for wives to submit to their husbands. Even singletons can benefit from the practice of adoration and respect for those whom they have the hardest time communicating with. Finding common ground with harder personality types is outstanding practice before getting married, so if you're single, instead of a spouse, consider applying the coming advice to the person you have the most trouble communicating with.

In marriage, a woman's willingness to respect her husband is a measure of her maturity and wisdom. Male or female, if you've ever cried out to God hoping marriage would be simpler, wallow no longer! God has carved a clear path to success! As God would have it, when a wife respects her husband, it disarms his ego. And when a husband disarms his ego, he is better able to give love to his wife.

A beautiful life does not just happen… it is built daily with love, laughter, sacrifice, patience, grace, and forgiveness. The simplest way to keep marital peace is to remember you married a good-willed human, as Emerson Eggerichs first coined in *Love and Respect*. If you genuinely believed your spouse to be malicious or to have evil intentions, I should hope you would not have decided to marry them! Deep down inside, you MUST know that your spouse's intents and purposes are pure. With this in mind, the next time you're driving and your spouse advises you to slow down or change lanes, remember s/he's good-willed and means well! Don't take offense and grow angry with him/her. Remind yourself that this person cares for you and wants to keep you and the family you've built safe.

The next time that your kids have a playdate planned with children whom your spouse deems to be bad company, cancel the playdate and be glad that s/he cherishes the wellbeing of your children! The next time you ask your spouse to take a trip and s/he advises saving money instead, heed their wisdom and don't plan the trip! The sage advice you so easily received from your spouse when you were dating is still good for you now that you're married! And please, when you don't get the outcome you desire, grow up and embrace that everything happens for a reason when God's in the center. Please don't plan a way around your spouse's wishes when s/he is not for your idea, like taking on an extra project or a new job to ensure you get your way.

The ninth of the Ten Commandments as relayed in Exodus 20 and Deuteronomy 5 is "You shall not give false witness against your neighbor" (NIV). This means two things: "do not lie when testifying in court." And, "do not lie." Period. I used to be infamous for bending the truth so things would turn out the way I wanted. If my husband closed a door, I'd find a window. If he finished a chapter, I'd find a whole new book. This created chaos and disharmony in my home and worst of all, it was not a good example to others, including our own children, of how to do marriage God's way. Please constantly be mindful of this responsibility the Lord is entrusting you with. Marriage needs to be honored by all, enjoyed by all, and shown off to the millennials so they'll quit shacking up and disobeying God's design! May all of us who are married decide daily to show ourselves, our children, and the world that marriage is SO GOOD!

In *Backup Singers to the Duet of Marriage*, Doug Fields shares that ten years ago the average age to get married in the U.S. was twenty. Today it's twenty-eight.[39] I want shirts that say something like "Happily Married" or "♥ Being Married!" We undoubtedly need to make marriage look better. Most statements out there on marriage are disparaging. Just Google some marriage t-shirts and you'll see what I mean. We can say all day long that we want to see marriages last but how we display marriage plays a huge part in that! Wouldn't you love to see our children giving marriage a good name too, and looking forward to it rather than dreading it?!

So whenever your spouse has input regarding your children, be grateful s/he is thinking of your future and your children's future! I know this is easier said than done, but be faithful. In Luke 16:10 Jesus says, "Whoever is faithful in small matters will be faithful in large ones; whoever is dishonest in small matters will be dishonest in large ones" (GNT). Your public blessings are determined by your private integrity.

Worldly spouses will empower you to stand firm and have the final say. Holy spouses will point you to Hebrews 9:27, which says, "People are destined to die once, and after that to face judgment" (NLT). Jesus postulated that people will be judged based on what they did during their lives. After the Judgment, Matthew 25 teaches us that the righteous will go to their eternal reward in heaven and the accursed will depart to hell (ESV). Armed with this knowledge, try to live each day knowing it could very well be your last and if it is, you'll want the security of knowing you selflessly stood by your spouse's side as God commands in His word. 1 Peter 3 provides the following instructions:

> Wives, in the same way, submit yourselves to your own husbands so that, if any of them do not believe the Word,

they may be won over without words by the behavior of their wives, when they see the purity and reverence of your lives. Your beauty should not come from outward adornment, such as elaborate hairstyles and the wearing of gold jewelry or fine clothes. Rather, it should be that of your inner self, the unfading beauty of a gentle and quiet spirit, which is of great worth in God's sight. For this is the way the holy women of the past who put their hope in God used to adorn themselves. They submitted themselves to their own husbands, like Sarah, who obeyed Abraham and called him her lord. You are her daughters if you do what is right and do not give way to fear.

Husbands, in the same way, be considerate as you live with your wives, and treat them with respect as the weaker partner and as heirs with you of the gracious gift of life, so that nothing will hinder your prayers (NLT).

Ephesians 5:33 extends this calling, stating: "Let the wife see that she respects and reverences her husband [that she notices him, regards him, honors him, prefers him, venerates, and esteems him; and that she defers to him, praises him, and loves and admires him exceedingly]" (AMP). One should note that wives are not excused from love any more than husbands are excused from submission. Husbands and wives are both equally called "to act out in marriage the same type of self-sacrificing, respectful, submissive love they would in any and all relationships within the believing community."[43] As God has taught me during this endeared wait, here are fifteen practical ways to propitiate your spouse AKA best friend on earth. As noted, if you're single, replace the word "spouse" with the name of a person whom you desire improved relations with. You can try these practices with them:

1. Get a shared Bible devotional app so you can grow closer to the Lord and each other.

2. With oil, ask the Holy Spirit to anoint your spouse while praying a Scripture-declaration from the free Shut Up, Devil app over them.

3. Pick a book in the Bible to read or listen to together for ten minutes a day.

4. Engage in a listening prayer together. You just pray and wait in silence for 10-12 minutes (preferably outdoors). You shut your eyes and open your spiritual ears. Once you hear a particular Scripture, impression, word, song, or picture, write or draw it in a journal and share with each other what you got. It's beautiful to watch how the pieces each of you get make better sense once put together! Here's a prayer template from Faithward.org that supports this process:

Father, we come to you in the name of Jesus Christ, your son, and according to James 1:5. We are seeking wisdom for __________________(your request). In the name of Jesus, according to Matthew 28:18 and Luke 10:19-20, we take authority over Satan and his fallen angels and command that they be rendered deaf, mute, and blind to our prayers, and removed from our presence. We submit our own voices to the shed blood of Jesus and command that our own thoughts be taken captive to the obedience of Christ, according to 2 Corinthians 10:5. We ask, Father, that only your Holy Spirit will speak to us now as we wait on you for wisdom, insight, and direction. And whatever you show us or direct us to do, we pray that we will quickly obey. In Jesus's mighty name, amen.[40]

5. Volunteer at church together.

6. Fast together.

7. Remember Dr. Leaf's 63-day brain detox that I described in Stride 6? Do it together.

8. Draw a Cross on a sheet of paper. Then across the cross, use a pencil to write some attitudes you each are struggling with (such as anger, bitterness, discouragement, clamor, offense, hopelessness, conceit, embarrassment, etc.), symbolically crucifying these attitudes on the cross. Then, in ink (darker than the pencil) write one of the fruits of the Holy Spirit (love, joy, peace, patience, kindness, goodness, faithfulness, gentleness, and self-control) on top of each of the bad attitudes that you wrote and pray together for God to strengthen you enough to convey this switch in your mind, heart, and actions. What you don't identify, you can't crucify!

9. Look for a Bible-based podcast or video study to watch/hear together.

10. Spend five minutes each in holding poses at the beginning or ending of each day. (See pics.) The first picture shows the husband as the connection receiver, and the second picture

shows the wife as the connection receiver.[71] Believe me when I say these boost bonding faster than a speeding bullet!

11. Google the 40-day love dare and do it. Watch the movie *Fireproof* before you do.

12. Take a vacation or staycation semi-annually (just the two of you). NO KIDS!

13. Go on a double date with an older Godly couple whose

relationship you admire.

14. Bring back your youthful vigor and play together! Ride bikes, speed on some go-karts, go for a run, plan a scavenger hunt, put together a puzzle, window shop at a home improvement store, play a card game, fly some kites, take some classes at your local library, knavishly guess which items around the house you took extreme close-up photos of, use your phone as a projector to watch a movie outside, swing on a park playground, grab some ice cream together at a fast food restaurant, paint at home while you watch a couples painting video on YouTube, etc.! Don't let money stop you from enjoying one another's company! You'll never get these years back! Delight in the spouse of your youth!

15. Exclusively for married readers: enjoy sex! In his bestselling book *Sexperiment*, Pastor Ed Young demonstrates that going from having sex once a year to once a month brings men as much happiness as an extra 50k annually! He also shares the stark reality that in a poll of 160,000 Christian dads, 79% are wanting more sex, 65% are watching porn—thus breaking the seventh commandment—and 50% are experiencing having their sexual advances rejected once per week or more. Pastor Young summarizes the top two problems in marriages with the acronym PMS which stands for

Problems=Money & Sex. He adds to this that the top trigger for these problems are children! He comically, yet truthfully, claims that KIDS stands for Keeping Intimacy at a Distance Successfully.[41] While men may be more likely to get it on even with kid noise in the background, women can't focus and be fully present if the kids are heard in the background. Each sound of their voices makes us feel like while we are trying to be good wives, we are dropping the ball as parents! Ahh!

Have you ever asked yourself what it is like making love to you? Is it exhilarating, or an inconvenience? Is it all about you, or do you try to pleasure your spouse too? Sex God's way is a huge part of becoming one flesh as conveyed in Ephesians 5:31 (NLT) and it's a wonderful way not to take your youth for granted as expressed in Proverbs 5:18-19 (NIV). When is the last time you read the erotic poem featured in the Song of Solomon? Ooh, is it steamy. As a woman, I especially appreciate the cherishment of the bride's body in Song of Solomon 7 (NIV) and what I perceive to be a nod to oral sex in Song of Solomon 4:16 (ESV). Anyone who twitches when I mention oral sex should read "Oral Blessings" by Chris Taylor on themarriagebed.com. In this article, Taylor shares excellent practical advice as well as a refreshing perspective on what it means to care of one another and make each other feel special.[42]

Sex is an excellent barometer to gauge the health of your marriage. Typically, when my husband and I mentor a couple in crisis, the first question we ask is how individually close or distant they feel from God. This is promptly followed with a second question about how often they are having sex. Couples who are upset and thus not communicating never tell us they're having sex. They'll tell us they were last intimate months or even years ago! Most of the time—granted outliers do exist—wives need time to talk with their husbands to feel bonded with them, whereas husbands need time to engage in intercourse with their wives to feel bonded with them. So, if a husband is feeling hurt, he'll avoid talking with his wife, and she'll avoid having sex with him. Likewise, if a wife is feeling hurt, she'll avoid having sex with her husband, and he'll avoid talking with her. But the good news is the opposite of this toxic cycle is also true. If a husband is feeling bonded, he'll eagerly talk with his wife, and she'll eagerly have sex with him. In this same way, if a wife is feeling bonded, she'll eagerly have sex with her husband, and he'll eagerly talk with her.

In short, this means you must operate counter-intuitively to achieve harmony in your marriage. If sex isn't high on your own list of needs, that is what your spouse needs you to work on. On the other hand, if conversation isn't high on your own list of needs, that is what your spouse needs you to work on. Sacrificially make the choice to do the opposite of what you feel like doing and your faith and your marriage will be rewarded. Be aware of intimacy robbers that the liar Satan uses. If you allow it, your thoughts will be swarmed with enemy attacks regarding previous relationships, abuse, abortions, social media, feeling like used goods, etc. With that being said, remember that your value is determined by God, NOT by how often or if ever your spouse makes a public post about you. And please, do not ask your spouse questions unless you're prepared to receive the answers to your questions. There are a lot of past-related topics that my husband and I decided to drop early in our marriage because we realized discussing them took us away from God. The more we pursued God, the less we cared to look backwards anyway. If you're up against deeper seated concerns regarding sex, give *Intimate Issues* a read by Linda Dillow. It will dramatically and permanently change your sex life!

Intimacy

In order to preserve a joyful marital (or premarital) relationship, one must learn to recognize Satan's most frequently used tactic of destruction: unforgiveness. Unforgiveness is the most productive demon operating in the kingdom of darkness. Tragically, because many aren't aware of the demon's fierce grip, homes and relationships are broken unnecessarily. Do not fall victim to releasing yourself from hardships that were meant to grow you, not to break you. Shame the devil, and learn to forgive! In *What's it like Being Married to Me?* Linda Dillow drives this point home with this compelling story about (un)forgiveness:

> Many of us have held a grudge against our husbands, but Rachel Jones takes the prize for being a champion grudge holder. She and her neighbor, David, had a lovers' quarrel. Every week for forty-two years, David slipped a love letter under Rachel's door in an attempt to mend the quarrel that parted them when both were thirty-two years old. Every letter was burned by the grudge-holding Rachel, and she repeatedly refused to speak to her suitor. Finally, despite the silent treatment, David summoned courage to knock on her door and propose and, to his surprise, she accepted. Both Rachel and David were seventy-four-years old when they finally got married. What did Rachel gain during her long years of silence? What did she achieve by failing to forgive? She gained loneliness, bitterness, and perhaps a sense of power over another person. Was her vigilant stance of "I'm right, and nothing will make me change my mind!" worth forty-two years of anguish? I wish she were still alive so we could ask her. I strongly suspect, however, that she would tell us that she had been a fool and had wasted years over an issue that mattered very little. A happy marriage is the union of two good forgivers who commit not to hold a grudge and nurse a hurt, but instead to freely forgive their mate, even though sometimes he or she does not deserve forgiveness.[44]

Peace before Increase

There's an old adage that says the most mature person forgives first. Following this line of logic, David was definitely the most mature person in this story. Work to forgive quickly as David did. Doing so will earn you greater intimacy with the Lord! Would you like to know what the happiest animal in the world is? It's a goldfish. Why? It's got a ten second memory. Let's strive to be more like goldfish. When we refuse to forgive, we're not believing God is as good as His Word says He is, and we're giving Satan the victory, but when we choose to forgive, we kick Satan out and give God the victory. Another testimony Dillow shares that greatly humbles me and clothes me in gratitude is this:

> The adornment a forgiving wife wears is a sweet fragrance that reminds others of the Lord Jesus. Her calm and gentle spirit, her tender smile, radiates peace and joy because forgiveness has set her free from resentment and anger. Long to be clothed with this adornment. My friend Katie already wears it. Eleven years ago, her world exploded without warning. The family she worked so hard to build and maintain was destroyed. It began with a phone call from the Children's Advocacy Center, asking her to come to the center about a matter involving her oldest daughter, Hannah. Once there, Katie received the worst news of her life. Hannah was accusing her father, Katie's husband, of sexually molesting her. Katie called me to come to pray with her. The anguish was indescribable for her and for both her daughters. She says, "That first day I didn't know if I would even stay married to Craig, or what my future would look like, but I did know that I would have to cling to God and trust Him in a deeper way than I ever had before."

Craig was arrested, pled guilty, and was later sentenced to a halfway house for ninety days. Additionally, he was given probation for five years, which included attending weekly counseling and a group therapy program for sexual offenders. This sentence meant Craig could not come home for several years. Because he repented and immediately went to their pastor to confess, Katie believed she needed to be willing to walk toward him with forgiveness. Psalm 51:12 became her prayer: Father, grant me a willing spirit! I'll let her tell you how God answered her prayer:

I [Katie] learned a lot about forgiveness watching Hannah. It took her two years of sobbing, screaming, and fighting before she could give up her anger and say from the heart, "I forgive you, Dad." I was still struggling. I was trying to forgive, but the shock of my husband's betrayal was so great, and my trust so destroyed, it took seeing my own sin before I could take the necessary steps to forgive Craig. [44]

How it pleases my soul to report that what could have ruined Katie ended up saving her and her family. To all who watched her going THROUGH and not AROUND this, she exemplified a willingness as a mother to model doing as she did, not only as she said. Her life reflected a deep intimacy with and reverence for Christ. Throughout her journey to forgiveness, the Lord revealed much to her, but these three lessons stand out in her memory:

First, I had to "get the log out of my own eye" (Matthew 7:3-5) in order to see my own sin and how I had pushed my husband away from intimacy. God showed me in Romans 2:11 that He does not have favorites. He wanted my healing, but He wanted Craig's healing too. How could I want God to forgive me and yet punish him?

Second, I learned firsthand that God's ways are above our ways (Isaiah 55:9). He called me to repair the breach in this relationship, even though I was not the one who blew a big hole in the wall. God stripped everything away that was important to me and put me in a place where I was utterly dependent on Him.

Third, I committed to doing whatever I could to be a blessing to my husband (1 Peter 3:8-18). How many ways are there to do this? I truly did find countless ways to bless my husband, starting with "a soft word turns away wrath."

As I sought to give a blessing to Craig, God blessed me and my family. Many thought this betrayal was too hard to repair. Craig and I lived apart for over five years, and during that time he received counseling and demonstrated to me, our family, and to his counselor that he was truly on the road to healing, so I felt it was safe to invite him back into our home. Eleven long years later, I stand in awe of my God who is the Healer and the One who can heal anything! I'm moved to tears as I compile this list of God's many blessings on our family:

* My marriage is completely restored and flourishing in all areas.

* My daughter is completely reconciled to her father, and she even asked him to walk her down the aisle at her wedding!

* Both our daughters are happily married, and my husband is a father to our young sons-in-law.

* Our family all attend church together.

* My husband and I have served our church by leading financial workshops and now teach a marriage Bible study for couples.

* I have had the privilege of walking with many women who are suffering betrayal by their husbands."[44]

I don't know what you may need to forgive your spouse for but when you hear a testimony like this, I pray it increases your hope that you can. You have to have hope before you can have faith! Try borrowing pain from your future by being quick to forgive today. This will catapult your intimacy with Christ and with your spouse. And remember, God will never ask you to forgive anyone for any more than He has forgiven you for. There is an African proverb that says "The camel does not see the bend in its neck," meaning we are often quicker to judge others than we are to judge ourselves. One more of Dillow's examples of forgiveness that has never left me is this example of a wife's remarkable choice to forgive her husband's sexual sins. I pray it blesses you as it has blessed me:

> All sin is difficult to forgive, but a husband's sexual sin touches a wife at the core of her being. There is a unique knowing when a wife opens herself up to her husband during sexual intercourse. She opens her soul, her body, and her emotions. Discovering her husband has "known" another woman pierces her in the core of her being. Connie knew this deep piercing. She tried to forgive, but when the images came again and again, she wondered if she really had. She wanted out of the roller-coaster ride of questioning whether she had really forgiven him. To move forward, Connie decided to cement in her mind that she had made the choice to forgive by acting out her forgiveness in a beautiful way. Here is what happened:

> I was shaking as I asked my husband to stand in front of me. I took off all of his clothes, and with a bottle of scented oil, I anointed his body.

> I touched his forehead: "I forgive your mind for thinking

thoughts of her."

I touched his ears: "I forgive your ears for listening to her."

I touched his hands: "I forgive your hands for touching her."

After anointing every part of his body, I came to his feet: "I forgive your feet for walking toward her." As the words came, tears cascaded down my face.

Relief flooded me. The past was truly in the past—for both of us.[44]

Incredible, right? Please don't read that and think "Good for Connie; I couldn't do that." The same Father living in Connie and strengthening her to extend such forgiveness lives in you! Think about not only how huge this is for you, but for your children, and for all of the future Christians who will learn from your brave decision. If a wife sees her body as 'hers' like the predominant culture teaches us, then she decides when, where, and how much she will give to her husband, but if she gives her body as a gift to her husband sexually, she'll want him to enjoy the gift. It is his gift. This choice changes everything!

In his book *Give & Take: The Secret to Marital Compatibility*, psychologist Dr. Willard F. Harley Jr. explores this further as he inspires readers to imagine a stool with a glass of water sitting on it. A husband is next to the stool and his wife is next to him. The wife is frozen, unable to move. Meanwhile, her husband is the only one who can get a glass of water for her. Harley elaborates:

The wife turns to her husband: "Honey, would you please pour me a glass of water? I am getting thirsty." The husband turns and responds, "I don't really feel like it right now. I am not in the mood; I'm a little tired; maybe in a couple of hours." Hours roll by. One more time, the wife turns to her husband "Honey, I am getting thirsty. Would you please give me a glass of water?" The husband responds, "Look, I told you I'm tired. I've had a long day, OK?" Then the wife begins to get angry. She can feel her temperature rising. She wants a glass of water badly at this point, so she begins to demand a drink of water. "I want a glass of water. You are the only one who can give me the glass of water. Give me some water." The husband looks at his wife, spins on his heels, and says you are not going to get any water with an attitude like that. Well, the husband returns to the scene about a day later and now the wife is livid. Finally, the husband says, "OK! Here is your water." When the wife is finally desperately gulping down the water, do you think she is really satisfied? Do you think her thirst is truly quenched? Not really. She is probably thinking or more like fearing that she is going to be thirsty again, and if she wants another drink of water, she had better watch what she says to her husband![45]

This illustration of husbands' irrefragable need for sex helps wives increase our understanding of their perspective in a memorable way. It brings our awareness full-circle, back to God's two greatest commandments, as found in Matthew 22:36-40, which are to "love the Lord thy God with all thy heart" and "love thy neighbor as thyself" (NKJV). When you learn to prioritize God, others, and then yourself, in that order, you begin to experience a true intimacy with the Lord.

Life Application Challenge 10: What do you think it's like being a friend to you? If you're married, what do you think it's like making love to you? Is this a responsibility God will see you carrying well or poorly today? To lead your love from sacrifice, write down one thing you are doing to serve your spouse (or a person you seek to grow closer to) every day for the next seven days. As a bonus, strive to laugh more! Focus on guarding your family time. Throughout the work week—between balancing work, school, after school or extra-curricular activities, taking care of pets, and other daily responsibilities—most families can only find about 37 minutes of quality time together.[68] How will you spend your 37 minutes? Park in the furthest parking spot to enjoy a prayer walk together on your way into stores and again on the way back to your car. Or allow others to pass in front of you in line and ask if you can pray for them. Those are just a couple of ideas.

<u>Lyrics to Family's Pick: "Tend"</u>

<u>by Bethel Music and Emmy Rose</u>

This song reminds my family not to gear our lives around natural acceptance. Divine acceptance is all that matters. "If all we have is God, we have everything we need," I often tell my brood. We must look first to God, not man, to show us where we need to make changes. As a family, we desire to embody Ephesians 2:8-9 which says "God saved you by His grace when you believed, and you can't take credit for this; it is a gift from God. Salvation is not a reward for the good things we have done, so none of us can boast about it" (NLT). Ever since my kids were small, we have

emphasized the family motto "Cruzes never quit." We work hard, yet we don't earn one another's love. It's a free gift that isn't based on performance. Often Husseim or I will pause to tell one of our arrows we are proud of who they are, not merely what they do. We want them to know how to abide in God's love, and not become spiritually paralyzed by focusing on "if only" thinking such as "if only I can get that next promotion," or "if only I can make that next purchase," or "if only I can finish one more page, THEN I'll be complete…" We strive to depend on God instead of allowing our mood or behavior to depend on our performance. Inevitably, we find that the more we depend on God, the more dependable we find He is.

In the landscape of my life
You don't rush through any season
You always take Your time
A careful hand, a gentle guide
You take what's dead away
And You prune what's running wild
So be the gardener of my heart
Tend the soil of my soul
Break up the fallow ground
Cut back the overgrown
And I won't shy away
I will let the branches fall
So what You want can stay
And what You love can grow
Through winter, I'm still alive
What You've planted in the dirt
You'll sustain what You have started
And You'll teach me to abide
Be the gardener of my heart
Tend the soil of my soul
Break up the fallow ground
Cut back the overgrown
And I won't shy away
I will let the branches fall
So what You want can stay
And what You love can grow, grow
Have Your way in me
Have Your way in me
Let it grow, let it grow, let it grow
I'll remain in You

Is ever reaching to the light
You prepare me for darkened
times
From the start until the ending
'Cause You know better
So be the gardener of my heart
Tend the soil of my soul
Break up the fallow ground
Cut back the overgrown
And I won't shy away
I will let the branches fall
So what You want can stay
And what You love can grow

You'll remain in me
And I will trust Your timing
I'll remain in You
You'll remain in me

Conclusion

Alas it is time for one final mnemonic device that will hopefully be witty enough to help you stain your memory with the ten foolproof ways the Lord has given me to give to you amid the splendor of my own Heaven-sent waiting season. Are you ready? Cue a drum roll, please:

Do	Declutter
Race	Roof busters
Excellently	Exercise
Because	Bible
Plans	Pray
Inevitably	Internalize
Ricochet	Raisin cakes
Supernaturally	Search
For	Fast
Lord God	Lighten up

There's much truth here. May we all continue giving every day our best, knowing for God's glory, changes to our plans will bounce off of us, not break us. As prompted in 1 Peter 5:8, we must "Be sober, be vigilant; because [our] adversary the devil, as a roaring lion, walketh about, seeking whom he may devour." (NKJV). We're above the devourer when we're activating the full authority deposited within us by God's Holy Spirit!

It is my sincerest prayer that this mnemonic—and the ten strides that it reminds you of—will help you to continue activating such authority long after your completion of this book. Your daily responsibility is to consecrate—meaning to connect yourself—to the Lord. If you do, by whatever means necessary, the Lord will take care of yesterday's healing *and* tomorrow's miracles. Know that whatever you don't acknowledge, you can't experience. So *fully* press in, eliminating busyness, leaning on others, getting active, absorbing the Word, fellowshipping with the Lord in prayer, internalizing the power invested in you, throwing away raisin cakes, searching for hope, fasting whatever steals your focus, and loosening your self-reliance.

GPS devices employ different routes, but they all lead to the same destination. In this same way, each of the strides can be thought of as distinct routes—all leading to the same destiny. Repeatedly executing each of these strides will power your ongoing, deepened connection to God like a cluster of batteries working in tandem can power a GPS.

When you're afraid, each stride will act as a rung on a ladder, one at a time increasing your confidence to command your heart to bless the Lord and to command your soul to trust in the Lord. However, your success 100% depends on you. As Paul Tripp is fond of saying, "no one is more influential in your life than you are because no one talks to you more than you do." When hard moments come, use the strides specifically to exhort yourself to hope in God as summoned in Psalm 103. Use them to center your thoughts on all that He has done, and on specific truths about the Lord.

Your circumstances may still be on hold, as are mine, but your peace needn't be. Don't tell God about your disturbances. Tell your disturbances about God! Don't tell God about your impatience. Tell your impatience about God! Don't tell God about your mind. Tell your mind about God! In the end, not knowing how this current glorious waiting season ends, and being at peace with that, is a tremendous win for the kingdom, as is my realization that my improved strength in the Lord is my greatest accomplishment *of all time*. Not my profession, not my abilities, not my accolades.

At long last, it appears that the most significant lesson the Lord has taught me in this breathing space is that the waiting season isn't for waiting at all. It's for setting new goals, building bolder faith, bettering life, helping others, and most importantly of all, abiding in God the Father—the one *true* source, and the only keeper of *real* peace. When we get to know that peace—HIS peace—we realize increase is inevitable, and there's no need to put a timer on it. His peace is ALL we need, and when we acquire it BEFORE increase, ALL the enemy thought he held over us will miraculously CEASE. Therein lies the inexhaustible power of peace before increase.

Notes

1. Lockyer, Herbert. All the Promises of the Bible. Zondervan, 2004.

2. Leaf, Caroline. "Mind Controls Matter." *Switch on Your Brain: The Key to Peak Happiness, Thinking, and Health*, BAKER Book House, 2018.

3. Upham, Becky, and By. "Is Stress Making You Sicker? Signs You Shouldn't Ignore." *EverydayHealth.com*, https://www.everydayhealth.com/wellness/united-states--of-stress/is-it- stress-it-serious/.

4. Explorer, Campus. "College Planning and Teen Parents: How to Help - Campus Explorer." *Campus Explorer* -, 11 Jan. 2023, https://www.campusexplorer.com/student-resources /college-teen/ #:~:text=Less%20than%20two%20percent%20ofgive%20birth%2 0as% 20a%20teenager).

5. Müller George. *A Narrative of Some of the Lord's Dealings with George Müller*, J. Nisbet & Co., London, England, 1856, pp. 1:271.

6. Rahman, Vanita, et al. *10 Minutes of Home Exercise a Day Boosts Health*, Healthline HealthNews,https://www.healthline

.com/health -news/how- adding-10-minutes-of-exercise-a-day-can-boost-your-health#:~:text=%E2% 80%9CWe%20 have%20 known%20that%20regular,organization %20that%20 promotes%20preventive%20medicine.

7. George T.B. Davis, Fulfilled Prophecies That Prove the Bible (Philadelphia: Million Testaments Campaign, 1931), pp. 30-33.

8. McDowell, Josh, et al. *Evidence That Demands a Verdict: Historical Evidences for the Christian Faith*. T. Nelson, 1999.

9. Fan, Ryan, and Scrinivas Rao. "To Read Better, Read Something Twice." *Medium*, Books Are Our Superpower, 6 May 2021, https://baos.pub/to-read-better-read-something-twice-15a666c2b00c.

10. Wiles, Jerry, and Tiana Wiles. Conquer Series: the Battle for Purity, Soul Refiner, https://www.conquerseries.com/

11. Wommack, Andrew. *A Better Way to Pray*. Harrison House, 2010.

12. Bevere, John, et al. *Hearing from God. Messenger International*, Hachette Book Group, https://www.messengercourses.com/hearing-god.

13. Murdock, Mike. *The Blessing Bible*. The Wisdom Center, 1986.

14. Peretti, Frank. *This Present Darkness*. Kingsway, 2006.

15. Lawrence, et al. *The Practice of the Presence of God: The Best Rule of a Holy Life*. Unboring Book Company, 2016.

16. Wommack, Andrew. *The Power of Imagination: Unlocking Your Ability to Receive from God*. Harrison House Publishers, 2019.

17. Shmerling, Robert. "12 Ways to Keep Your Brain Young." *Harvard Health*, 13 May 2022, https://www.health.harvard.edu/mind-and-mood/12-ways-to-keep-your-brain-young#:~:text=Any%20mentally%20stimulating%20activity%20should,%2C%20painting%2C%20and%20other%20crafts.

18. Lambersky, Sarah. *How to Manage Your 40,000 Negative Thoughts a Day and... - Financialpost*. https://financialpost.com/entrepreneur/three-techniques-to-manage- 40000-negative-thoughts.

19. "Power Posing: Fake It until You Make It." *HBS Working Knowledge*, 20 Sept. 2010, hbswk.hbs.edu/item/power-posing-fake-it-until-you-make-it.

20. *Why Scholars Just Can't Stop Talking about Sarah and Hagar - U.S. News ...*, www.usnews.com/news/religion/articles/2008/01/25/why-scholars-just-cant-stop-talking-about-sarah-and-hagar. Accessed 15 Oct. 2023.

21. Grudem, Wayne. "The Holy Spirit." *Just Between Us*, justbetweenus.org/everyday-faith/the-holy-spirit. Accessed 14 Oct. 2023.

22. Working on calm. "Five Lessons from the Happiness Advantage." *Five Lessons From The Happiness Advantage -*, 26 Jan. 2023, workingoncalm.com/five-lessons-from-the-happiness-advantage/.

23. Harley, Willard F. *His Needs, Her Needs: Building a Marriage That Lasts*. Revell, a Division of Baker Publishing Group, 2020.

24. Frederick, Ryan, and Selena Frederick. *Fierce Marriage: Radically Pursuing Each Other in Light of Christ's Relentless Love*. Baker Publishing Group, 2018.

25. Brewer, Jack. "Issue Brief: Fatherlessness and Its Effects on American Society." *Home*, americafirstpolicy.com/latest/issue-brief-fatherlessness-and-its-effects-on-american-society#:~:text=This%20number%20is%20a%20major,%25%2C

%20according%20to%20Pew%20Research. Accessed 15 Oct. 2023.

26. Bet-David, Patrick, and Greg Dinkin. *Your next Five Moves: Master the Art of Business Strategy*. Gallery Books, 2021.

27. Lifeway Research. "Mother's Day Church Attendance Third among Holidays, Father's Day Last." *Lifeway Research*, 29 Apr. 2021, research.lifeway.com/2012/05/11/mothers-day-church-attendance-third-among-holidays-fathers-day-last/.

28. Cady, Nick. "The Impact on Kids of Dad's Faith and Church Attendance." *Theology for the People*, 3 June 2019, nickcady.org/2016/06/20/the-impact-on-kids-of-dads-faith-and-church-attendance/#:~:text=According%20to%20data%20collected%20by,will%20become%20a%20regular%20worshiper.

29. "Developing Shared Spiritual Intimacy." *Focus on the Family*, 19 Jan. 2022, www.focusonthefamily.com/marriage/healthy-marriage-traits/developing-shared-spiritual-intimacy/.

30. "How Complaining Rewires Your Brain for Negativity." *TalentSmartEQ*, 21 Aug. 2022, www.talentsmarteq.com/articles/how-complaining-rewires-your-brain-for-

negativity/#:~:text=Research%20from%20Stanford%20University%20has,brain%20areas%20destroyed%20by%20Alzheimer's.

31. Griffith, Taylor. "Fasting Health Benefits: The Science behind This Treatment Method." *Healthline*, Healthline Media, 29 Sept. 2018, www.healthline.com/health/fasting-and-cancer.

32. Richter, Amy, and Rachael Ajmera. "8 Health Benefits of Fasting, Backed by Science." *Healthline*, 13 Mar. 2023, www.healthline.com/nutrition/fasting-benefits.

33. Bevere, John, and Addison Bevere. *The Holy Spirit: An Introduction: An Interactive Study of the Person of the Holy Spirit.* Struik Christian Media, 2017.

34. "Stress Management Stress Basics." *Mayo Clinic*, Mayo Foundation for Medical Education and Research, 8 Apr. 2022, www.mayoclinic.org/healthy-lifestyle/stress-management/ in-depth/stress-basics/hlv-20049495.

35. "Stress Management Stress Basics." *Mayo Clinic*, Mayo Foundation for Medical Education and Research, 8 Apr. 2022, www.mayoclinic.org/healthy-lifestyle/stress-management/in-depth/stress-basics/hlv-20049495.

36. Providence Seniors Health Team, et al. "Can Laughter Help You Live Longer?" *Expert Tips and Advice for Living Your*

Healthiest Life, 13 Oct. 2022, blog.providence.org/elderly-care/can-laughter-help-you-live-longer.

37. Dunbar, R I M, et al. "Social Laughter Is Correlated with an Elevated Pain Threshold." *Proceedings. Biological Sciences*, U.S. National Library of Medicine, 22 Mar. 2012, www.ncbi.nlm.nih.gov/pmc/articles/PMC3267132/.

38. Cunningham, Ted. *A LOVE THAT LAUGHS: Lighten up, Cut Loose, and Enjoy Life Together*. Tyndale House Publishers, 2020.

39. "Backup Singers to the Duet of Marriage Archives." *Living on the Edge*, livingontheedge.org/broadcast-series/backup-singers-to-the-duet-of-marriage/?media=daily. Accessed 15 Oct. 2023.

40. Harrison, Jim. "Listening Prayer Helps You Hear God More Clearly. Here's How." *Faithward.Org*, 24 Aug. 2023, www.faithward.org/listening-prayer-hear-god/.

41. Young, Ed, and Lisa Young. *Sexperiment*. FaithWords, 2012.

42. "Oral Blessings." *The Marriage Bed*, 8 Apr. 2021, themarriagebed.com/oral-blessings/.

43. Michael Gorman, *Cruciformity: Paul's Narrative Spirituality of the Cross* (Eerdmans 2001) 265. Each of the verbs used to describe these responsibilities—"submit" (vv. 22, 24), "respect"

(v. 33) and "love" (vv. 25, 28, 33)—is drawn from the general responsibilities expected of all believers stated in 5:2 and 5:21.

44. Dillow, Linda. *What's It like to Be Married to Me?: And Other Dangerous Questions*. David C Cook, 2011.

45. Harley, Willard F. *Give & Take: The Secret to Marital Compatibility*. Fleming H. Revell, 1996.

46. Earls, Aaron. "More Americans Are Reading the Bible. Now What?" *Lifeway Research*, 28 May 2021, https://research.lifeway. com/2021/05/28/more-americans-are-reading- the-bible-now-what/.

47. Evans, Tony. "Real Faith." *Facebook*, 18 Sept. 2020, https://www.facebook.com/drtonyevans posts/ faith-is-measured-by-your-feet-not-your-feelings-its-measured-by-what- you-do-not/3619033431443064/.

48. Hampton, Debbie, et al. "How Writing Improves Your Brain and Helps You Heal." *The Best Brain Possible*, 21 Oct. 2021, https://thebestbrainpossible.com/writing-improves- brain-heal-emotions-health-journaling/#:~:text=Benefits%20of%20Writing% 20For%20Your%20Brain%20and%20Body&text=A%20brain%20 imaging%20study%20by,anger%2C%20and%20pain%20less%20i ntense.

49. Institute, Dent Neurologic. "22 Facts about the Brain: World Brain Day." *Dent Neurologic*, 17 Aug. 2022, www.dentinstitute.com/22-facts-about-the-brain-world-brain-day/.

50. *Btms.Htnutricion.Com*, btms.htnutricion.com/.

51. Nelson, Thomas. "Redeeming Gomer: The Price." *TIME in the Word Ministries*, 22 May 2017, https://timeintheword.org/2017/05/23/redeeming-gomer-the-price/.

52. Renfer, Kristin. "Forsaking the Lord For...raisin Cakes?!" *So I Fix My Eyes*, https://www.soifixmyeyes.com/hosea/forsaking-the-lord-forraisin-cakes.

53. Roach, Stacy. "8 Bible Verses on Exercise {Add Worship to Your Workouts}." So Very Blessed, 22 May 2019, https://soveryblessed.com/8-bible-verses-exercise/.

54. Scipioni, Jade. "This Simple Tactic Can 'Trick' Your Brain into Feeling Happier, Researchers Say." *CNBC*, CNBC, 22 May 2021, https://www.cnbc.com/2020/08/21/simple-trick -that-can-make-you-happier-according-to-research.html.

55. "Putting a Finger on Our Phone Obsession." *Dscout.Com*, dscout.com/people-nerds/mobile-touches. Accessed 15 Oct. 2023.

56. Allen, Jennie. *Get out of Your Head: Stopping the Spiral of Toxic Thoughts*. WaterBrook, 2020.

57. Sharon, et al. *Sharon's Blog*, 1 May 2012, sharon.soundoffaith.org/2012/05/01/did-you-know-speaking-in-tongues-can-improve-your-health/.

58. Mackenzie, Sarah, and Christopher A. Perrin. *Teaching from Rest: A Homeschooler's Guide to Unshakable Peace*. Classical Academic Press, 2015.

59. Cloud, Henry. *Changes That Heal: Four Practical Steps to a Happier, Healthier You*. Zondervan, 2018.

60. GotQuestions.org. "Praying in Tongues." *GotQuestions.Org*, 4 Nov. 2006, www.gotquestions.org/praying-in-tongues.html.

61. Hagee, John. "The Decision to Pray with Power." *Jhm.org*, www.jhm.org/Articles/2019-05-01-the-decision-to-pray-with-power.

62. Eggerichs, Emerson. *Love & Respect: The Love She Most Desires, the Respect He Desperately Needs*. Christian Large Print, 2010.

63. Scott LaPierre. "Male Leadership in the Bible Is God's Pattern Even with Deborah (1 Timothy 2:12 and Judges 4)." *Scott*

LaPierre, 20 June 2023, www.scottlapierre.org/male-leadership-in-the-bible/.

64. George, Jim, and Elizabeth George. *A Couple after God's Own Heart: Building a Lasting, Loving Marriage Together*. Harvest House Publishers, 2012.

65. Bowen, Will. *A Complaint Free World: How to Stop Complaining and Start Enjoying the Life You Always Wanted*. Harmony, 2024.

66. Bevere, Lisa. *Fast Forward,*.Revell, a Division of Baker Publishing Group, 2020.

67. Louie, Dexter, et al. "The Laughter Prescription: A Tool for Lifestyle Medicine." *American Journal of Lifestyle Medicine*, U.S. National Library of Medicine, 23 June 2016, www.ncbi.nlm.nih.gov/pmc/articles/PMC6125057/.

68. Renner, Ben. "American Families Spend Just 37 Minutes of Quality Time Together per Day, Survey Finds." *Study Finds*, 1 Apr. 2022, studyfinds.org/american-families-spend-37-minutes-quality-time/.

69. Bevere, John. *Honor's Reward: How to Attract God's Favor and Blessing*. Faith Words, 2007.

70. "Where Are You, God?" *Billy Graham Evangelistic Association*, 3 Feb. 2022, billygraham.org/story/where-are-you-god-billy-grahams-answers-for-hard-times/.

71. Yerkovich, Milan, and Kay Yerkovich. How We Love: Discover Your Love Style, Enhance Your Marriage. WaterBrook, 2017.

About the Author

Amanda Kay Cruz, Ph.D., is a passionate believer, wife, and homeschool mom of five. After birthing her first child at age fifteen, the Lord equipped her with the fortitude and support to finish high school at age sixteen, college at nineteen, her master's at twenty-three, and her doctorate at twenty-five. Now thirty, she has spent half of her life working in secondary and higher education as a teacher of English, P-16 Integration, and Special Education coursework. She and her husband, Husseim, fervidly serve as marriage ministry specialists at The Family Church in Texas's Rio Grande Valley, right on the Texas/Mexico border. Along with her family, Amanda enjoys studying God's Word, serving others, cruising, thrifting, and baking anything with chocolate. Her family's mantra, "Cruzes never quit," stems from their firm belief in Psalm 57:6 which declares: "Enemies set traps for my feet and struck me down. They dug a pit in my path, but fell in it themselves" (NIV). Time and time again. Amanda has watched God's favor outweigh all opposition in her life.